The Cold War in Universities

New Perspectives on the Cold War

Series Editors

Jussi M. Hanhimäki (*Graduate Institute Geneva*)
Marco Wyss (*Lancaster University*)

Advisory Board

Nigel Ashton (*The London School of Economics and Political Science*)
Mark P. Bradley (*The University of Chicago*)
Anne Deighton (*University of Oxford*)
Mario del Pero (*Centre d'histoire de Sciences Po, Paris*)
Bernd Greiner (*Berlin Center for Cold War Studies*)
Tanya Harmer (*London School of Economics and Political Science*)
Hope M. Harrison (*The George Washington University*)
Wolfgang Mueller (*University of Vienna*)
Andrew Preston (*University of Cambridge*)
Sergey Radchenko (*Cardiff University*)

VOLUME 9

The titles published in this series are listed at *brill.com/npcw*

The Cold War in Universities

U.S. and Soviet Cultural Diplomacy, 1945–1990

By

Natalia Tsvetkova

BRILL

LEIDEN | BOSTON

Cover illustration: American University, Cairo, Egypt.

The Library of Congress Cataloging-in-Publication Data is available online at http://catalog.loc.gov

Typeface for the Latin, Greek, and Cyrillic scripts: "Brill". See and download: brill.com/brill-typeface.

ISSN 2452-2260
ISBN 978-90-04-47177-1 (hardback)
ISBN 978-90-04-47178-8 (e-book)

Copyright 2021 by Natalia Tsvetkova. Published by Koninklijke Brill NV, Leiden, The Netherlands.
Koninklijke Brill NV incorporates the imprints Brill, Brill Nijhoff, Brill Hotei, Brill Schöningh, Brill Fink, Brill mentis, Vandenhoeck & Ruprecht, Böhlau Verlag and V&R Unipress.
Koninklijke Brill NV reserves the right to protect this publication against unauthorized use. Requests for re-use and/or translations must be addressed to Koninklijke Brill NV via brill.com or copyright.com.

This book is printed on acid-free paper and produced in a sustainable manner.

Contents

Abbreviations IX

Introduction 1
1   The Cold War, Cultural Diplomacy, and Universities   4
2   Universities in Cultural Cold War Studies   25
3   Archival Documents: What They Reveal   29
4   Theoretical Discussion: Realism, Constructivism, Americanization/
    Sovietization, Response Concept, or Fear?   31

1   **Europe**
    Opposition of "Conservative" Professors to U.S. and Soviet
    Transformations in German Universities   37
    1   Introduction   37
    2   U.S. and Soviet Cultural Offensive in Universities of Divided
        Germany: Making a Pliable Professor   40
        2.1   *Facing the Old Professors: U.S. and Soviet Perceptions*   42
        2.2   *Purging Rectors*   46
        2.3   *Purging Professors*   49
        2.4   *Pliable Professors?*   54
        2.5   *U.S. and Soviet Institutions in German Universities*   61
    3   Opposition of "Conservative Professors" to U.S. and Soviet
        Reforms   66
        3.1   *U.S. Advisors and Opposed Professors*   66
        3.2   *Soviet Advisors and Opposed Professors*   73
    4   Conclusion   84

2   **Middle East and Central Asia**
    Americanization, Sovietization, and Resistance in Afghanistan   86
    1   Introduction   86
    2   Kabul University Under the Control of the United States   89
        2.1   *Promoting the Faculty of Engineering*   89
        2.2   *English as the Language of Instruction*   95
        2.3   *Turmoil and Termination of Projects*   98
        2.4   *Aftermath...*   101
    3   Kabul University Under Soviet Control   102
        3.1   *Purging Everything "American"*   102

VI   CONTENTS

4   Professors and Students at Kabul University: Resistance to
     Americanization and Sovietization   108
     4.1   *Professors against U.S. and Soviet Advisors*   108
     4.2   *Students against U.S. and Soviet Advisors*   114
5   Conclusion   118

3   **Africa**
     When Development and Professors Erased U.S. and Soviet
     Transformations in Universities of Ethiopia   121
     1   Introduction   121
     2   U.S. Advisors at Haile Selassie I University: Under the Pressure of
          Ethiopianization   125
          2.1   *Building a University Scattered across the City*   125
          2.2   *Faculty of Education: Between Success and Failure*   128
          2.3   *Ethiopianization: A Clash between Local and U.S.*
                Professors   130
          2.4   *Anti-Americanism of Students: Undermining American*
                Transformations   134
     3   Soviet Advisors at Bahar Dar Polytechnic Institute: Caught
          between Sabotaged Professors and Loyal Students   136
          3.1   *The Ethiopian Government versus Soviet Advisors*   136
          3.2   *Professors: Sabotage against Russians*   141
          3.3   *Students: Between Government Repression and Soviet*
                Marxism   147
     4   Conclusion   152

4   **Asia-Pacific**
     Sabotage of Academics against U.S. and Soviet Strangers in
     Vietnam   156
     1   Introduction   156
     2   Making Teachers of English: U.S. Education Policy in Saigon   159
          2.1   *The University of Saigon and the Faculty of Pedagogy:*
                Making a Teacher   160
          2.2   *U.S. Advisors at Schools: Building Infrastructure*   166
          2.3   *Successes, Failures, and Consequences of American*
                Reforms   169
     3   Making Teachers of Russian: Soviet Education Policy in
          Hanoi   173
          3.1   *Pedagogical Institute of Foreign Languages at Hanoi:*
                Making a Teacher of Russian Language   173

    3.2   *Soviet Advisors at Schools: Teaching Children*   179

    3.3   *Successes, Failures, and Consequences of Soviet Reforms*   183

4   Conclusion   186

5   Latin America and Caribbean
Fear in U.S. and Soviet University Policy in Guatemala and Cuba   187

1   Introduction   187

2   The Policy of "Low Gringo Visibility" at Guatemalan Universities   191

    2.1   *Beginnings of U.S. Cultural Diplomacy before the Cold War*   191

    2.2   *Imposing Social Service at San Carlos University: Extending the Functions of a Traditional University*   195

    2.3   *Fear and a Policy of Low Gringo Visibility*   200

    2.4   *Leaving the Traditional University: The Shift to Alternative Academies*   204

3   The Policy of Appeasement by "Russo Soviético" in Cuba   207

    3.1   *Approaching the Universities of Latin America*   207

    3.2   *Soviets at the University of Havana: Fear of Loss*   210

    3.3   *Soviets at Alternative Academies: Facing Opposition and Denial*   216

4   Conclusion   225

Conclusion   228

Bibliography   233

Index   250

Abbreviations

GARF	Russian abbreviation for State Archive of the Russian Federation
GDR	German Democratic Republic
HICOG	Office of the US High Commissioner for Germany
HSIU	Haile Selassie I University
NARA	National Archives Records Administration
OMGUS	Office of the US Military Government in Germany
RGANI	The Russian State Archive of Modern History
RGASPI	Russian State Archive of Social–Political History
SED	German abbreviation for Sozialistische Einheitspartei Deutschlands, Socialist Unity Party of East Germany
SMAD	German abbreviation for Sowjetische Militäradministration in Deutschland, Soviet Military Administration in Germany
USAID	United States Agency for International Development
USIA	United States Information Agency
USOM/Vietnam	United States Operations Mission in Vietnam

Introduction

Universities, students, and professors form a significant cluster of actors in any country's cultural diplomacy, public diplomacy, and soft power policy. As bearers and transmitters of new ideas, they are the locomotives of cultural interaction between countries. As such, they are also attractive targets for governmental policy aimed at promoting national values, political stances, models of education, and even certain disciplines in other countries. Time after time, the world's leading countries have thus engaged universities in their cultural and public diplomacy, especially as objects of foreign policy.

This book describes how two such leading countries—the United States and the Soviet Union, now mostly Russia—aspired to transform overseas academic institutions according to their political aims during the Cold War. From the 1940s to the 1980s, U.S. and Soviet attempts to impose certain values, disciplines, teaching models, structures, statutes, and personnel at foreign universities were often foiled, however, by sabotage, ignorance, and resistance on the part of the local academic elite, particularly professors. In telling that history, the book discusses both U.S. and Soviet university policies on a global scale by covering the most fascinating cases from countries in five regions—Europe, the Middle East, the Asia-Pacific area, Africa, and Latin America—that played strategic roles in the Cold War. Across its chapters, the book provides evidence that neither the United States nor the Soviet Union could ultimately sway foreign universities toward becoming pro-U.S. or pro-Soviet. On the contrary, and perhaps as the book's most important finding, each superpower's essential policy, in the process of circulating through various universities worldwide, changed in profound ways, from being imperial and unilateral at first to becoming more cooperative and dialogue-based by the end of the Cold War.

Amid the decades-long struggle of the superpowers, U.S. and Soviet policy at universities abroad also endured clashes, misunderstandings, and even outright negation on the part of professors. In parallel, the attitudes of both U.S. and Soviet policymakers toward overseas faculty shifted from arrogance to resentment and even to fear, and they eventually realized that local repudiation of political aims in their university policies could be fertile ground for cultivating cooperation and development. After wading through the academic dissonance, the policymakers at last recognized that it was impossible to implement and enforce such rigid, self-serving policies at foreign universities. Over time, their policymaking experience across such a range of countries, typically marked by conflicts with unrelenting local communities that defended local traditions in education and sought to stop the spread of American and

© NATALIA TSVETKOVA, 2021 | DOI:10.1163/9789004471788_002

Soviet values, brought about fascinating transformations in both superpowers' cultural diplomacy, which became better tailored to each country and far friendlier to universities there. The academic communities at institutions that U.S. and Soviet policymakers attempted to Americanize or Sovietize were finally able to temper the superpowers' ambitions, and the top–down politics of the two superpowers changed under the influence of grassroots communities—namely, groups of professors.

The journey of U.S. and Soviet cultural diplomacy at universities around the world ended contrary to the expectations of both superpowers. Their success with distinct policies, first applied in 1945 in particularly severe, inflexible reforms at universities in occupied Germany, seemed to assure the United States and the Soviet Union of their imperial justification in imposing rival ideologies in foreign communities. From there, the policies were transferred to states in the Middle East and Central Asia, Africa, and the Asia-Pacific area, where U.S. and Soviet reformers soon began confronting fierce opposition from local academic bodies—opposition that caused both governments to doubt their capacity to fully realize their competing goals. Finally, in Latin America and the Caribbean, both U.S. and Soviet reformers recognized that they risked losing their hard-won political influence unless they abandoned aspects of their projects and instead adopted a policy of cooperation with local academic communities. In that way, political fear heavily impacted U.S. and Soviet university policies abroad.

In terms of cases examined, the book covers countries in which the United States and the Soviet Union clashed: divided Germany, Afghanistan, Ethiopia, both Vietnams, and Cuba as well as Guatemala. By extension, each case concentrates on established institutions of higher education at which policies of Americanization or Sovietization were put into practice. Case countries were selected not only for their pivotal positions in the strategies of Cold War policy but also with reference to the availability of archival documents that would allow writing a complete story of each case, from its unique beginning to the end of the Cold War. The documents that have been studied reveal unusual shifts in U.S. and Soviet education policies in action overseas. Under the pressure of professors at foreign universities, both superpowers went from complete confidence in their power, strength, and capability to transform the institutions in light of their rival objectives, to the realization that their reforms aimed at realizing Americanization or Sovietization were doomed to fail.

Such dramatic frustrations for U.S. and Soviet policies are depicted in each chapter throughout the book. Chapter 1 begins the journey in occupied Germany, whose academic communities were destabilized by defeat followed by denazification and where universities were under the complete control of

INTRODUCTION   3

the triumphant powers. There, the United States and the Soviet Union became increasingly assured of their justifications in fundamentally transforming German universities according to their competing values and educational models, In short order, the military occupation of Germany, the country's division, and the ideological struggle rapidly unfolding between the superpowers fueled the development of exceptionally harsh policies at German universities.

Thus confident that they could transform universities in any country, the United States and the Soviet Union pushed their projects to the Middle East/Central Asia, where new lines of Cold War containment were being drawn. Chapter 2 describes how the superpowers, each seeking to contain the other's influence in the region while promoting its own national brand of liberal democracy or socialism, sought to Americanize or Sovietize universities in Afghanistan by eroding the clan-based system and local traditions in education, among other social institutions. However, their agents faced unexpected resistance on the part of local academic communities, which dealt a crippling blow to their ability to change universities not only in Afghanistan but in Lebanon, Egypt, Turkey, and Syria as well.

Chapter 3 shifts focus to Africa, where the attempted transformation of local universities under the policies of Americanization and Sovietization was stifled by the need to develop infrastructure for higher education: classrooms, dormitories, even entire campuses. Ignoring ideology and propaganda, however, the Ethiopian academic community carefully selected projects proposed by the superpowers that would instead serve local purposes. Experiences in Africa during the Cold War profoundly influenced the perceptions of U.S. and Soviet experts, who began questioning their power to achieve Americanization or Sovietization at foreign universities aside from completing a handful of construction projects.

Next, chapter 4 describes how in the Asia-Pacific area, particularly in Vietnam, the two superpowers experienced unprecedented setbacks to their policies of education reform abroad. Facing Americanization and/or Sovietization, local academic communities reacted with resistance, sabotage, and even contempt. The reluctance of the Vietnamese to acquire knowledge about disciplines imposed by the foreign projects baffled advisors of both countries, who, despite losing focus, persisted in seeking reforms even as civil war ravaged the country.

Last, as recounted in chapter 5, in the Latin American/Caribbean nations of Guatemala and Cuba the two superpowers faced another extraordinary problem: their own concern about losing political influence. The denial of U.S. reforms in Guatemala and of Soviet ones in Cuba, both led by local professors, was so strong that under the Cold War conditions riddling the region the superpowers were compelled to submit to unruly academic communities and largely abandon their attempts at transformation. After all, the possible loss of a valuable client–partner far exceeded any advantages that could be gained by Americanizing or Sovietizing local universities.

Of course, such fluctuations in both U.S. and Soviet policies were neither linear nor sequential but coincided in parallel fashion. Even so, at the end of all attempted transformations in each foreign state, the superpowers' policies of reform, no matter how harsh, were restricted by local academic communities. Although once-intrepid soldiers convinced of the justice of instituting their ideals at occupied German universities, the reformers gradually became cautious diplomats who doubted whether their models of education and their disciplines from back home should, or even could, be transplanted overseas. In every case—in Germany, Afghanistan, Ethiopia, Vietnam, Guatemala, and Cuba—groups of professors were the ones who dulled the appetite of the reformers and made their policies bend to the needs, if not the will, of local universities.

To clarify that phenomenon, some essential details about the context of the Cold War, the university policies of the United States and the Soviet Union in other countries, the origins of our book in terms of historiography, our primary sources, and our major theoretical assumptions must be provided.

1 The Cold War, Cultural Diplomacy, and Universities

From the 1940s to the 1980s, world politics was framed by a political, economic, military, and cultural confrontation between the United States and the Soviet Union. This rivalry dominated world politics until the end of the 1980s and affected almost every aspect of culture, education, and everyday life in numerous other countries around the world. This conflict was fought on every continent on the globe with different periods of strong levels of both hostility and reconciliation. Historians still debate the Cold War in terms of the macro problems it caused on micro histories. Without delving too deeply into the complicated story of the Cold War context, which has been reconstructed and articulated by highly reputable scholars, we mention here that, in general, the Cold War was a rivalry for global influence between the United States and the Soviet Union.[1] The soft and hard methods included the establishment

---

[1] Among the best studies on the Cold War are: John Lewis Gaddis, *The Cold War: A New History* (New York: Penguin Press, 2005); John Lewis Gaddis, *We Now Know: Rethinking Cold War History* (New York: Oxford University Press, 1997); Melvyn P. Leffler and Odd A. Westad, *The Cambridge History of the Cold War*. Vols. 1–3 (Cambridge: Cambridge University Press, 2011);

INTRODUCTION

of military alliances, an arms race, propaganda campaigns, guerrilla warfare, political assassinations, and relative instruments, such as cultural diplomacy and developmental aid. To maintain the allegiance of their partners during that conflict, both superpowers imposed their values and rival models of politics, economics, and education around the world. As their ideological struggle became an increasingly significant factor in active cultural expansion, initially in Europe and later in Asia, Latin America, and Africa, the political and military contest known as the Cold War turned into the so-called Cultural Cold War.

The Cultural Cold War can be roughly divided into three periods. The first period of the 1940s and 1950s involved the introduction of a new apparatus and projects of cultural diplomacy, including arts, exchanges, sports, tourism, and information in both the United States and Soviet Union. The divided parts of Europe were in the epicenter of the cultural rivalry between both superpowers during the first period. The second period can be defined from the 1960s to the early 1970s, when the Cold War realized its global impact by embracing countries in Africa, Asia, and Latin America. Foreign aid to developing countries cemented cultural diplomacy projects as a part of a modernization process. This new cultural diplomacy based on the development and transformation policy was designed to ensure a political orientation of new sovereign states of the South towards either Washington or Moscow. The third period is the mid-1970s to the late 1980s, when Détente and the Helsinki Accords—and, later, a new cultural diplomacy of Ronald Reagan—contributed to political reforms in Eastern Europe and the Soviet Union. Undoubtedly, these three periods are defined with reservations, but they fix some new points in the cultural diplomacy of the Cold War.

The period of ideological confrontation between the United States and the USSR during the Cold War is often called the Golden Age of cultural (or public) diplomacy.[2] The confrontation enhanced the introduction and generous governmental funding of a new strategy, mechanisms, and various projects to spread opposing values around the world.[3] However, before the Cold War, the

---

David Foglesong, The American Mission and the "Evil Empire": The Crusade for a "Free Russia" since 1881 (New York: Cambridge University Press, 2007). Historiography review about debates on the Cold War in: Michael F. Hopkins, "Continuing Debate and New Approaches in Cold War History," Historical Journal 50, no. 4 (December 2007): 913–34.

2 Richard T. Arndt, The First Resort of Kings: American Cultural Diplomacy in the Twentieth Century (Washington, D.C.: Potomac Books, 2005).

3 Charles A. Thomson and Walter H. C. Laves, Cultural Relations and U.S. Foreign Policy (Bloomington: Indiana University Press, 1963); Frank Ninkovich, The Diplomacy of Ideas: U.S. Foreign Policy and Cultural Relations, 1938–1950 (New York: Cambridge University Press, 1981); Johnston Gordon, "Revisiting the Cultural Cold War," Social History 35, no. 3 (August 2010): 290–307.

cultural diplomacy of both also existed, but most of the projects were in the hands of private sponsors. American missionaries developed cultural diplomacy in terms of teaching local communities and translating indigenous languages in the Middle East and Africa. Later, during the Progressive Era, famous for its rise of American philanthropy as a social and international institution, charitable foundations set the first international projects. For example, the Carnegie Endowment for World Peace promoted ideas of peace and international organizations.[4] The involvement of the United States in the First World War and the necessity of developing its national instruments of informational engagement abroad led to the establishment of a Committee on Public Information known as the Creel Committee. George Creel aimed to challenge negative images of America abroad by opening libraries and arranging tours for journalists and university professors. The Committee was not long lasting and ceased to exist by 1919 without receiving funds from Congress. A new threat from Germany to U.S. interests in Latin America in the 1930s turned out to be the focal point for cultural diplomacy. Private cultural projects turned out to be under the control of the government. In 1938, a Division of Cultural Relations was established within the Department of State to stop the instillation of Nazi ideas into the Americas.[5] In Soviet Russia, cultural diplomacy was based on tours by artists, pianists, and poets, but since the mid-1920s, the government-sponsored agency known as the All-Union Society for Cultural Relations with Foreign Countries (VOKS) began. Projects and events arranged by this agency continue today to cause debates between supporters of the concept that the Soviet cultural diplomacy was part of Russia's humanitarian mission promoting grassroots connections, and supporters of the idea that VOKS was more a political than a cultural agency applying pressure and intelligence and designated as a sharp power.[6] The Second World War intensified information projects by both. The Voice of America counteracted German propaganda and turned out to be one of the most effective parts of cultural diplomacy during

---

4 Merle Curti, *American Philanthropy Abroad* (New Brunswick, NJ: Transaction Books, 1963); Robert Arnove, *Philanthropy and Cultural Imperialism: The Foundations at Home and Abroad* (Bloomington: Indiana University Press, 1982); More about the U.S. missionary movement and American charities in the Middle East in: Robert Daniel, *American Philanthropy in the Near East, 1820–1960* (Athens, Ohio: Ohio University Press, 1970).

5 William Glade, "Issues in the Genesis and Organization of Cultural Diplomacy: A Brief Critical History," *Journal of Arts Management, Law & Society* 39, no. 4 (Winter 2009): 240–59.

6 Jean Fayet, "VOKS: The Third Dimension of Soviet Foreign Policy," in *Searching for a Cultural Diplomacy*, ed. Jessica Gienow-Hecht and Mark Donfried (New York: Berghahn Books, 2013), 33–49; On the concept of sharp power, see: Christopher Walker, "What Is 'Sharp Power'?" *Journal of Democracy* 29, no. 3 (2018): 9–23.

INTRODUCTION

the Cold War beginning in 1942. The same story is referred to as Radio Moscow, which expanded its broadcast in all European languages with the help of refugees during the war, and was a focal part of Soviet Cold War diplomacy.

However, it was the Cold War, with its containment strategy to deter the rival's values, and its offensive strategy to gain geostrategic aims around the world, which extensively developed cultural diplomacy. During the first period of the cultural Cold War, the governmental apparatus of cultural diplomacy was completely built, conserving most of its agencies until the end of the Cold War.

In the United States, all cultural diplomacy programs were controlled by the Office of International Information and Cultural Affairs at the Department of State, established in August 1945. The famous public law on cultural, informational, and educational exchanges of 1948, known as the Smith-Mundt Act, laid a foundation for the future division of the office into two bureaus, notably the Bureau for International Information, and the Bureau for Educational and Cultural Affairs. For the first time the act proclaimed the introduction of global cultural diplomacy in terms of funding for a wide variety of projects around the world. Until that moment, the Fulbright Program was the only project with real global impact. But the program mostly embraced academic exchanges.[7] The growth of misunderstanding between Moscow and Washington, the Sovietization of the countries of Eastern Europe, and concern over the spread of communist ideas in the United States through exchanges were reasons for congressmen to allow exchanges only with potential allies of the United States. The Eastern Bloc was removed from the list of target countries. Finally, the National Security Council's Report 68, entitled "U.S. Objectives and Programs for National Security," adopted after the start of war on the Korean peninsula, coined educational, cultural, and informational programs as a part of the containment strategy to deter the ideology of the USSR in the world.[8]

The Soviet Union did not lag behind in terms of a scope of its cultural diplomacy and apparatus. The International Department, the Agitation and Propaganda Department, the Department of Science and Higher Education, and others at the Central Committee of the Communist Party were responsible for connecting cultural diplomacy and real politics. They supervised international public organizations such as the World Peace Council, the World Federation of

---

7 For example: Sam Lebovic, "From War Junk to Educational Exchange: The World War II Origins of the Fulbright Program and the Foundations of American Cultural Globalism, 1945–1950," *Diplomatic History* 37, no. 2 (2013): 280–312.

8 John Lewis Gaddis. *Strategies of Containment: A Critical Appraisal of American National Security Policy During the Cold War* (New York: Oxford University Press, 2005).

Trade Unions, and The Women's International Democratic Federation. However, until now, some records, i.e., of the International Department have been only partially declassified, and still little is known about the real political advocacy projects that engaged leaders in some countries.[9] Few new and fascinating studies on this topic reveal the influence of the Soviet Union on elections and political movements through cultural diplomacy.[10] The Council of Ministers of the Soviet Union and its departments for cultural relations, as well as the Ministry of Education, the Ministry of Foreign Affairs, the Soviet embassies, Soviet cultural centers abroad, the Commission on the Visits Abroad, later known as State Committee of the USSR on Foreign Tourism, the Komsomol's Bureau Sputnik, and other agencies were involved in cultural diplomacy. At the bottom of the chain, it was the Union of Soviet Societies of Friendship and Cultural Relations with Foreign Countries known better as the SSOD that replaced VOKS in 1958. Current scholarship has smoothed previous arguments about strong ideological and political frames of cultural projects of the agency illustrating how the SSOD built people-to-people diplomacy.[11] Despite numerous and detailed studies on the apparatus of Soviet cultural diplomacy, there are still blind spots. For example, the Soviet Committee for the Cultural Affairs with Compatriots Living Abroad, often referred to in documents as *Rodina*, which engaged Russian emigrés in different countries, has been barely introduced to the Cultural Cold War Studies.[12]

Current studies on the Cultural Cold War of the first period are represented by a variety of narratives and concepts, and among the main areas of the studies the following should be noted: U.S. arts diplomacy; U.S. informational projects; regions and countries in the U.S. cultural diplomacy; U.S.-Soviet exchanges; and, separately, Soviet cultural diplomacy.

U.S. arts diplomacy is one of the most popular areas in historiography. Music, films, exhibitions, posters, books, and everything related to *cultural*

---

9   Russian State Archive of Modern History, Moscow, Russia. Records group 10. International Conferences and Negotiations with Communist and Workers' Parties, 1956–1988. Partially declassified.

10 Simo Mikkonen, "Interference or Friendly Gestures? Soviet Cultural Diplomacy and Finnish Elections, 1945–56," *Cold War History* 20, no. 3 (2020): 349–65.

11 John McNair, "Winning Friends, Influencing People: Soviet Cultural Diplomacy in Australia, 1928–1968," *Australian Journal of Politics and History* 61, no. 4 (2015): 515–29; Simo Mikkonen, "The Finnish-Soviet Society: From Political to Cultural Connections." In *Nordic Cold War Cultures: Ideological Promotion, Public Reception, and East-West Interactions*, eds. Valur Ingimundarson and Rosa Magnusdottir (Helsinki, Aleksanteri Institute, 2015): 109–31.

12 State Archive of Russian Federation, Moscow, Russia. Records group 9651. *Soviet Society for Cultural Relations with Compatriots Living Abroad (Rodina Society), 1955–1992.*

INTRODUCTION   9

presentations had a huge impact on recipients. But if earlier scholars unreservedly argued that jazz won the Cold War, current estimations have been more balanced, unbiased, and have not belittled the power and impact that Soviet cultural diplomacy had on target audiences. Today, researchers compare American jazz or rock music with Soviet classical music in terms of their impact, for example, on European consumers, who are reported to have been exposed to the high culture provided by the Soviets.[13] Nevertheless, these are no reasons to neglect an enormous impact of American jazz diplomacy and tours of bands to Germany, Poland, or other states.[14] A tour of the Dave Brubeck Jazz Quartet to Poland in 1958, for example, opened a dialogue between American jazzmen and the public that led the development of the jazz movement in Eastern Europe and in the Soviet Union.[15] Cinema is also prominently featured in the studies on the Cultural Cold War. However, no clear methodological perceptions of American or Soviet films and their efficiency has been introduced. How would we assess the impact of American Westerns on the Soviet audience or Soviet films on foreign audiences? The statistics on the number of viewers does not provide variable methods to conclude that cinema made changes in hearts and mind.[16] The questions on the cinema in the Cold War are more and more often reviewed in terms of its consumerism but not in terms of its political and ideological effect.

The intensification of containment in Europe, the Middle East, and Asia— and the concern of both Washington and Moscow that the values and ideology of their counterpart could win the hearts and minds of people, change a political system, and bring a loss of geostrategic gains—all led to the reestablishment of propaganda, and various information projects in terms of radio, pamphlets, leaflets, mobile cinemas, and libraries, translated literature, which

---

13 Cf.: Walter Hixson, *Parting the Curtain: Propaganda, Culture, and the Cold War, 1945–1961* (New York: St. Martin's, 1997); Daniella Fosler-Lussier, "Music Pushed, Music Pulled: Cultural Diplomacy, Globalization, and Imperialism," *Diplomatic History* 36, no. 1 (2012): 53–64.

14 Pierangelo Castagneto, "Ambassador Dizzy: Jazz Diplomacy in the Cold War Era," *Americana: E-Journal of American Studies in Hungary* 10, no. 1 (2014), accessed March 05, 2020, http://americanaejournal.hu/vol10jazz/castagneto; Graham Carr, "Diplomatic Notes: American Musicians and Cold War Politics in the Near and Middle East, 1954–60," *Popular Music History* 1, no. 1 (2004): 37–63.

15 Keith Hatschek, "The Impact of American Jazz Diplomacy in Poland During the Cold War Era," *Jazz Perspectives* 4, no. 3 (2010): 253–300.

16 Natalia Tsvetkova, Ivan Tsvetkov, and Irina Barber, "Americanization versus Sovietization: Film exchanges Between the United States and the Soviet Union, 1948–1950," *Cogent Arts & Humanities* 5, no.1 (2018): 1–17; Nick Cull, "The Cold War on the Silver Screen," *Diplomatic History* 33, no. 2 (2009): 357–59.

were to be the primary and cohesive parts of cultural diplomacy. Notorious campaigns by the Truman administration, known as mass letters writings, tried to persuade Italians not to vote for communists during the elections of 1948 or the Campaign of Truth of 1951, which made political advocacy in cultural diplomacy a priority.[17] The logic led to the establishment the U.S. Information Agency (1953–1999), one of the most effective agencies of the Cold War, and still the most popular among the relevant studies. Today, scholars have written a comprehensive story of the agency, giving various interpretations of its projects. The USIA's famous directors, such as T. Sorensen or E. Murrow, became icons of U.S. public diplomacy. The first introduced new approaches to the shaping of effective programs based on aspirations of target audiences, and the latter was able to expand the activities of the USIA in countries of the South and promoted ethics and unbiased news in international broadcasting.[18]

Being a core tenet in the culture war, information projects and propaganda attracted researchers. The scholarship has accumulated a number of investigations on U.S. campaigns or on the institutions of international broadcasting like the Voice of America. The most popular theme is the broadcasting to Eastern Europe that served as a catalyst for dissidents' movements and protests, including the Hungarian uprising of 1956.[19] Scholars have connected the strategies issued by the National Security Council (i.e., Report by the National Security Council on the Coordination of Foreign Information Measures of 1947), psychological operations, and informational campaigns with cultural

---

17 Edda Martinez and Edward A. Suchman, "Letters from America and the 1948 Elections in Italy," *The Public Opinion Quarterly* 14, no. 1 (1950): 111–25; Kaeten Mistry, "The Case for Political Warfare: Strategy, Organization and US Involvement in the 1948 Italian Election," *Cold War History* 6, no. 3 (2006): 301–329; Tobe Rider, "A Campaign of Truth: The State Department, Propaganda, and the Olympic Games, 1950–1952," *Journal of Cold War Studies* 18, No. 2 (2016): 4–27.

18 Theodore Sorensen, *The Word War: The Story of American Propaganda* (New York: Harper & Row Publishers, 1968); Gregory Tomlin, *Murrow's Cold War: Public Diplomacy for the Kennedy Administration* (Lincoln: Potomac Books, 2016); Nicholas Cull, "'The Man Who Invented Truth': The Tenure of Edward R. Murrow as Director of the United States Information Agency During the Kennedy Years," *Cold War History* 4, no. 1 (2003): 23–48; Wilson Dizard Jr., *Inventing Public Diplomacy: The Story of the U.S. Information Agency* (Boulder, CO: Lynne Rienner Publishers, 2004); Nicholas Cull, *The Cold War and the United States Information Agency: American Propaganda and Public Diplomacy 1945–1989* (Cambridge, UK: Cambridge University Press, 2008).

19 For example: Mark Pittway, "The Education of Dissent: The Reception of Voice of Free Hungary, 1951–1956," in *Across the Blocs: Cold War Cultural and Social History*, eds. Rana Mitter and Patrick Major (London: Frank Cass, 2004), 97–116; Arch Puddington, *Broadcasting Freedom: The Cold War Triumph of Radio Free Europe and Radio Liberty* (Lexington: The University Press of Kentucky, 2015).

INTRODUCTION

diplomacy.[20] Washington and Moscow initiated world-scaled campaigns revisited by scholars in terms of their efficiency. However, the historiography neglects projects on engagement of representatives of Islam in Iraq, Iran, and Saudi Arabia as a part of cultural diplomacy.[21]

U.S. cultural diplomacy in terms of regional dimension is a way to know about details on success and failures in the policy aimed at promoting ideas and values abroad. Europe, or rather, Western Europe, occupies a special place both in U.S. cultural diplomacy of the Cold War and in its historiography, as much as it was cultural diplomacy that contributed to the establishment and further maintaining of the transatlantic partnership between European countries and the United States of America. The most popular aspects of U.S.–European public diplomacy can be named as follows: the engagement of European elite through education and information programs; the introduction of U.S. management and the cooperation with European businessmen in the framework of U.S. economic assistance; the rivalry with the Soviet Union for the minds and hearts of intellectuals and youth in Europe.[22] It was the Congress for Cultural Freedom, established by the U.S. government, that contributed enormously to the creation of the transatlantic partnership uniting elite, intelligentsia, and the youth around American values.[23] The scholarship knows in detail how the United States built the alliance through information activities in all European countries, including the Netherlands, Norway, Spain and Ireland, and others.[24] Moreover, cultural diplomacy was aimed toward not allowing young people and intellectuals to fall into the left movement and communism.

---

20 Kenneth Osgood, "Form before Substance: Eisenhower's Commitment to Psychological Warfare and Negotiations with the Enemy," *Diplomatic History* 24, no. 3 (2000): 405–33; Giles Scott-Smith, "Confronting Peaceful Co-existence: Psychological Warfare and the Role of Interdoc, 1963–72," *Cold War History* 7, no. 1 (2007): 19–43.

21 NARA. Records Group 59. Records of the Department of State. Decimal Files, 1950–1954. Box 16.

22 Frances Saunders, *Who Paid the Piper? The CIA and the Cultural Cold War* (London: Granta, 1999); Manuela Aguilar, *Cultural Diplomacy and Foreign Policy: German-American Relations, 1955–1968* (New York: Peter Lang Inc., 1996); Volker Berghahn, *The Americanization of West German Industry, 1945–1973* (Leamington Spa: Berg, 1986); Richard Aldrich, "The Struggle for the Mind of European Youth: the CIA and European Movement Propaganda, 1948–1960," in *Cold-War Propaganda in the 1950s*, ed. Gary Rawnsley (London: Palgrave Macmillan, 1999), 183–203; Giles Scott-Smith, "Mending the "Unhinged Alliance" in the 1970s: Transatlantic Relations, Public Diplomacy, and the Origins of the European Union Visitors Program," *Diplomacy & Statecraft* 16, no. 4 (2005): 749–78.

23 Giles Scott-Smith, *Politics of Apolitical Culture: Congress for Cultural Freedom, and the CIA and Post-War American Hegemony* (London: Routledge, 2002).

24 See the selected chapters about the U.S. public diplomacy in European counties in: Kenneth Osgood and Brian Etheridge, *The United States and Public Diplomacy: New Directions in Cultural and International History* (Leiden: Martinus Nijhoff Publishers, 2010).

Finally, tourism was exploited to enhance contacts between Americans and Europeans and duty-free goods and cheap tickets are said to have been introduced to attract ordinary Americans to travel. Hence, the U.S. cultural diplomacy and tourism in Europe is often associated with the seeding of a consumer society and its political consequences in Europe.[25]

Therefore, some researchers estimate the U.S. cultural diplomacy in Europe as a success in terms of creating and promoting the transatlantic partnership, deterring communist and leftist ideas through engagement of moderates, and building a more or less politically loyal society.[26] But some researchers have raised questions about cultural imperialism and a reaction from recipients of the U.S. cultural diplomacy and its products in Europe. The discourse about the cultural imperialism has been rooted in the 1960s after disclosure of publications about the connections between the government and the cultural projects aimed at intelligentsia and students in Western Europe that pushed the criticism of U.S. foreign policy by the leftists and revisionists.[27] The concept was entrenched in scholarly literature and blamed the U.S. government in the unfolding of the Cold War, in misunderstanding of Russia, and in exploiting culture as an instrument of imperialism.[28]

In Cultural Cold War Studies, cultural imperialism in its traditional interpretations depicts the spread of values by political and economic powers at the expense of local cultures.[29] A significant shift in the perception of the concept was the writings by Jessica Gienow-Hecht who proposed to view the concept of cultural imperialism as the main foundation for concepts such as Americanization, Westernization, globalization, or cultural transfer firmly fixed in the scholarship after the end of the Cold War. All of them are said to have been derived from the concept of cultural imperialism, and their popularity among scholars has been caused by changes in international context and scholarly discourse.[30] The adopters of the concept of cultural imperialism have switched

---

25   Christopher Endy, *Cold War Holidays: American Tourism in France* (Chapel Hill: The University of North Carolina Press, 2004).

26   Giles Scott-Smith, "Maintaining Transatlantic Community: US Public Diplomacy, the Ford Foundation and the Successor Generation Concept in US Foreign Affairs, 1960s–1980s," *Global Society: Journal of Interdisciplinary International Relations* 28, no. 1 (2014): 90–103.

27   See, for example: "How the CIA Turns Students into Traitors," *Ramparts* (April 1967): 38–40.

28   Christopher Lasch, *The Agony of American Left* (New York: Alfred A. Knopf, 1969); Christopher Lasch, "The Cultural Cold War," *The Nation* (11 September, 1967): 198.

29   John Tomlinson, *Cultural Imperialism: A Critical Introduction* (Baltimore: Johns Hopkins University Press, 1991).

30   Jessica Gienow-Hecht, "Academics, Cultural Transfer, and the Cold War – A Critical Review," *Diplomatic History* 24, no. 3 (Summer 2000): 465–95.

INTRODUCTION   13

to a more pliable discourse about liberal imperialism and pan-Americanism. The United States, according to proponents of this idea, was an empire by invitation that pursued a policy of liberal imperialism to contain the ideology of communism that accelerated the development of democracy.[31] Consequently, the U.S. cultural diplomacy in Europe has been more often discussed in terms of Americanization and so-called partial Americanization, implying that American values or technological innovations were Europeanized and societies successfully resisted the cultural supremacy of the United States.[32]

Cultural, scientific, and academic exchanges between the United States and the Soviet Union were a miniature of the global ideological Cold War.[33] In 1958, the first cultural agreement between the two was approved, but exchanges were limited for a long time. The most prominent researcher and memoirist on the topic is Yale Richmond, a former staff member of the Department of State and of the U.S. Informational Agency during the Cold War. In his works, he shows how the Soviet elite, including its young members, were involved in U.S. exchange programs, and how the programs affected the fate of the USSR.[34] Festivals, exhibitions, and other large-scale public events between the two were a prominent part of U.S.–Soviet exchanges and a part of the studies in the field of Cultural Cold War.[35] If the U.S. exhibitions in Moscow and Leningrad in 1959 have been well studied, then U.S. exhibitions in different cities

---

31   Peter van Ham, "Power, Public Diplomacy and the Pax Americana," in *The New Public Diplomacy: Soft Power in International Relations*, ed. Jan Melissen (New York: Palgrave Macmillan, 2007), 47–66.

32   Simona Tobia, "Introduction: Europe Americanized? Popular Reception of Western Cold War Propaganda in Europe," *Cold War History* 11, no. 1 (2011): 1–7; Brian McKenzie, *Remaking France: Americanization, Public Diplomacy, and the Marshall Plan* (New York: Berghahn Books, 2008); Ruth Oldenziel and Karin Zachmann, *Cold War Kitchen: Americanization, Technology, and European Users* (Cambridge, Mass.: MIT Press, 2011).

33   For example: Victor Rosenberg, *Soviet-American Relations, 1953–1960: Diplomacy and Cultural Exchange during the Eisenhower Presidency* (Jefferson, NC: North Carolina: McFarland & Company, 2005); Reinhold Wagnleitner, "The Empire of the Fun, or Talkin' Soviet Union Blues: The Sound of Freedom and Cultural Hegemony in Europe," *Diplomatic History* 23, no. 3 (1999): 499–524; Yale Richmond, *Cultural Exchange and the Cold War: Raising the Iron Curtai* (University Park PA: Penn State University Press, 2003).

34   Yale Richmond, "Cultural Exchange and the Cold War: How the West Won," *American Communist History* 9, no. 1 (2010): 61–75; Yale Richmond, *Practicing Public Diplomacy: A Cold War Odyssey* (New York: Berghahn Books, 2008).

35   Susan Reid, "Who Will Beat Whom? Soviet Popular Reception of the American National Exhibition in Moscow, 1959," *Kritika: Explorations in Russian and Eurasian History* 9, no. 4 (2008): 855–904; Ellen Mickiewicz, "Efficacy and Evidence: Evaluating U.S. Goals at the American National Exhibition in Moscow, 1959," *Journal of Cold War Studies* 13, no. 4 (2011): 138–71.

14 INTRODUCTION

of the Soviet empire have been neglected in the scholarship and researchers' approach to it.[36] The exhibitions are often viewed in terms of the opposition of consumer society and socialistic economy as it was manifested during the famous kitchen debates between Richard Nixon and Nikita Khrushchev during the U.S. exhibition in Moscow in 1959.[37]

The Soviet cultural diplomacy is a distinctive track in the historiography. For a long time, the theme has been studied in a one-sided manner due to a lack of access to archival records.[38] Today, the Soviet cultural diplomacy is under a new revision by researchers who apply new approaches, theories, and revealed new narratives about arts, diplomacy, tourism, exchanges, home fronts, *Sovietophilia*, and much more. The concept of the triumphalism of the U.S. cultural diplomacy over the Soviet one, popular in the studies in the 1990s–early 2000s, has been gradually fading in the historiography. However, current studies on institutions and projects of Moscow's cultural diplomacy highlight its weaknesses and draws a conclusion about the reasons for the cultural defeat of the USSR in the Cold War. Often, the concept of triumphalism is replaced by theses about *Pax Sovietica* determined by the rising of the Soviet soft power after the Second World War in terms of the victory over fascism, the popularity of the ideas of socialism and communism in various countries, and the turn of the youth of the Third World countries towards Moscow as the center of a revolutionary movement. Moreover, a bomb and a space program have contributed to a so-called global Sovietization. Music tours, youth festivals, Soviet exhibit pavilions, information campaigns, etc., promoted the Soviet ideology on a global level. All of these factors contributed to the expansion of Soviet ideas and *Pax Sovietica*.[39]

However, cultural diplomacy was not only seen through large-scale exhibitions or festivals; in most cases, it was a variety of grassroots stories at the level of interaction between individuals. The shift to studies of microhistory and the microcosm of the Soviet cultural diplomacy has resulted in the introduction of

---

36 NARA. Records Group 306. *U.S. Information Agency. Office of Research and Media Reaction.*

37 Sarah Phillips and Hamilton Shane, *The Kitchen Debate and Cold War Consumer Politics: A Brief History with Documents* (New York, NY: Macmillan Higher Education, 2014).

38 Frederick Barghoorn, *The Soviet Cultural Offensive: The Role of Cultural Diplomacy in Soviet Foreign Policy* (Princeton: Princeton University Press, 1960).

39 Lewis Siegelbaum, "Sputnik Goes to Brussels: The Exhibition of a Soviet Technological Wonder," *Journal of Contemporary History* 47, no. 1 (2012): 120–36; Margaret Peacock, "The Perils of Building Cold War Consensus at the 1957 Moscow World Festival of Youth and Students," *Cold War History* 12, no. 3 (2012): 515–35; Vladimir Paperny, "Hot and Cold War in Architecture of Soviet Pavilions," in *Architecture of Great Expositions 1937–1959: Messages of Peace, Images of War*, eds. Rika Devos, Alexander Ortenberg, and Vladimir Paperny (Farnham, UK: Ashgate, 2015), 81–98.

INTRODUCTION 15

a paradigm about a multilevel and multipolar interaction between participants in the cultural diplomacy that created a space for a dialogue. Grassroots actors of the cultural Cold War, including tourists, participants in citizens' diplomacy or people-to-people diplomacy, and various civic organizations erased political boundaries in the Cold War. Technology transfers and a trade between the West and the East eroded the hostility of the ideological confrontation. This led to leaks in the Iron Curtain, and later, to its breaking down.[40]

A reflection of this dimension of the cultural diplomacy is laid in the studies about the Cold War's tourism or constructed images.[41] Perceptions of each other at the microlevel, for example, such as the studies on perceptions of the Soviet Union by Icelandic farmers, have opened up a new understanding of the effectiveness or ineffectiveness of cultural diplomacy.[42] The studies on tourism have introduced new narratives on academic tourism and tours by artists, who published memories, notes, and travelogues that had a significant impact on the construction of the image of Western countries among the Soviet population as a consumer paradise, and, at the same time, on the construction of the image of a Soviet society among citizens of Western countries, and among young people and the leftists in particular, as a source for promoting progressivism and socialism.[43] These studies have introduced other unique phenomenon as *Sovietophilia*. A communication of foreign intellectual elites with politicians of the Soviet Union during the Cold War is defined as the *intellectual Sovietophilia* or the fellow travelers. Why did European intellectuals like Pablo Picasso or Romain Rolland turn a blind eye to the problems of the Soviet system? The Sovietophilia is explained by the fusion of the leftists' culture and the Soviet ideology in terms of antifascism, progressive humanism, and global justice. And this phenomenon has a huge impact of the image of the Soviets abroad.[44]

---

40 Sari Autio-Sarasmo and Katalin Miklóssy, *Reassessing Cold War Europe* (New York: Routledge, 2011).

41 See, for example: Patryk Babiracki and Kenyon Zimmer, *Cold War Crossings: International Travel and Exchange across the Soviet Bloc, 1940s-1960s.* (College Station, TX: Texas A&M University Press, 2014); Gleb Tsipursky, "Active and Conscious Builders of Communism: State-Sponsored Tourism for Soviet Adolescents in the Early Cold War, 1945–53," *Journal of Social History* 48, no. 1 (2014): 20–46.

42 Sigurjóón Baldur Hafsteinsson and Tinna Gréétarsdóóttir, "Screening Propaganda: The Reception of Soviet and American Film Screenings in Rural Iceland, 1950–1975," *Film History* 23, no. 4 (2011): 361–75.

43 Michael David-Fox, *Showcasing the Great Experiment: Cultural Diplomacy and Western Visitors to the Soviet Union, 1921–1941* (New York: Oxford University Press, 2014); Michael David-Fox, "The Fellow Travelers Revisited: The Cultured West through Soviet Eyes," *The Journal of Modern History* 75, no. 2 (2003): 300–335.

44 Michael David-Fox, "The 'Heroic Life' of a Friend of Stalinism: Romain Rolland and Soviet Culture," *Slavonica* 11, no. 1 (2005): 3–29.

16   INTRODUCTION

The other area of Soviet cultural diplomacy can be also placed in the discourse on microhistory studies. This is an interaction of Soviet officials with Russian immigrants in the United States and European countries. This part of cultural diplomacy, as has been indicated above, was referred to as the Rodina agency, whose records have been barely studied by historians. The Soviet officials skillfully exploited emotions of the immigrants about their former homeland to encourage them to become a part of the Soviet soft power through visits to the homeland and publications about the positive sides of a Soviet life. However, the cooperation with the officials in exchange for free-of-charge travel to the USSR undoubtedly raises a new question about the ethics of cultural diplomacy.[45]

The second period of cultural diplomacy can be defined as the 1960s–early 1970s, when the Cold War became global in countries of the South. Decolonization and newly created states in Asia, Africa, Latin America, and the Middle East and pushed the United States and the Soviet Union into expanding their rival powers in all these regions, making allies and supporting national movements, military coups, etc. The policy required soft power resources to keep the loyalty of new friends and to carry out necessary reforms in political, economic, and education spheres, based on their ideological preferences. Each of the superpowers sought to get such a category of countries into its alliance by creating a counterbalance to the counterpart in a particular region. Foreign aid turned out to be a reliable part of this policy, along with the cultural diplomacy that contributed to the development projects educating civic and military specialists and introducing new projects designed to transform societies in the Third World. However, until now, these projects have been poorly studied in comparison to the projects of the first period of the Cold War.[46]

Nikita Khrushchev's times were the beginning of the global Soviet cultural diplomacy. It included foreign aid, modernization, training of foreign students carried out within the framework of the struggle for the countries of the Third

---

45   The topic is discussed in: Ieva Zake, "Controversies of US–USSR Cultural Contacts During
      the Cold War: The Perspective of Latvian Refugees," *Journal of Historical Sociology* 21, no.
      1 (2008): 55–81; Simo Mikonnen, "Mass Communications as a Vehicle to Lure Russian
      Émigrés Homeward," *Journal of International and Global Studies* 2, no. 2 (2011): 45–61.
46   Michael E. Latham, *Modernization as Ideology: American Social Science and "Nation Building" in the Kennedy Era* (Chapel Hill: University of North Carolina Press, 2006); See the
      details about the origins of the theory of modernization in the U.S. experts' community
      during the Kennedy administration: Nils Gilman, *Mandarins of the Future: Modernization
      Theory in Cold War America* (Baltimore: Johns Hopkins University Press, 2007). Debates
      about the modernization and colonization are in Patrick Williams, *Colonial Discourse and
      Post-Colonial Theory: A Reader* (New York: Columbia University Press, 2011).

INTRODUCTION

World, which shaped a new cultural diplomacy of Moscow, and was followed by a new round of clashes between Americanization and Soviet globalization.[47] For the Soviets, it was an absolutely new policy as much as Russia did not have independent philanthropic foundations and wide-scoped projects in the field of foreign aid before. In contrast, as mentioned earlier, in the United States, foreign aid and privately sponsored philanthropy with international impact manifested themselves long before the Cold War. During the Cold War, the Rockefeller, Ford, Carnegie and, later, MacArthur foundations made a significant contribution to the modernization of Third World countries. They introduced social sciences in Latin America and Africa, donated to construction projects along with UNESCO and Europeans, and funded vocational training and culture programs.[48] They acted independently but in the most cases coordinated their projects with the U.S. government, which operated in the Third World through the Agency for International Development and the Peace Corps.[49] The U.S. government created its own Marshall Plan for developing countries in terms of a newly adopted Foreign Aid Act and established these agencies in 1961. The development aid implied the conduct of infrastructure projects building factories, schools, hospitals, and, at the same time, of projects in education and culture. The Soviet Union introduced similar programs, but failed to establish a new ministry or agency for foreign development programs. They were financed and implemented by different departments, depending on the projects' content.

The historiography continues its debates about the impact of the Cold War on foreign aid. Some researchers argue that the foreign aid was not politically determined.[50] Other researchers consider the aid policy to Third World countries in terms of interdependence theory and neo-Marxism or in terms of the

---

47   David Engerman, *Staging Growth: Modernization, Development, and the Global Cold War* (Amherst: University of Massachusetts Press, 2003); Jeremiah Wishon, "Soviet Globalization: Indo-Soviet Public Diplomacy and Cold War Cultural Spheres," *Global Studies Journal* 5, no. 2 (2013): 103–14; Odd Arne Westad, *The Global Cold War: Third World Interventions and the Making of Our Times* (Cambridge: Cambridge University Press, 2005).

48   See, for example: Giles Scott-Smith, "Aristotle, US Public Diplomacy, and the Cold War: The Work of Carnes Lord," *Foundations of Science* 13, no. 3/4 (2008): 251–64; Tim Mueller, "The Rockefeller Foundation, the Social Sciences, and the Humanities in the Cold War," *Journal of Cold War Studies* 15, no. 3 (2013): 108–35.

49   Edward Berman, *The Influence of the Carnegie, Ford and Rockefeller Foundations on American Foreign Policy: The Ideology of Philanthropy* (Albany: State University of New York Press, 1983).

50   Michael E. Latham, *The Right Kind of Revolution Modernization, Development, and US Foreign Policy from the Cold War to the Present* (Ithaca: Cornell University Press, 2011); Herbert Feis, *Foreign Aid and Foreign Policy* (New York: Dell Publishing. Co., 1966).

concept of social capital reproduction put forward by critical sociology.[51] For them, the foreign aid programs moved social engineering and reproduction of prospective pro-Soviet or pro-American elite serving the human capital formation for national economics.[52] Some studies continue to argue that the foreign aid and related programs in the field of training specialists, creating universities and schools, and reeducating teachers or journalists must be evaluated in terms of cultural imperialism.[53] But it should not be forgotten that during the Cold War, foreign societies were not passive recipients of the American or Soviet projects of cultural diplomacy and development. The analysis shows that Third World countries welcomed technological innovations from both superpowers, but restrained their ideology. For example, Egypt agreed to Soviet contributions for the construction of the Aswan Dam, but was very cautious about the work of Soviet specialists in universities. Therefore, the concept of cultural imperialism should be considered through the open and hidden resistance of local recipients. The current scholarship calls for a unbiased analysis of the development policies introduced by the United States and the Soviet Union. The latest studies on Soviet aid argue that the Soviet Union did not exercise any ideological pressure and helped more than it indoctrinated.[54] The same evaluations are heard about the Peace Corps and from American then-youth who traveled to different countries following the initiative of John Kennedy, and contributed more to the development rather than to the dissemination of the political culture.[55]

Exploring cultural diplomacy as a part of foreign aid, military training, and education should not be forgotten. These programs were introduced long before the Cold War. Moscow introduced the program training the military

---

51   Pierre Bourdieu, "Cultural Reproduction and Social Reproduction," in *Power and Ideology in Education*, ed. Jerome Karabel and A. H. Halsey (New York: Oxford University Press, 1977), 487–510; Patrick Williams, *Colonial Discourse and Post-Colonial Theory: A Reader* (New York: Columbia University Press, 2011); Natalia Tsvetkova, "International Education during the Cold War: Soviet Social Transformation and American Social Reproduction," *Comparative Education Review* 52, no. 2 (2008): 199–217.

52   Viswanathan Selvaratnam, "Higher Education Co-Operation and Western Dominance of Knowledge Creation and Flows in Third World Countries," *Higher Education* 17, no. 1 (1988): 41–68; Brad Simpson, "Indonesia's Accelerated Modernization and the Global Discourse of Development, 1960–1975," *Diplomatic History* 33, no. 3 (2009): 467–86.

53   Martin Carnoy, *Education as Cultural Imperialism* (New York: McKay, 1974).

54   Tim Kaiser, et al., "Educational Transfers in Postcolonial Contexts: Preliminary Results from Comparative Research on Workers' Faculties in Vietnam, Cuba, and Mozambique," *European Education* 47, no. 3 (2015): 242–59.

55   Stanley Meisler, *When the World Calls: The Inside Story of the Peace Corps and Its First Fifty Years* (Boston: Beacon Press, 2011).

INTRODUCTION

from Afghanistan in the mid-1920s, and President Franklin Roosevelt brought similar programs to Latin America.[56] Military training can also be attributed to cultural diplomacy, as military officers studied English or Russian, got acquainted with culture, and absorbed the basics of political culture. The programs were part of U.S. military assistance overseas, and, in the Soviet Union, they were controlled by the Ministry of Defense. The Cold War expanded the practice of military education and sometimes they replaced traditional cultural diplomacy programs such as happened in the countries of the Middle East, whose elite was suspicious of both the U.S. and Soviet culture and education. Military advisors in Washington and Moscow were forced to expand programs of military training, technology, and weapons transfers, reducing programs in the fields of culture and education in exchange for temporal political loyalty of the local elite.[57]

The third period of the Cultural Cold War can be associated with the period of Détente in U.S.-Russia relations, with the interactions between the countries of Western and Eastern Europe during the 1970s, and extending into the 1980s, when the Soviet empire and its cultural diplomacy began to fade out. The political relaxation between the United States and the Soviet Union in the beginning of 1970s and the establishment of economic and cultural contacts between the West and the East in Europe cemented a new political climate that led to the signing of the famous Helsinki Accords in 1975. A variety of cultural agreements provided a new channel for Americans coming to Eastern European countries, and Ronald Reagan's new policy offensive in the fields of education, information, and culture contributed to the final shaking off of Soviet ideology within the Eastern Bloc.[58] It would seem that such a fascinating shift in the Cultural Cold War must have brought plenty of new research. However, the cultural diplomacy of the 1970s and early 1980s were not studied well. In the historiography, the ideological confrontation between the United States

---

56   Russian State Military Archive. Records group 37837. Red Army Personnel Department.

57   Minutes of the Meeting of the Special Group. May 28, 1964. In *Foreign Relations of the United States. Vol. XXI, 1964–68* (Washington, D.C.: GPO, 2000), 517–20.

58   Peter Schweizer, *Reagan's War: The Epic Story of His Forty-Year Struggle and Final Triumph over Communism* (New York: : Doubleday Publishing, 2003); Daniel Thomas, "Human Rights Ideas, the Demise of Communism, and the End of the Cold War," *Journal of Cold War Studies* 7, no. 2 (2005): 110–41; David Foglesong, *The American mission and the "Evil Empire:" The Crusade for a "Free Russia" since 1881* (New York: Cambridge University Press, 2007); Nicholas Cull, *The Decline and Fall of the United States Information Agency: American public diplomacy, 1989–2001* (New York: Palgrave Macmillan, 2012); Yale Richmond, "Cultural Exchange and the Cold War: How the West Won," *American Communist History* 9, no. 1 (2010): 61–75.

20   INTRODUCTION

and the Soviet Union has mostly been transformed into a broader question on the interaction between West and East. The construction of images through radio propaganda and films, the perception of the "Other," and the issues of historical memory have been discussed in the historiography. The Détente and the Helsinki Accords are said to have built bridges between the West and the East, while Europe is considered a single transnational unit including its "capitalist" and the "socialist" parts. Constructivist approaches dominate in studies, and the discourse on the realism, confrontation, cultural imperialism, and propaganda are seen to be part of the studies about the first periods of the Cold War.[59]

However, scholarship knows a few details of how cultural diplomacy has contributed to, for example, Jimmy Carter's human rights concept introduced to foreign policy. The president is known to have applied cultural diplomacy to disseminate his ideas, including the introduction of a new, international educational program, the Initiatives to Protect Human Rights, and of the expansion of aid programs for journalists and teachers.[60] Despite the intrigue of Ronald Reagan's policy in Eastern Europe in the 1980s, studies about it and, i.e., its main driver as the National Endowment for Democracy, created by the president to support and develop open democratic institutions in communist countries, are also exceptional.[61] It is known that Ronald Reagan returned the containment strategy to foreign policy, introducing tougher instruments for undermining the Soviet Union, such as sanctions against pipeline policy of the Soviets in Europe, the development of the dissident movement, and a crusade for free, democratic institutions.[62] This list of economic, political, and educational instruments was aimed at cracking down on Soviet control in Eastern Europe. The well-known directive NSDD–54, "United States Policy Toward Eastern Europe" of 1982 designated "the primary long-term U.S. goal in Eastern Europe is to loosen the Soviet hold on the region and thereby facilitate its eventual reintegration into the European community of nations.[63] The President's

---

59   Simo Mikkonen and Pia Koivunen, *Beyond the Divide: Entangled Histories of Cold War Europe* (New York: Berghahn Books, 2015); Annette Vowinckel, Marcus Payk, and Thomas Lindenberger, *Cold War Cultures: Perspectives on Eastern and Western Societies* (New York: Berghahn Books, 2012).

60   *Department of State Bulletin* (May 23, 1977), 505, 507.

61   A good start for exploring the topic: Kate Geoghegan, "A Policy in Tension: The National Endowment for Democracy and the U.S. Response to the Collapse of the Soviet Union," *Diplomatic History* 42, no. 5 (2018): 772–801.

62   National Security Council, "National Security Decision Directive 32. "U.S. National Security Strategy, May 20, 1982," accessed July 08, 2020, www.fas.org.

63   National Security Council, "National Security Decision Directive 54. U.S. Policy Toward Eastern Europe, September 2, 1982," accessed July 08, 2020, https://fas.org/irp/offdocs/nsdd/nsdd-54.pdf.

INTRODUCTION 21

project, known as *The Democracy*, entirely revised U.S. cultural diplomacy. Cultural diplomacy was no longer considered a vehicle to spread ideas, as it was previously regarded, but as a way to build a democratic infrastructure, including free press, trade unions, political parties, universities, and various other structures, which would allow the citizens of the countries of the communist alliances to approach a new political future. Finally, the president revived the work of the Voice of America and Radio Free Europe/Liberty, which were in a deplorable situation after a period of Détente. The content of the broadcasting and the target audience were revised. The news highlighted failures in social or economic policy of the Soviet Union, and the life of ethnic minorities and religion in the USSR, disseminated in the Ukrainian, Armenian, Georgian, and Azerbaijani languages.[64] At the Geneva Summit in November 1985, the U.S. president clearly intended to propose "dramatic increases in people-to-people exchanges, programs to share information," etc.[65] The proposals touched the re-education of Soviet primary and secondary school teachers, the introduction of new methods of teaching English and history, and short-term studies of students specializing in the social sciences and arts in American universities, and were supported by Mikhail Gorbachev.[66] These questions provided a bulk of new archival documents but discussed less than the beginnings of the Cultural Cold War.

The important component of cultural diplomacy turned out to be children's and citizens' diplomacy that facilitated a new stage in communication between people of the United States and the Soviet at the micro level.[67] Hundreds of Soviet students and schoolchildren sponsored by private U.S. funds visited America. Moreover, the Reagan administration managed to expand the exchange programs for students from Eastern Europe enormously. The number

---

64 Laurien Alexandre, *The Voice of America: From Détente to the Reagan Doctrine* (Norwood, NJ: Ablex Publishing Corporation, 1988).

65 National Security Council, "National Security Directive 194. Meeting with Soviet Leader in Geneva: Themes and Perceptions. October 25, 1985," accessed July 08, 2020, https://fas .org/irp/offdocs/nsdd/index.html.

66 Public Papers of President Ronald W. Reagan, "Statement by Principal Deputy Press Secretary Speaks on Soviet–United States Cultural and Educational Exchanges. August 05, 1986," accessed July 08, 2020, http://www.reagan.utex.edu/archives; National Security Council, "National Security Decision Directive 223. Implementing the Geneva Exchanges Initiative, April 02, 1986," accessed July 08, 2020, https://fas.org/irp/offdocs/nsdd/nsdd -223.htm; John Kelley, "U.S. Public Diplomacy: A Cold War Success Story?" *The Hague Journal of Diplomacy* 2 (2007): 53–79.

67 Margaret Peacock, "Samantha Smith in the Land of the Bolsheviks: Peace and the Politics of Childhood in the Late Cold War," *Diplomatic History* 43, no. 3 (2019): 418–44; David Foglesong, "When the Russians Really Were Coming: Citizen Diplomacy and the End of Cold War Enmity in America." *Cold War History* 20, no. 4 (November 2020): 419–40.

of Eastern European students in the USA tripled in 1985 and quadrupled in 1989 compared with the number of students from 1975–1976.[68] The U.S. Information Agency was able to extend the Fulbright, Humphrey, and International Visitor programs to Soviet youth and representatives of non-governmental organizations newly established in the Soviet Union during the perestroika period. By the end of the 1980s, the Reagan administration succeeded in mobilizing the active part of the population and returning confidence in the United States as a power that would support the countries of Eastern Europe in the event of a new wave of protests.

In June 1989, during his visits to Poland and Hungary, then-President George H.W. Bush, announced that the new democracies would be supported through financial assistance and a variety of public diplomacy programs. In November 1989, the famous act known as the Support Eastern Europe Democracies or SEED was signed by George H.W. Bush, and in 1990 the former allies of the anti-Hitler coalition signed an agreement on the unification of Germany and, finally, in 1991, the USSR collapsed. These dates are considered be the end of the Cold War, and starting from this point, U.S. cultural diplomacy, more often called public diplomacy, was aimed at building democratic societies in Eastern Europe and Eurasia.[69] These events can be considered as the logical end of the Cultural Cold War.

Among the items in the toolkit of the Cold War's cultural diplomacy were universities and education projects that played their roles in the ideological confrontation. In the attempt to spread liberal democracy and socialism, the transfer of military and economic aid went hand-in-hand with universities. Strengthening the military potential of allies was impossible to imagine without the training of foreign military personnel; the development of the political system in countries abroad (based either on the American or Soviet model) was the main goal of government training programs; economic and social development implied the education of cadres in the field of economics, politics, pedagogy, the social sphere, etc.; and the bridging between the countries of the communist or Western alliances was possible through apolitical exchange programs.

---

68 National Council of Educational Statistics, "Digest of Educational Statistics 1997," accessed April 14, 2001, http://nces.ed.gov/pubs/digest97/d97t410.html.

69 National Security Council, "National Security Directive 23. US Relations with Soviet Union. September 22, 1989," accessed July 08, 2020, https://fas.org/irp/offdocs/nsd/nsd23.pdf; U.S. Congress, "Support Eastern Europe Democracies. Public Law 179, 101 Congress. November 28, 1989," accessed July 08, 2020, https://www.congress.gov/101/statute/STATUTE-103/STATUTE-103-Pg1298.pdf.

INTRODUCTION

Local universities that fostered prospective elite were involved in the U.S. and Soviet foreign aid projects and cultural diplomacy to make an impact on professors and students. Education, science, and a university were evaluated for effective transfer of values and turned out to be among the most important parts of the cultural diplomacy efforts, along with music diplomacy, tourism, and exchanges.[70] Universities embraced various layers of foreign societies, including students, professors, scientists, politicians, and leaders of non-governmental organizations. The expansion of a number of educational institutions in foreign countries in the frameworks of development aid laid a foundation for both superpowers to contribute to forming new social capital with a certain set of values.[71] Projects in education, and in construction in particular, stemming from either the United States or the Soviet Union were welcomed by recipients as long as the projects supported modernization, development, and progress. The United States and the Soviet Union used this unique opportunity and tried to accompany their development projects by imposing their rival values through disciplines, propaganda, etc. However, the recipient countries did not always accept Americanization and Sovietization and effectively restrained their political intentions.[72]

Both superpowers elaborated a special governmental education policy aimed at implementing such crucial reforms in universities under the guise of a revision of academic programs, curricula, student body, administrative structures, etc. in order to make them more suitable for instilling the American or Soviet political culture into a foreign society. At universities outside the United States and the Soviet Union, both Washington and Moscow orchestrated transformations patterned on U.S. or Soviet models by establishing new departments in the fields of liberal arts and Marxist philosophy, by revising study plans for academic degrees, by introducing new disciplines in political science, Marxism, American studies, Soviet history, English, and Russian, and by re-educating teaching staff. All of these actions contributed both to modernization as well as the Americanization/Sovietization of national education in different countries. Despite differences in their political systems and culture, however, both superpowers pursued similar political ends by influencing

---

70   For example: Chay Brooks. "The Ignorance of the Uneducated": Ford Foundation Philanthropy, the IIE, and the Geographies of Educational Exchange," *Journal of Historical Geography* 48 (2015): 36–46.

71   Tom Griffiths and Euridice Charon Cardona, "Education for Social Transformation: Soviet University Education Aid in the Cold War Capitalist World-System," *European Education* 47, no. 3 (2015): 226–41.

72   Stefan Paulus, "The Americanisation of Europe after 1945? The case of the German Universities," *European Review of History* 9, no. 2, (2002): 241–53.

the orientation of local academic elite toward either the U.S. or Soviet value system and model of education.

Both governments, however, recognized that the key to success for their reforms depended on the favorable position of the people associated with the university, and the professoriate in particular. For both Americans and Soviets, it became evident that the revision of universities could be successfully implemented by establishing a loyal and friendly professoriate that, moving forward, would implement and maintain the educational plans of either the Americans or Soviets. All transformations touched on the personal life and academic careers of professors who worked at universities. They were left with the choice of reacting either positively or negatively to the reforms and this, in turn, would enormously influence the lasting effects of the transformations.

Making their revision at universities in foreign countries, the United States and the Soviet Union faced unanticipated criticism on the part of professors. Among other actions, they resisted the introduction of new departments for the disciplines of, for instance, political science or Marxism, did not want to have to shift their traditional research interests to American studies or the history of proletarian revolutions, and refused to deliver classes in English or to study Russian. That segment of university faculty, often called the *conservative professoriate* by both superpowers, became the "gravediggers" of numerous reforms sought by Washington or Moscow, and, more importantly, the saviors of some local traditions of university education. Professors at universities in Europe, Latin America, Africa, and Asia turned out to be the primary defenders of national university traditions.

Although universities have always played a political role in national development and in the system of international relations, historians have neglected to analyze the professoriate as a group with the power to have impact on high politics. By comparison, students have often attracted the attention of researchers, due to not only the variety of historical documents available that refer to student activism but also the publicity of students' actions. The reactions of professors to reforms prompted by the superpowers at local universities, however, rarely penetrated beyond their institutions in their day and have been rarely discussed since, largely because the corpus of sources referring to the interactions of local professors and U.S. or Soviet experts has remained limited.

The scholarship has not yet proposed a comprehensive analysis of these hidden relationships between the USA/USSR and key universities in different regions. Neither has the behavior of the professoriate as a staunch defender of national and sometimes archaic traditions of their university education that restrained both modernization and/or Americanization/Sovietization

INTRODUCTION   25

received serious scholarly attention. The experience of the universities that endured the cultural influence from either Washington or Moscow and the consequences of the superpowers' transformations and impositions should be incorporated into the studies of Cold War cultural diplomacy and beyond. However, the scholarship has gained some general insights in understanding of a place and role of universities in the Cultural Cold War.

2   Universities in Cultural Cold War Studies

Studies on the Cultural Cold War and the cultural diplomacy have gained attention of scholars from such diverse disciplines as political science, international relations, cultural studies, sociology, development studies, and finally, history and its various areas, such as the history of specific countries and regions and the history of specific historical periods. Each field of knowledge brings its own methodology, including various theories and research methods, as well as its own context for exploring the cultural diplomacy and education policy. Consequently, the scholarship has obtained some fascinating interdisciplinary studies that examine universities through approaches, theories, and sources from various disciplines but that have not heretofore been applied to the studies.

Political science and the study of international relations, for example, consider universities as an instrument of national security, foreign policy, and official diplomacy, and draw on theoretical backgrounds such as realism, liberalism, or constructivism to the study of the history of education. From this perspective, universities and education become a cohesive part of cultural diplomacy, public diplomacy, and soft power, making the academic world part of a political game on both local and international levels for followers of these disciplines. While adherents of realism and liberalism agree that education as a part of public diplomacy or soft power helps promote foreign policy aims, followers of constructivism argue that education and academic exchanges in particular shape a system of values and norms that, in turn, shape identity, perceptions, and social, political, and economic constructs of the world.[73]

---

73   Giles Scott-Smith, "Mapping the Undefinable: Some Thoughts on the Relevance of Exchange Programmes Within International Relations Theory," *Annals of the Academy of Political and Social Science* 616 (2008): 173–95; Carol Atkinson, "Does Soft Power Matter? A Comparative Analysis of Student Exchange Programs 1980–2006," *Foreign Policy Analysis* 6, no. 1 (2010): 1–22.

Critical sociology and comparative and international education view education as a driver for the reproduction of the elite as well as ideologies and culture. Education reinforces the existing dominant culture and social structure on both local and international levels and contributes to ideological incorporation. Researchers have shown, for example, how educational policy can be effective by selecting and reproducing social strata in different countries.[74]

Development studies explore education systems in terms of their modernization or transformation in unique historical periods. The decolonization of the 1940s–1960s and the West's subsequent assistance in education in the developing world is the most popular subject. Recently, specialists in the field have studied Soviet aid programs in education.[75]

History embraces diverse forms of research and views on universities from the position of its cultural, family, and social functions. Historians typically launch their research from the standpoint of definite historical periods, using them to place the research subject in various historical contexts and assess what is happening with education under the effects of these contexts.

Historians who study a period of European and global history named the *Cultural Cold War* are taking a close look at the history of universities. Researchers are renewing studies on educational exchanges, exploring the Americanization of European universities, and opening a new study on how and why some new educational institutions were established in the context of the Cold War. New archival documents have unleashed a flow of these new findings, but at the same time, theoretical comprehension of the events relative to the history of education in the Cold War period has been scarce. Most research has centered around such anthropological concepts as Americanization/Sovietization, cultural imperialism or cultural transfer, and others. Moreover, all these studies rarely take into account the response of the local community to the actions of outside powers. New studies focusing on response theory reveal some limitations of educational reforms undertaken by, for example, the United States or the Soviet Union in client countries, due to sabotage and the aspirations of the local academic corporation to retain national educational traditions and keep them out the hands of the superpowers.[76]

---

[74] Natalia Tsvetkova, "International Education during the Cold War: Soviet Social Transformation and American Social Reproduction," *Comparative Education Review* 52, no. 2 (2008): 199–217.

[75] Tom Griffiths and Euridice Charon Cardona, "Education for Social Transformation: Soviet University Education Aid in the Cold War Capitalist World-System," *European Education* 47, no. 3 (2015): 226–41.

[76] Giles Scott-Smith, "Networks of Influence: U.S. Exchange Programs and Western Europe in the 1980s," in *The United States and Public Diplomacy: New Directions in Cultural and*

INTRODUCTION   27

Examining the policy of both United States and the USSR towards universities during the Cold War, most scholars have emphasized transformations that occurred inside national American or Soviet universities, neglecting the influence of both superpowers on higher educational institutions located in Europe, Latin America, Africa, and Asia. Despite a wide corpus of archival sources, this part of the cultural diplomacy of both superpowers has been overlooked by scholars of the Cultural Cold War and of international relations. However, a few previous investigations touched the policies of both American and Soviet governments at universities abroad to some extent, and they must be noted here. The discussions about American and Soviet policies of transformations at foreign universities can be found among numerous books and papers on academic exchanges, foreign assistance, cultural diplomacy, university-to-university partnership, and so on.

American and Soviet policies toward universities all over the world are mentioned in numerous scholarly writings about academic exchanges. The exchanges between professors and students sponsored and managed by the governments are reviewed from different perspectives. Some scholars interpret the state-to-state educational exchanges as a political instrument for shaping a favorable elite, other researchers look at them as a driver for university cooperation, while a third group views the exchanges between academics as a source of new knowledge and technologies.[77]

Examples of American/Soviet reforms at universities in different countries have been touched on, with the American policy definitely having been studied more profoundly than the Soviet one. The most illustrative example is a study on the Americanization of universities in Great Britain. The authors conclude the Americanization has been rolled back, and national traditions have survived.[78] This group of studies also includes the establishment of American

---

      International History, ed. Kenneth Osgood and Brian Etheridge (Leiden: Martinus Nijhoff Publishers, 2010), 345–70; Giles Scott-Smith, "The Free Europe University in Strasbourg," *Journal of Cold War Studies* 16, no. 2 (2014): 77–107; Natalia Tsvetkova, *Failure of American and Soviet Cultural Imperialism in German Universities, 1945–1990* (Leiden, Netherlands: Brill, 2013); Esra Pakin, "American Studies in Turkey during the Cultural Cold War," *Turkish Studies* 9, no. 3 (2008): 507–24.

77   Yale Richmond, "Cultural Exchange and the Cold War: How the West Won," *American Communist History* 9, no. 1 (2010): 61–75 Zachary Abuza, "The Politics of Educational Diplomacy in Vietnam," *Asian Survey* 36, no. 6 (1996): 618–31; Chay Brooks, "The Ignorance of the Uneducated": Ford Foundation Philanthropy, the IIE, and the Geographies of Educational Exchange," *Journal of Historical Geography* 48 (2015): 36–46.

78   Jean Bocock, et al., "American Influence on British Higher Education: Science, Technology, and the Problem of University Expansion, 1945–1963," *Minerva: A Review of Science, Learning & Policy* 41, no. 4 (2003): 327–46.

colleges and universities abroad. The American University of Beirut, American colleges in Turkey, the American University in Cairo, etc. are still the most common themes in the scholarship.[79] In addition, the scholarship is enriched by the investigations into the establishment of institutions such as the Free University in Berlin. A recent shift in the scholarship has been the study of the Cultural Cold War in relation to the existence of dissident universities in the countries of Eastern Europe such as the Flying University in Poland and some universities-in-exile.[80]

The Soviet transformations of foreign universities are studied by researchers whose research interests include development aid or foreign assistance during the Cold War. As a rule, the researchers analyze only special cases of Soviet educational policy abroad. The most illustrative example is the research about Soviet preparatory departments established at the universities of client countries during the Cold War. The authors have found that these departments trained several generations of doctors, engineers, and builders, and Soviet educational policy contributed more to the development of economics than to implanting Soviet ideology.[81]

Two views on the university diplomacy of the superpowers in the Third World dominate recent scholarship. The first view argues that the development aid proposed by the American/Soviet governments for universities abroad instilled the locals with solely American or Soviet ideologies. The second approach is more balanced and argues that both powers contributed to the development of national economies through their university policies. However, all similar studies neglect the reception and attitudes of the local academic corps toward the imposed transformations and revisions that occurred at national universities under the control of either American or Soviet experts.

The introduction of new disciplines such as American studies/Soviet history, English/Russian languages, Political Science/Marxism, etc. are also subjects of study by scholars. The most popular theme is the introduction of American Studies to European universities. The previous scholarship did not look closely at the same situation that surrounded the introduction of this discipline at universities in Africa, Latin America, and Asia that fell under American influence. The available documents witness vague reactions on the part of university academics.

---

79   Betty Anderson, *American University of Beirut: Arab Nationalism and Liberal Education* (Austin: University of Texas Press, 2012).

80   Hanna Bucznska-Garewicz, "The Flying University in Poland, 1978–1980," *Harvard Educational Review* 55, no. 1 (1985): 20–33.

81   Tim Kaiser, et al., "Educational Transfers in Postcolonial Contexts: Preliminary Results from Comparative Research on Workers' Faculties in Vietnam, Cuba, and Mozambique," *European Education* 47, no. 3 (2015): 242–59.

INTRODUCTION

The final group of studies that can be referred to deal with the theme of American/Soviet policies towards students. Active and open positions of the students towards both American and Soviet actions at universities have survived in documents, accounts, memoirs, and so on, that have opened wide prospects for historians to reconstruct a policy of both the American and the Soviet sides toward the students. Hence, the relationship between the students, on the one hand, and the American or Soviet political powers, on the other, have been well documented by historians.[82]

To sum up this overview of American and Soviet policy towards universities around the world during the Cold War, several important issues can be identified. Numerous questions relative to the behavior of the professoriate and everyday communication between American/Soviet visiting experts and the local university community, are still beyond the sight of current studies of the Cultural Cold War. Recent studies about Cold War universities need to be chronologically expanded. Most of the studies have centered on the era of the 1950s and 1960s, neglecting the period of the 1970s and 1980s when the transformations proposed by both powers were actually rolled back at local universities. The scholars have focused their studies on the Cultural Cold War in Europe, neglecting other regions and crucial countries where the United States struggled with Moscow for dominant influence at universities. Vietnam, Ethiopia, Afghanistan, Egypt, and Guatemala are a few of the countries where both Washington and Moscow encountered negative reactions of professors against prospective reforms at their local universities. A comparative historical analysis of the university policy of both superpowers can demonstrate the extent to which the rival states sought to exploit opportunities to implant their ideologies in oversees societies and the degree of success they achieved at revising local traditions at universities.

This book, thus, offers a narrative on education policy as a part of the cultural diplomacy in terms of the history of international relations and, more narrowly, in terms of the Cold War based on archival records.

3 Archival Documents: What They Reveal

This book was written with reference to archival documents retrieved from the records of the U.S. Agency for International Development, the U.S. Department of State, and others located in the National Archives in College Park, Maryland; and from the Arkansas University Library in Fayetteville; from the records of

---

82   Oscar Garcia, "A Complicated Mission: The United States and Spanish Students during the Johnson Administration," *Cold War History* 13, no. 3 (2013): 311–29.

the Soviet Ministry for Higher Education maintained by the State Archive of the Russian Federation in Moscow; and from the records of the Communist Party Apparatus located in the Russian State Archive of Modern History and the Russian State Archive of Social–Political History, also in Moscow.

Both American and Russian archives keep reports, letters, memories, and other formal and informal documents prepared by American and Soviet advisors, who worked in universities around the world. These advisors were professors from American or Soviet universities and are called *advisors, consultants,* or *visiting professors* in the documents. They were principal reformers of foreign universities and, at the same time, had front-line encounters with the disagreements, restraints, and resistance to their activities from both professors and students in foreign countries. Advisors recorded their impressions, successes, and failures relative to transformations in the variety of documents sent to either Washington or Moscow. However, these documents have still not been fully examined by historians. All the archival materials cited in the book are, therefore, introduced for the first time to the historical science.

The history of U.S. and Soviet policies at universities overseas is largely determined by analyzing official government documents that contribute to immensely popular theses about the success of those education policies and their effectiveness in both achieving political goals and promoting rival values. Without a doubt, top-level government documents, including the reports of the Soviet Ministry of Foreign Affairs and the U.S. Department of State, along with the strategies, plans, and letters of various government departments, can give a historian some important details for understanding the nature of rival U.S. and Soviet policies at universities abroad. However, other types of documents—the reports, letters, memoranda, and notes of U.S. and Soviet advisors and professors sent to transform universities in specific countries—reveal a different level of cultural diplomacy practiced by the superpowers. Those documents showcase micro-level interaction between the U.S. and Soviet advisors, on the one hand, and, on the other, academic communities of teaching staff and students. The advisors often disclose how they, as U.S. or Soviet government representatives, were able or, in many cases, unable to interact with local communities entrenched in different cultures and how they, as vessels of American or Soviet values and models of education, sought to instill those values at universities with starkly different traditions in education, communication, and culture. Those documents more fully capture the absolute disruption of policies of Americanization and Sovietization, as well as of the superpowers' political goals at universities in foreign countries during the Cold War. Such documents therefore allow a historian to apply other methods of research derived from concepts of constructivism, identity theory, and other frameworks.

INTRODUCTION   31

4   Theoretical Discussion: Realism, Constructivism, Americanization/
         Sovietization, Response Concept, or Fear?

This book does not endorse one theory or concept over another for understanding the roles of professors at foreign universities in U.S. and Soviet education policy during the Cold War. On the contrary, each case presents an opportunity to discover a variety of possible concepts that may enrich discussions on the topic. Each chapter of the book includes some paragraphs on the specific theories that were applied. However, added to that, some general theoretical insights on the topic will be briefly provided as well. The events depicted in the book require discussing the nature of U.S. and Soviet education policies as part of foreign policy and diplomacy aimed at achieving objectives of national security during the Cold War. For such a macro-level discussion, a look at theories in international relations studies, especially realism, constructivism, fear, cultural imperialism, Americanization, and Sovietization can be illuminating. At the micro-level, by contrast, the education policy implemented by U.S. and Soviet advisors either clashed with or engaged the local academic elite, who responded to the policy in kind. In that light, the discussion can also proceed with respect to response theory. Lastly, the concept of political fear seems applicable for discussing U.S. and Soviet education policies as practiced in specific countries.

The international relations studies consider education as an instrument of foreign policy and draw on theoretical backgrounds such as realism and constructivism in studying the history of education. While followers of realism agree that education as a part of public diplomacy or soft power helps to promote foreign policy aims, followers of constructivism argue that education shapes a system of values and norms and social, political, and economic constructs of the world. The constructivism offers insights in the binary system of perception as constructed in such terms as "we/they," "strangers," or "another" that is widely applied in the study of international relations.[83] So, in our case, the macro policy of both superpowers can be analyzed through the concept of realism as much as both sought to realize political goals, and the micro policy in terms of daily communication between advisors arrived at universities in foreign countries and local professors can be analyzed through the concept of constructivism as much as values of the advisors and their political goals clashed with interests and ideals of local professors.

83   Ted Hopf, "The Promise of Constructivism in International Relations Theory," *International Security*, 23, no. 1 (1998): 171–200.

Concerns, anxiety, and the concept of political fear discussed in the studies on foreign policy decision making might be applicable for the understanding of the U.S. and Soviet policy at the universities. In the studies of foreign policy, the political fear is connected to the concern of actors regarding a geopolitical control, security, and coexistence. The political fear is caused by uncertain intentions of a country towards others that make the country follow a more aggressive or more cooperative policy.[84] Here, the fear of loss the political influence in some client countries in Latin America pushed the United States and the Soviet Union to make their reforms very soft. The superpowers were forced to revise or deny their own projects to appease the professorate. Consequently, the cultural diplomacy, and Americanization/Sovietization turned out to be limited by the political fear.

A more anthropological approach referred to well-known concepts such as Americanization and Sovietization and relative theses about hegemony and cultural imperialism. The most general of those concepts is cultural imperialism, which traditionally refers to the policy of a power that exalts and spreads its culture in a foreign country at the expense of the native culture or cultures.[85] The other conceptual framework often employed in analyzing the cultural Cold War embraces other well-known notions about Americanization and Sovietization. The traditional definition of Americanization denotes the implantation of values or norms of U.S. society in another country.[86] Sovietization, bound to ideas about Soviet cultural imperialism, implies the implantation of Soviet models in the economic, political, educational, and cultural systems of another country.[87]

The concept of Americanization has aroused heated discussions among commentators and historians since the early 1900s, when British journalist William Stead published his famous book, *The Americanization of the World,* and argued that Americanization would be inevitable and a global process. Since that time, the literature has elaborated a general definition of the term: "Americanization" is a process of cultural and socio-cultural adaptation to the

---

84   Renato Cruz de Castro, "Explaining the Duterte Administration's Appeasement Policy on China: The Power of Fear," *Asian Affairs: An American Review* 45, no. 3/4 (2018): 165–91.

85   Jessica Gienow-Hecht, "Shame on US? Academics, Cultural Transfer, and the Cold War—A Critical Review," *Diplomatic History* 24, no. 3 (2000): 465–95.

86   Richard Kuisel, *Seducing the French: The Dilemma of Americanisation* (Berkeley: University of California Press, 1993).

87   Simo Mikkonen and Pia Koivunen, *Beyond the Divide: Entangled Histories of Cold War Europe* New York: Berghahn Books, 2015); Artemy M. Kalinovsky, *Laboratory of Socialist Development: Cold War Politics and Decolonization in Soviet Tajikistan* (Ithaca: Cornell University Press, 2018).

INTRODUCTION   33

standards set by the society of the United States. Since the end of the Cold War, the concept has become very popular among researchers who discuss these questions based on Globalization/Localization, Americanization/Anti-Americanism, and Cultural Transfer/Cultural Imperialism theses.

However, scholars are still debating questions such as how to investigate and measure the complex process of Americanization. This question relates to the methodological problems of the research: how to separate Americanization process from modernization or globalization, how to avoid the stereotypical image of Americanization substituted often by the discourse of cultural imperialism of the United States, how to measure the empirical facts in order to provide strong evidence that Americanization has or has not happened, and how to evaluate the degree of Americanization in different countries. Two groups of discussions centered on the Americanization concept can be identified. One group of researchers defends the thesis that some countries, mostly in Europe, have been entirely Americanized, while another group argues that Americanization of Europe has been only partial and thus that it is necessary to raise the question of the Europeanisation of American ideas, culture, and values.[88] For example, France or Germany were not entirely Americanized because the processes of Frenchification and Germanization of American values took place.[89]

While Americanization is mostly treated as a process of a more-or-less two-way, mutual cultural exchange, Sovietization is evaluated unconditionally by most scholars as Soviet expansion, imperialism, and hegemony in subjugated nations. Researchers draw a sign of equality between such phenomena as Soviet cultural imperialism and Sovietization. The general definition of the Sovietization concept implies a transformation of politics, culture, and education based on the Soviet model. Previous research on the question mainly concerns Soviet transformations in the countries of Eastern Europe and the former Soviet Union. Researchers argue that Sovietization was the implantation of

---

88   Richard Pells, *Not Like US: How Europeans Have Loved, Hated, and Transformed American Culture since World War II* (New York: Basic Books, 1997); Reinhold Wagnleitner, *Coca-Colonization and the Cold War: Cultural Transmission of United States in Austria after the Second World War* (Chapel Hill: University of North Carolina Press, 1994); Giles Scott-Smith, *Politics of Apolitical Culture: Congress for Cultural Freedom, and the CIA and Post-War American Hegemony* (London: Routledge, 2002); Rolf Lunden, *Networks of Americanization: Aspects of American Influence in Sweden* (Uppsala, Stockholm: Almqvist & Wiksell International, 1992).

89   Anne Paulet, "To Change the World: The Use of American Indian Education in the Philippines," *History of Education Quarterly* 47, N no. 2 (2007):173–202; Jessica Gienow-Hecht, *Transmission Impossible: American Journalism as Cultural Diplomacy in Post-War Germany, 1945–55* (Baton Rouge: Louisiana State University Press, 1990); Richard Kuisel, *Seducing the French: The Dilemma of Americanization* (Berkeley, 1993).

34 INTRODUCTION

communist ideas in a political culture, educational institutions, and in life as a whole. For example, the imposition of Soviet ideas implied enhancing the power of communists in societal life and, more narrowly in terms of education, the indoctrination of students through reading communist literature and studying Russian. The researchers studying the Soviet reforms in higher education in Eastern European countries in terms of Sovietization, reiterate these theses. The higher educational systems in Czechoslovakia, East Germany, and Poland appeared to be faithful reproductions of the Soviet model. However, the outcomes of Sovietization were different in these three countries and had their limits. Sovietization was successful in East Germany and it nearly failed in Poland.[90]

These concepts can be justified to explain the informational, cultural, and educational policies imposed by both United States and Soviet Union during the Cold War. However, in most cases, the concepts do not take into consideration the behavior, attitudes, and resistance of local university people to U.S. and Soviet transformations at foreign universities. The book shows that advisors of both countries were able to change university structures, introduce new management, and develop a new infrastructure for students and teaching staff. However, they could not transform traditional ways of teaching, force the professoriate to teach new courses, or compel students to study new subjects. The professors and students were not passive recipients of such policies but resisted the values imposed by the superpowers. Neither superpower could subdue the localism and conservatism of universities that preserved some traditional, local features specific to local universities. So, another concept might be appropriate for to explain this.

A response theory shifts the focus from the policies of superpowers to reactions and attitudes on the receiving end of such policies and perhaps better approximates the realities of the Cultural Cold War. Theses on the resistance of local societies to values from other countries have been sounded in reception studies that have introduced the theory of resistance or response theory.[91] Reception studies have shifted from the theme of cultural expansion to the theme of local reactions to it and seem to challenge the concepts of cultural imperialism, Americanization, and Sovietization, which envision a one-way street of hegemonic domination, and suggest instead a project of intentions

---

90   John Connelly, *Captive University: The Sovietization of East German, Czech, and Polish Higher Education, 1945–1956* (Chapel Hill: The University of North Carolina Press, 2000), 3.

91   Bassam Tibi, "Culture and Knowledge: The Politics of Islamization of Knowledge as a Postmodern Project? The Fundamentalist Claim to De-Westernization," *Theory, Culture & Society*, no. 12 (1995): 1–24.

INTRODUCTION   35

without guaranteed outcomes.[92] However, such investigations remain rare, and professors, the chief agents of resistance to both U.S. and Soviet transformations have been neglected in studies on the Cultural Cold War. The response, reception, and resistance studies can perhaps best explain the essence of cultural or educational policies during the Cold War. Such studies illuminate the consequences of the policies of the superpowers as reflected in behavior on the receiving end of such policies. Further investigations have also found that both American and Soviet cultural influences in other countries were successfully restrained and limited by local elites during the Cold War.[93] As demonstrated in this book, investigating how professors at universities interacted with advisors from the United States or the Soviet Union can illuminate reasons for the success and failure of the education policies of the superpowers that can, by extension, stir new discussions about how local communities engage in enacting and enforcing policies that restrain or deny the transfer of culture, education, and values by foreign states.

In terms of theoretical and methodological implications, the book lies at the crossroads of cultural diplomacy, public diplomacy, development aid, cultural studies, education, international relations, and foreign policy. Moreover, the questions discussed in the book can make use of concepts such as cultural imperialism, Americanization/Sovietization/response theory based on the anthropological approaches developed in history and cultural studies. The macro- and micro-level analysis is very appropriate for evaluating the different layers of U.S. and Soviet policies. The first layer was the official policy proposed by the superpowers, while the second represents the local level of the receiving institutions and their national educational programs.[94]

Hence, the book offers a new perspective in the study of the Cultural Cold War by examining the ideological contests that took place over higher education. Comparative historical analyses that make use of new archival documents that open a window on everyday communications between American/Soviet visiting experts and the local teaching staff and students, and the attitudes and behavior of local university people, can open up a deeper understanding

---

92 Barbara Reeves-Ellington, "Vision of Mount Holyoke in the Ottoman Balkans: American Cultural Transfer, Bulgarian Nation-Building and Women's Educational Reform, 1858–1870," *Gender & History* 16, no. 1 (2004): 146–71.

93 Natalia Tsvetkova, *Failure of American and Soviet Cultural Imperialism in German Universities, 1945–1990* (Leiden: Brill, 2013).

94 Natalia Tsvetkova, "Universities During the Cultural Cold War: Mapping the Research Agenda," in *Entangled East and West: Cultural Diplomacy during the Cold War*, ed. Simo Mikkonen, Jari Parkkinen, and Giles Scott-Smith (Berlin: De Gruyter Oldenburg, 2018), 132–56.

of the mechanisms of the Cultural Cold War. It will be worthwhile to further study the reactions of local university officials toward the imposed reforms brought by Washington and Moscow to the universities of different countries. The research of the phenomenon of resistance by the inhabitants of the ivory tower could also explain the motives of the university people to preserve conservative traditions of local education against modernization, which came along with the American and Soviet reforms. It can be concluded that a comprehensive comparative study of both American and Soviet policies at key universities in European, African, Asian, and Latin American countries could alter our understanding of how the Cultural Cold War, as a realm of contesting discourses and narratives on modernization, affected individuals and institutions in the field of education in different ways around the world, triggering different responses in turn.

CHAPTER 1

Europe

Opposition of "Conservative" Professors to U.S. and Soviet Transformations in German Universities

1 Introduction

After the end of World War II, occupied Germany was at the core of the military, economic, and cultural confrontation between the United States and the Soviet Union. Although Germany was known to be divided into four occupied zones in 1945, when three of the zones were consolidated shortly afterward, two new, antagonistic German states were created, wherein the military administrations of the victorious countries were established and reserved the right to implement policy according to their national goals. Throughout the Cold War, universities in the Federal Republic of Germany (West Germany) and in the German Democratic Republic (East Germany) were regarded by the rival superpowers as sources ripe for creating a new pro-U.S. and pro-Soviet elite and thus became primary targets for U.S. and Soviet reforms. Drawing on the models of their education systems at home, the superpowers sought to bring about profound, often uncompromising transformations at the occupied universities. Although seven German universities were located in the initial U.S. zone, once the occupation was lifted in the mid-1950s, 54 universities in Germany would come under U.S. influence in West Germany over the course of the Cold War. The Soviet Union, by comparison, controlled six universities, soon to be seven, in its East German zone.[1]

The course of German universities during the Cold War was determined by the ideological rivalry between Soviet socialism and American liberal democracy. The divided Germany turned out to be the epicenter of the political and cultural confrontation between the two rival divergent ideologies. At the time, Germany's economic and technological potential, geopolitical position in Europe, and its possible alliance either with the Western or Eastern blocs could ensure a strategic preponderance for one ideological camp over the other in the confrontation between the Soviet Union and the United States. West and East Germany, respectively, supported by the United States and the Soviet

---

1 Sari Autio-Sarasmo and Katalin Miklóssy, *Reassessing Cold War Europe* (New York: Routledge, 2011).

© NATALIA TSVETKOVA, 2021 | DOI:10.1163/9789004471788_003

Union, became important geostrategic pieces in Europe that could allow one of the opposing sides to win this politico-cultural confrontation.[2]

In terms of the policy of the United States and the Soviet Union at universities during the Cold War, divided Germany is an exceptional case. Unlike the other case countries discussed in subsequent chapters, the occupation of Germany by the triumphant countries, as well as their agreements concerning the nation's denazification, allowed the military administrations of both Washington and Moscow to enact spiteful policies toward German universities and their academic communities, especially in early years of occupation. Upon becoming responsible for transforming the occupied universities, military officers did not heed any of the opinions or perspectives of local professors but regarded faculty members as enemies who required thorough denazification, even to the point of exclusion from university life. In a certain light, U.S. and Soviet reforms at German universities resembled purges. As described in the next chapter, although Soviet-occupied Afghanistan would experience similar purges in the 1980s, such policies were mere shadows of the ones first pursued by both superpowers in Germany.

Indeed, Germany was the first country where, for first time in history, two countries attempted to revamp universities in other states according to their national values, political cultures, and models of education. Before Germany's occupation began in 1945, neither world power had ever modified foreign universities as a means to render them pliable in cultural offensives against the other. As a consequence, university policy developed for that purpose did not exist in foreign policy arsenals of the United States or the Soviet Union. Germany's defeat, occupation, and denazification all seemed to justify the profound revision of disciplines, departments, media, faculty, and students at German universities and, in the process, uprooting German traditions of higher education. Facing a vacuum at German universities after eliminating courses, professors, departments, and books, the military officers of the victorious countries had only their own national models of education as guidance to fill the void.

A comparative study of U.S. and Soviet policies in force at German universities refutes the widespread view that soft, liberal Americanization was diametrically opposed to harsh Soviet cultural imperialism. On the contrary, as this chapter illustrates, the difference in American and Soviet values and culture did not affect the rival goals of the superpowers designed for higher education in Germany. Although the content of the curricula and disciplines instilled by U.S. reformers differed from their Soviet counterparts, the approaches and

---

2 Wilfried Loth, "The German Question from Stalin to Khrushchev: The Meaning of New Documents," *Cold War History* 10, no. 2 (May 2010): 229–45.

methods of their competing policies did not. Indeed, with the same goal of eradicating national features of German education, both superpowers used hard as well as soft power in order to promote their rival models of education. The theory of realism elaborated by international relations studies and the theory of cultural imperialism can be appropriate to look at the U.S. and Soviet cultural diplomacy in Germany. The realism considers education as an instrument of national security and foreign policy and the cultural imperialism implies the uprooting of local traditions. From this perspective, the education policy of both victorious powers became the cohesive part of their cultural diplomacy, public diplomacy, and soft power, making the German academic world be a part of the political game on both local and international levels.[3]

The effects of their rival reforms did not largely differ either. U.S. and Soviet reforms pursued by establishing new departments and institutions, as well as by introducing new disciplines and themes for research, similarly affected the work and life of professors at German universities. The policy of the superpowers aimed at reconstituting university senates, limiting the autonomy of faculties or mobilizing the ivory tower of the university to meet the needs of society irritated professors, who found themselves under tremendous pressure from the new political rulers. Compared with the professorate in other countries where U.S. or Soviet reformers would arrive, they also found themselves in a unique situation. Thoroughly humiliated by denazification, German professors faced the difficult choice of surrendering to the proposed reforms or, at the expense of the cost of protecting their universities from foreign influence, shielding their universities from the introduction of political science or Marxism, as well as American studies or Russian history, and the publication of books about the U.S. or Soviet political systems. The question of the relationship between professors at German universities during the Cold War, on the one hand, and the United States or the Soviet Union, on the other, is central to understanding the university policy of the superpowers, even if the question continues to be underestimated.[4] Newly declassified documents allowed for

---

3 Jan-Otmar Hesse, "The 'Americanisation' of West German Economics after the Second World War: Success, Failure, or Something Completely Different?" *European Journal of the History of Economic Thought* 19, no. 1 (2012): 67–98; Heinz Ickstadt, "Uniting a Divided Nation: Americanism and Anti-Americanism in Post-War Germany," *European Journal of American Culture* 23, no. 2 (June 2004): 157–70.

4 It must be recognized that both U.S. and Soviet policy toward Germans who occupied positions such as professors, associate professors, assistant professors, and lecturers at German universities after the end of the Second World War has not been analyzed to any great depth in the literature. These Germans, however, had a very large impact on the final results of the transformations proposed by both powers in the 1970s and 1980s. However, the scholarship in

40   CHAPTER 1

an examination of this aspect of both American and Soviet education policy in
Germany during the entire period of the Cold War.

This chapter will consist of two parts. The first part will investigate and compare the specific policies of the United States and the Soviet Union at the German universities that mainly touched professors. The second part will reveal
how the opposition of the professoriate undermined both American reforms in
West Germany and Soviet reforms in East Germany. The chapter will end with
a conclusion about the main successes and failures of the policy conducted by
the United States and the Soviet Union in German universities.

2   U.S. and Soviet Cultural Offensive in Universities of Divided
         Germany: Making a Pliable Professor

After the end of the Second World War and during the period of occupation,
the United States initially controlled universities in Heidelberg, Munich, Erlangen, Frankfurt, Marburg, and Würzburg. After the division of the University of
Berlin in 1948, the US also gained control of part of this university called the
Free University. The history of the universities in Berlin, Heidelberg, Munich,

---

the field of cultural diplomacy has still made no attempt to describe the American and Soviet
education policies in the two German states beyond the occupation period, and more importantly, they have not compared American and Soviet activities in the universities of West
and East Germany for the entire period of the Cold War, 1945–1990. See, the most visible
works on the U.S. or Soviet policy at the German universities: Andrey Nikitin, *The Activity of
the Soviet Military Administration in the Democratization of German Higher Education, 1945–
1949*. PhD diss. (Moscow: Moscow State Historical Archival Institute, 1986); Geoffrey Giles,
"Reeducation at Heidelberg University," *Pädagogik Historica* 33, no. 1 (1996): 201–19; Helen
Liddell, "Education in Occupied Germany: A Field Study," *International Affairs (Royal Institute of International Affairs 1944–)* 24, no. 1 (1948): 30–62; James Tent, *Mission on the Rhine:
Reeducation and Denazification in American–Occupied Germany* (Chicago: University of Chicago Press, 1982); John Connelly, *Captive University: the Sovietization of East German, Czech,
and Polish Higher Education, 1945–195.* (Chapel Hill: The University of North Carolina Press,
2000); Manfred Heinemann, *Hochschuloffiziere und Wiederaufbau des Hochschulwesens in
Deutschland 1945–1949. Die sowjetische Besatzungszone* (Berlin: Akad.–Verlag, 2000); Nikita
Bogatyrev, *Democratization of German Schools after the Liberation of Germany: Materials of
the Ministry of Education in Thüringen, 1945–1949*. PhD diss. (Moscow: Academy of Education
Sciences, 1951); Norman Naimark, *The Russians in Germany: a History of Soviet Zone of Occupation, 1945–1949* (Cambridge, MA: The Belknap Press of Harvard University Press, 1995);
Nikoly Vorobjev, *Higher Education in the Democratic Republic of Germany* (Rostov: University
of Rostov Press, 1972); Wilhelm Geck, "Student Power in West Germany: The Authority of the
Student Body and Student Participation in Decision–Making in the Universities of the Federal Republic of Germany," *The American Journal of Comparative Law* 17, no. 3 (1969): 337–58.

EUROPE 41

Erlangen, Frankfurt, Marburg, and Würzburg stretched back to the late fourteenth century,[5] and their international recognition as centers of science and philosophy had long been established by the community of the professoriate of these universities. These universities were supervised by a special division (Education and Religious Affairs Office) established within the American Military Administration. The initial work of the Education and Religious Affairs Office was supervised by Colonel John Taylor. He had a doctorate in education from the Columbia Teachers College at Columbia University. Every university was under control of an American military officer called a curator. After the official lifting of the occupation in 1952 and through the end of the Cold War, all 54 universities opened in West Germany during the period from the 1950s through the 1980s were targets of American public diplomacy. American diplomats accredited in Bonn, the American diplomatic mission located in West Berlin, and all American consulates established in West Germany supervised the German universities.

During the period of 1945–1955, the Soviet occupation authorities and their Education Division controlled German universities in Berlin, Halle, Leipzig, Greifswald, Jena, and Rostock. The head of the Education Division was Professor Pjotr Zolotukhin, a former rector at Leningrad University and a future rector of the Moscow Pedagogical Institute. During the following years of the Cold War, the Soviet diplomats and the Soviet Houses of Culture, which were located throughout East Germany, oversaw all seven universities that existed in East Germany at the time. The Soviet Military Administration also accommodated a department for education. Unlike their U.S. counterparts, Soviet officers created the German Administration for Education, which was later consolidated within East Germany's Ministry of Education. In time, the interaction of the Soviet and German agencies smoothed the Sovietization and even prompted the "Germanization" of Soviet transformations.

Both superpowers elaborated a special education policy aimed at transforming the German universities in order to make them more suitable for installing American or Soviet political culture in a divided German society. Despite the differences in the political systems and culture of the two superpowers, they pursued similar political goals, maintaining the orientation of Germans toward either the American or Soviet value system. Components of German university life such as organizational structure, statutes, rectors, curriculum, student body, student units, holdings in the university libraries, teaching methods, and the professoriate became the primary targets of both American and Soviet policy.

---

5   The oldest universities were Heidelberg and Würzburg, established in 1386 and 1402 respectively. Other universities were created from the sixteenth through the nineteenth centuries.

2.1 Facing the Old Professors: U.S. and Soviet Perceptions

In planning their reforms, both powers had their own perceptions of the German universities and professoriate. The American government considered the German teaching staff as too elitist, closed, and too intellectually oriented. The Department of State, from its side, indicated that the German professors assigned too much emphasis on philosophy and theoretical scholarship in their concept of a university education, and neglected society's significant problems. German universities, as compared to American universities, seemed to be institutions that were too removed from public life to be able to play, let alone implement, any social role. It was decided to convert the ivory tower into an egalitarian democratic university.[6]

While the American experts considered the content of German academic programs to be far too removed from public life, and too philosophical and aristocratic, the Soviet specialists noted other features of the German academic process that they deemed subject to revision: a lack of control, a lack of detailed study plans (known as a curriculum), and a lack of detailed plans for every course, known as a syllabus. With the absence of a curriculum and syllabus, the Soviets believed that the German system needed to be revised.

The military officers and civilians, hereafter called "advisors" and "consultants," invited from either U.S. or Soviet education initiatives regularly assessed German professors in a negative light. The occupation of Germany, the country's defeated status, and even suspicions of lingering Nazi ideology stoked the antagonistic attitudes of U.S. and Soviet advisors toward professors in divided Germany. At the same time, the advisors were not involved in developing or modernizing universities in Germany as would be the case in Asia, Africa, and Latin America from the 1960s to the 1980s, largely because the concept of foreign aid did not exist in the education policies implemented by either superpower in Germany. For that reason, German professors were viewed not as a target audience to be helped, improved, or developed, but as the bearers of Nazi ideology, conservatism, and conformism.

For both powers, a German professor was viewed as a conservative or reactionary force who was old and resistant to change.[7] The staff of the Education

---

6   Higher Education Branch. Some Ideas Concerning the Reforms of the Universities [1946], box 128, records group 260, Records of US Occupation Headquarters. World War II. Office of Military Government of the United States (hereafter OMGUS), Berlin. Education and Cultural Relations Branch, 1945–49, National Archives Records Administration (hereafter NARA).

7   Higher Institutions. Annual Report. OMGUS Land Wuerttemberg–Baden [sic] (SEP), 19 August 1946, box 913, records group 260, Records of US Occupation Headquarters. World War II. Office of OMGUS Württemberg–Baden. Records of Education and Cultural Relations Division, 1945–1949, NARA; Reports on the Implementation of the Plans by the Educational

EUROPE   43

Division at the American Military Administration called this segment of the
professoriate the *Old Professors* and described them as a conservative force.
When they described university professors, experts at the University Education Branch noted the following conservative characteristics:

> They are generally quite old and quite tradition-minded. The profes-
> soriate is overweighed with persons devoted to humanistic studies
> and not very sensitive to modern problems. They realize little how far
> back the German higher institutions [sic] have slipped and know little
> about higher education in America. The older professors are in general
> those most resistant to change, most wedded to the old curricula, most
> attached to traditional methods of teaching, least cognizant of training
> students for effective citizenship, least aware of the social responsibilities
> of higher education, and least democratic in general.[8]

Another document states:

> German universities are now composed largely of men and women of
> advanced age who [sic] by the very nature of things lack the initiative
> and energy to rebuild the universities and adapt them more closely to the
> needs of present day life [sic] in Germany.[9]

Their close work and personal contacts with German professors convinced
American advisors that a change in basic attitudes could not realistically be
expected in the near future. While formally proclaiming their acquiescence
to the American reforms in the curriculum, in actuality the professoriate
neglected to offer lectures in political science and American studies. The
American experts were therefore compelled to develop these new disciplines
outside of the traditional German faculties by establishing independent
institutes.

  Division at the Sowjetische Militäradministration in Deutschland (hereafter SMAD), 1947,
  folder 3, entry 55, records group P–7317, The Files of the Soviet Military Administration in
  Germany, State Archive of the Russian Federation (hereafter GARF), p. 95.
8 Letter from E& RA, Sep. 2, 1948 [sic], box 917A, records group 260, NARA.
9 Report from George F. Zook, Chairman U.S. Education Mission to Germany to Lieutenant
  General Lucius D. Clay, Deputy Military Governor. Office of Military Government for
  Germany, September 20, 1946, box 702, records group 260, Records of US Occupation. High
  Commissioner for Germany (hereafter HICOG). Office of OMGUS, Hessen. Education and
  Cultural Relations Division, 1947–48, NARA.

The documentary sources for Soviet policy towards these German members of the faculty are more extensive than those for American policy in this area. To the extent that Soviet experts, educationalists, military officers, and diplomats who stayed on in Germany sent numerous and detailed reports to Moscow concerning the behavior of German professors, and their interrelations with the Soviet authorities and German communists, these archives hold a generous number of documents dealing with the relationship between the Soviet Military Administration and German professors and are quite sufficient for our purposes.

The Soviet Military Administration also evaluated the German professoriate as "old and reactionary professors of advanced age whose typical mood appears to be aloof, suspicious, expectant, and skeptical with respect to everything new as well as negative in relation to the occupation authority."[10] Similar to U.S. experts, Soviet ones reported that some reactionary professors, typically exceeding 70 years of age, impeded the implementation of reforms. However, unlike the Americans, who did not want to establish confidence in such a deep-seated part of the university community but instead wanted to establish separate institutions in order to avoid contact with conservative professors, the Soviet specialists tried to win over that part of the academic community. In fact, older professors received huge financial grants and grocery stipends from the Soviets; their salaries were increased tenfold, and their quotas for food rations and firewood were raised as well.[11] By the mid-1950s, Soviet diplomats confirmed that their efforts had cultivated a certain loyalty, even friendly relationships, with the older professoriate. For Moscow, one motive behind those efforts was to gain the formal consent of the conservative part of German universities as a means to facilitate the introduction of new disciplines, especially Soviet history and Russian literary studies.[12]

The Soviet officers believed that understanding the three pillars of the life and academic activity of the professoriate, that is, their methods of teaching, philosophical views, and political position, was the key to their policy of creating new and pliable professors and thus to the final success of Soviet reforms. Establishing contacts with the professoriate and winning over their minds were considered the primary ways of carrying out reforms without bloodshed.

---

10   Report on Political Attitudes of Intelligentsia [in Germany], 1946, file 273, entry 1, records group P–7133, The Main Office of the Soviet Military Administration in Germany, Sachsen–Anhalt, GARF, p. 305.

11   Reports on the Examination of the Activities of German Higher Educational Institutions, of their Democratization, and of the Establishment of the Socialist Unity Party in German Universities, 1949, file 12, entry 54, records group P–7317, GARF, p. 60.

12   Reports on the Results of the Inspection of German Universities, 1949, file 11, entry 54, records group P–7317, GARF, p. 86–87.

In their initial communication with this academic corporation, the Soviets embarked on their policy by learning about the German professoriate *per se*. Monitoring the positions, views, and mood of the German university professoriate was the means the Soviets would use to understand them and to establish friendly and cooperative relations with them. The Soviet interpretation of the professors' philosophical positions, values, and thoughts about the communist regime therefore constituted a very important part of Soviet policy.

In contrast to the Americans, who considered the opinions, views, and mood of the professoriate as not that paramount, the Soviet reformers based their initial reforms upon private conversations with the German intelligentsia which were aimed at persuasion. All professors who delivered lectures in the departments of philosophy, theology, classics, and other departments of the arts received an order from the Soviet authorities to complete and return a detailed questionnaire and, moreover, to write a report entitled "My worldview." The questionnaire was elaborated on by those Soviet military officers who had specialized in philosophy before the Second World War. By encouraging the professoriate to prepare this report, the Soviet officers were trying to clarify what was the philosophical credo and political thinking of every professor in the zone. However, most of the professors were opposed to this and the results of the "poll" of those professors who agreed to fill in the questionnaire demonstrated to the Soviets that almost all the professors stood for a position known as idealism. This was the term used to designate any philosophical currents considered as un-Marxist thought by Soviet officers.[13] The Soviets were dissatisfied with the results because to shift professors away from the stance of idealism to that of Marxism was considered be more difficult than shifting them from National Socialism to communism.

Along with this came the monitoring of attitudes towards the new political regime among university professors. The results of this assessment were also deplorable as far as the Soviets were concerned. Strongly suspicious attitudes on the part of the German intelligentsia towards the Soviet regime became a sad fact of life for the Soviets:

> For professors, it is difficult to free themselves from the well-known prejudices with respect to the cultural and political values of Russia. Even leftists share visceral prejudices against Russians, particularly Russian soldiers.[14]

---

13   Reports on the Implementation of the Plans by the Educational Division at the SMAD, 1947, file 3, records group P–7317, GARF, p. 121.

14   Report on Political Attitudes of Intelligentsia [in Germany], 1946, file 273, records group P–7133, p. 305.

46   CHAPTER 1

This suspicious and negative attitude towards the Soviet regime would remain the main feature of the political position of German university faculty, as noted by Soviet diplomats and educators who lived and worked in East Germany during the entire period of the Cold War.

Undoubtedly, those descriptions of professors make reference to the behavior of German academic circles, which, facing pressure, harassment, and dismissals owing to the policy of occupying authorities in U.S. and Soviet zones and, later, in West and East Germany, sought to restrain either American or Soviet reforms.

2.2   *Purging Rectors*

The universities of divided Germany under U.S. control each accommodated a curator, the U.S. Education Officer, sent by the U.S. Military Administration to assess the institutions for Americanization. The officer was tasked with exposing students' and faculty members' sympathetic connections with the fallen Nazi regime, replacing rectors if they refused to cooperate with the new authorities. More importantly, however, rectors were responsible for urging each university's senate to adopt a new charter with new articles about the introduction of egalitarian universities, and, most controversially, the reduction of the power of professors.[15]

For the most part, German universities were unenthusiastic about the proposals of U.S. authorities during the occupation. Only the University of Heidelberg, where renowned philosopher Karl Jaspers had a position, immediately accepted all of the proposals. Indeed, Jaspers became an active promoter of U.S. ideas and conducted the purge of the faculty that led to the dismissal of several esteemed physicians, biologists, and even the rector.[16] Bavarian universities suffered persecution more than the other universities because of their strong resistance to American reforms and because of the conservatism of their rectors. The staff of the U.S. administration encountered a tough rebuff from the Senate and professors who did not want to revise the charter in terms of the American proposals. Consequently, most members of the university faculty in Munich and Erlangen were fired by the curator.[17] By the mid-1950s, the

---

15   Military Government Regulation. Reopening of Universities and Institutions of Higher Learning. 25 October 1945, box 128, records group 260, NARA.

16   Reopening of Theological Faculty. Heidelberg University. Headquarters Seventh Army, 4 October 1945, box 917A, records group 260, NARA.

17   Political Report (University of Munich). American Consulate General. Munich. November 20, 1946, reel 7, records group 59, General Records of the Department of State (hereafter, records group 59), Confidential Central Files. Germany. Internal and Foreign Affairs 1945–1969, microfilm, NARA.

U.S. authorities managed to insert new articles in the charters, but professors were able to retain their power in terms of revisions on disciplines, study plans, and educational programs.

Disloyal rectors were replaced, however. This happened with the famous physician Karl Bauer, a specialist in oncology and rector of the University of Heidelberg. He was the first postwar rector and, together with his friend Karl Jaspers, prepared for the reopening of the university. However, the American authorities were alerted to the negative position that Karl Bauer had taken concerning denazification and to his resistance to purging university professors. Bauer actually kept many professors and students who were former members of the Nazi party. Besides these sins, the rector was for some reason disliked by the famous American reformer Edward Hartshorne, a specialist on German education from Harvard University, and by an officer of the Counter Intelligence Corps, Daniel Penham, a German-Jewish émigré. It was found that the rector had been able to hide certain information about his life during the Nazi regime. This information concerned his scholarly works on racial hygiene. As a result, the Americans began a persecution of the rector in the hope that Bauer would resign his position. However, the rector began his own campaign against these American experts, declaring publicly that there were no scientists without close associations with the Nazi Party during the period of the Third Reich. American documents show that on November 15, 1946, Rector Bauer was removed. His place was occupied by another professor who also lost his position soon after. A case similar to the Bauer one occurred at the University of Munich. The American authorities appointed the philosopher and dean of the philosophy faculty, Albert Rehm, as the new rector. The professor had not been an active supporter of the Nazi party, which influenced his selection from among other figures. However, it later became clear that the rector did not feel any sympathy towards the United States either, since he was deeply conservative. He publicly questioned whether the German university system could really learn anything from the American educational system. Consequently, the American authorities stated that the rector was frustrating the American democratization process, and they ordered the Bavarian Educational Ministry to remove Rehm from his post and replace him with another professor who was, in turn, also replaced thereafter.

Similar trends unfolded at the universities in the Soviet part of Germany, where rectors and deans were replaced by individuals in favor of Soviet reforms.[18] This policy was articulated at the end of March 1948, and by the end

---

18   Reports on the Control over the Activities of German Higher Educational Institutions, 1948, file 6, entry 55, records group P–7317, GARF, p. 143.

of October 1948 the rectors of Jena, Halle, Greifswald, and Leipzig Universities were replaced through official elections by the university senates. This marks a very important difference from the American policy towards rectors. Although the American Military Administration conducted a softer policy towards them, the US authorities themselves nominated and replaced the rectors during the initial years of occupation. The Soviets successfully implemented this replacement policy through the university senates. Their success was determined by the fact that some influential professors (such as Valter Markov,[19] Eduard Winter,[20] and many other scholars and professors) in every university actually supported Soviet policy, and some of the apolitical professors were convinced by the Soviets to elect a predefined kind of rector.

The most difficult situation emerged at the University of Jena where the rector, Fredrich Hund, one of the most famous specialists in quantum theory,[21] adhered to a firm standpoint against Soviet reforms. Due to his position, the new statute was not accepted, new students from lower social groups were not enrolled, and new courses were not introduced. One of the Soviet officers, the chief of the Education Division of the Soviet Military Administration in Thüringen, Nikita Bogatyrev, who later defended a dissertation about Soviet reforms in Thüringen, decided to replace Hund without coming to any agreement with the Soviet central agencies in Berlin. He suddenly burst in on a meeting of the senate of University of Jena, which shocked the senior professoriate, and declared that the senate had to replace the rector and, if not, then the senate would be dissolved. The reasons for the replacement, as N. Bogatyrev stated, were "mistakes" purposely made by Hund when enrolling new students. Finally, the senate agreed under duress and the rector was replaced by a new one, the communist Otto Schwarz.[22] However, the professors of the University of Jena sent a letter to the central office of the Soviet Military Administration

---

19   Walter Markov (1909–1993) was a historian and a member of the SED. He taught at Leipzig and Halle Universities after the end of the Second World War. He was expelled from the SED because of his support for the Titoist movement. Markov was famous for Slavic studies and for his studies on the French revolution.

20   Eduard Winter (1896–1982) was a historian and professor at Halle University. From 1948–1951 he was rector of Halle University and in 1951 became director of the Eastern European History Institute at Humboldt University.

21   Friedrich Hund (1896–1997) was a physician and a professor of theoretical physics. He was rector of Jena University in 1948. After his replacement by the Soviet authorities, he became a professor at Frankfurt University in the American Zone in 1951. He was very famous for his contributions to quantum physics.

22   Otto Schwarz (1900–1983) was a botanist. He had emigrated to Turkey during the Nazi regime. After the war he became a member of the SED and a professor at Jena University. From 1948–1951 and from 1958–1962, he was rector of Jena University.

EUROPE

in Berlin concerning the attack by this Soviet officer, and N. Bogatyrev was disciplined and sent back to Moscow. Otto Schwarz kept his position, but Hund was compelled to flee to the Western zone. Later, the Soviets realized the loss of this famous physicist and presented Hund with the National Prize of East Germany for his outstanding findings in quantum physics.[23] Hund's case and Bauer's case, which occurred in the American zone, were often discussed in documents, articles, and recollections that bear witness to the serious challenges to American and Soviet cultural diplomacy.

2.3 *Purging Professors*

However, professors who were denazified endured harsh treatment, including dismissal with the possibility of reinstatement after a period of several years. Denazification was severe in the U.S. zone, where officials sought to dismiss all professors affiliated with the Nazi regime, all of whom were thought to jeopardize classes and educational programs at the universities. The Soviet authorities, in contrast, did not conduct such strict forms of denazification, for they believed that German professors could rid themselves of Nazism without being exiled from their universities. In U.S.-controlled universities, the selection of professors for dismissal tasked the U.S. curators with establishing special commissions comprised of faculty to identify colleagues known to collaborate with Nazis. Such commissions made the environment at universities particularly hostile. Some rectors even asked the U.S. Military Administration to cease the humiliating project of denazification on the basis that finding professors who had not been affiliated with Hitler's party would be impossible.[24] The petitions were not heard. Up to 50 percent of professors were dismissed from all the universities, and the most massive layoffs happened at the universities in Bavaria, where up to 70 percent of faculty left universities. According to documents, some American and European scientists occupied vacated seats.[25]

An American Education Officer, special agents, and professors who cooperated with the Occupation Administration were responsible for purging the universities of Nazis. For submission to the American Education Officer, a special committee at the university formulated plans covering the nominations of those lecturers whom they considered academically and politically

---

23 Manfred Heinemann, "Interview mit Pjotr I. Nikitin," in *Hochschuloffiziere und Wiederaufbau des Hochschulwesens in Deutschland 1945–1949. Die sowjetische Besatzungszone,* ed. Manfred Heinemann (Berlin: Akad.–Verlag), 75–146.

24 Letter. Der Rektor Universität Heidelberg to Military Government Office at Heidelberg University. June 30, 1947, box 917A, records group 260, NARA.

25 Political Report (Dismissals at University of Erlangen). Letter from American Consulate General Munich to Department of State. February 7, 1947, reel 7, records group 59, NARA.

acceptable, along with a list of the university personnel who had already been excluded or should be excluded for political reasons. Hence, those German professors who participated in committees such as these contributed to the American program of denazification. Their activity, however, created a platform for conflict and tense situations among the professors in the universities themselves. The first purge began in 1945. Initially, the Americans supposed that denazification could be carried out through recommendations made by these committees as well as through investigations based on the *Frageboren*, a questionnaire filled out by the university people, along with additional investigations made by secret and anonymous agents of the Counter Intelligence Corps, a special intelligence agency for hunting down members of the Nazi Party. Archival records mention that there was no time to conduct personal interviews or to do any thorough investigations. All the initial *Fragebogen* were quickly examined by these special agents, and those professors who fell into the automatic arrest category as having been active members of the Nazi Party since 1933, were interned; all other people initially remained in the universities. As a result, after the reopening of the universities, classes began with many professors who had been involved with the Nazis and who believed in National Socialism.

In 1946, a new investigation or purge began, because the agents had received information that there were still professors who continued to give lectures from the standpoint of nationalism and racism. In one of the reports, an American agent indicated that

> a tremendous mistake was made in opening the University of Heidelberg in 1945 without consideration for the fact that University of Heidelberg, as well as all of the German Universities had been, over a period of twelve years, Nazified to the core. It will require at least another six months of careful, methodical investigation before it can be said that the elements of potential threat to the security of the American Occupation have been removed.[26]

Another reason for this second purge was determined by resistance on the part of the administration of the universities to dismissing these professors. At the University of Würzburg, the military officers learned that many lecturers still remained in the university, contrary to the instructions for denazification

---

26   Screening of Heidelberg University. Report of Progress. 307th Counter Intelligence Corps Detachment Headquarters Seventh United States Army. Daniel Penham, 23 February 1946, box 917A, records group 260, NARA.

EUROPE   51

previously issued by the Education Branch of the American Military Administration. An officer of the University Education Branch pointed out this viola-
tion to a Vice Rector and advised him to dismiss those professors without any
further delay. The Vice Rector suddenly opposed this order and was therefore
himself replaced by the American Military Administration "because of his failure to carry out denazification directives."[27] Rectors of German universities
appealed to the American authorities requesting that a stop be made to this
denazification "which was inimical to the best interest of the universities."[28]
Professors who personally sent letters to the American authorities complained
in them about the uncertainty of their futures but were not heard.

The Würzburg, Erlangen, and Munich universities were considered the most
reactionary universities by the Military Administration. The notion of "reactionary universities" implied their nationalistic and anti-American positions.
These universities were the last to be reopened because they were the first to
completely give themselves over to the National Socialists during the rise of
Hitler. Hence, screening was conducted there several times. The philosophy
and law faculties of these universities were the hardest hit by denazification of
any other department. The percentage of dismissals was the highest, with half
of the standing faculty discharged.[29] The University of Erlangen suffered the
most: out of the total teaching staff then employed, 70 percent were dismissed.

On the contrary, other German states such as Baden-Württemberg, and in
particular the University of Heidelberg located there, became the first to "have
felt the might of the American denazification on its back."[30] This oldest of the
universities, and the one with a strong international reputation, was opened in
September 1945, after a purge of 184 professors out of 376.[31] However, the dismissal of almost half of the teaching staff compelled the rector to complain to
the American authorities about the state of affairs in the university in order to
impede denazification. Addressing his letter to the American administration,
he wrote:

---

27   Reopening of Würzburg University. Letter from Business Manager, Würzburg University
      to Office of Education and Religion Military Government Würzburg, 19 October, 1945, box
      57, records group 260, Records of US Occupation Headquarters. World War II. Office of
      OMGUS, Bavaria. Office of Education and Cultural Relations Division, 1945–49, NARA.
28   Letter. Der Rektor der Universität Heidelberg to Military Government. Report, January 28,
      1946, box 917A, records group 260, NARA.
29   Denazification of Würzberg University. Civil Administration Division. APO–319.1,
      OMGUS, 7 December 1946, box 134, records group 260, NARA; Political Report (Dismissals
      at University of Erlangen). Letter, February 7, 1947, reel 7, records group 59, NARA.
30   Higher Institutions. Annual Report, box 913, records group 260, NARA.
31   Ibid.

By denazification the staff has been reduced to about half its size. The remaining half consists, to almost two-thirds, of old, partly too old professors [*sic*]. Some of them were undernourished for a considerable time; many are weakened or even sickly. Many bear the signs and the consequences of the mental suffering of the Nazi time [*sic*]. The problem is made especially difficult by the fact that precisely the middle generations are affected with particular severity by denazification. In these very generations the means of bait and pressure of the Party were immense, so that the individual could hardly escape them sometimes [*sic*]. German science has suffered a great number of bleeding [*sic*] one after the other. Denazification may be compared with a great operation performed on an organism already weakened considerably. One will understand that precisely the German anti-Nazis, who, at the same time the preservation of science is nearest to their hearts, plead that the operation should not be more dangerous than the illness for which is performed. Precisely those who hate the real Nazis ardently ask all the more for grace those who merely lost their way and for those who, in our opinion, taken a false step [*sic*].[32]

Rector Bauer made an effort to protect scientists and professors from denazification. However, after the second purge in his university in 1946, the rector, as a former member of the Nazi Party and the administrator "who tried in every way to soften and, if possible, to nullify the denazification," was discharged by the Occupation Administration.[33] There is no doubt that this program of denazification devastated the universities and contributed to the interruption of normal academic activity. It may well be that the American officers understood the level of severity of their program, although no direct record of this in the documents has been found.

However, a new policy that followed the program of purges may be evidence that the American authorities decided to shift away from this policy of purges when they began to allow former Nazis to return to the universities in 1947 and 1948. After the wave of dismissals, a process of reemployment, called reinstatement in the documents, was elaborated and began in 1947 and 1948. This policy was aimed at returning nominal members of the Nazi Party to academic institutions. All the professors who had been dismissed were given

---

32 Ibid.

33 The agents of the CIC even suggested hanging the rector: CIC Investigation of Heidelberg University. Memorandum from to Director Col. Dawson. OMG Wuerttemberg–Baden [*sic*], n/d, box 917A, records group 260, NARA.

the opportunity to submit a petition for reinstatement in the universities. The program of reemployment lasted during the entire period of occupation. On the whole about 30–40 percent of dismissed faculty members had returned to academic life by 1955. It is possible that some of the rejected persons were later able to be reinstated in the universities during the 1960s through the 1970s. In addition, this program was accompanied by supervision of the academic and teaching activities of every reinstated professor, which implied checking the content of courses, as well as a policy of isolating deviant or disagreeable professors, along with the promotion of pliable members of the faculty. Every reemployed professor was put under the control of the American University Officer, who supervised the content of courses delivered by these professors. The procedure for this supervision of courses was as follows: the rectors of German universities submitted to the American University Officer a list of courses together with a brief description of their content and the names of the instructors; only after the officer gave his approval were the proposed courses or lectures announced by the lecturers. The research and scholarly activities of the reinstated community of professors were placed under the control of the American officers. At the end of each semester, the universities reported on these activities to the officer.

The Soviet Union adopted a slightly different attitude toward German professors. For one, denazification was far milder in the Soviet part of Germany; screening the faculty for Nazi sympathies began in May 1945 and ended in September 1946. In a sense, Soviet denazification was superficial compared with the U.S. policy of cleansing that persisted for years. One reason for such leniency was that many professors escaped from the Soviet zone—roughly 60 percent by 1946—which compelled Moscow to make compromises with the faculty: out of more than 2,000 members of the university faculty that comprised the universities in 1945, only about 800 members remained in 1946.[34] The percentage of former members of the Nazi Party who were allowed to remain in the universities by the Soviets varied from 36 percent to 47.9 percent. Pjotr Nikitin, the Chief of the Higher Education Division, mentions in his memoirs that all the professors purged earlier were reinstated in their previous positions between 1946 through 1949.[35] For another, the Soviet authorities believed that reforming the views of professors who did not leave East Germany was realistic. The officers arranged conversations with each professor in order to change his or her mind about Marxism. Another reason is that the

---

34　Natalia Tsvetkova, "Why is Cultural Imperialism Impossible?: The US and USSR Policy in German Universities during the Cold War," *Ab Imperio*, no. 2 (2017): 144–75.

35　Heinemann, "Interview mit Pjotr I. Nikitin," 140.

Soviet Union, similar to the United States, planned to forge a new generation of professors who would be pliable to the superpower's ideology. To attract the professoriate, special propaganda campaigns and discussions about the nature of Marxism were even organized at the universities. Consequently, the institutions agreed to add a few classes on Marxism–Leninism in philosophy courses.[36]

According to the Soviet final evaluation of the implementation of denazification

> 611 representatives of German higher educational institutions were purged under the terms of denazification. However, 650 new teachers for the universities were trained by the Soviet authorities up to and including 1948, so that the average number of lecturers in eighteen institutions varied from 1,303 to 1,380 persons, which was 57% of the number of lecturers in 1940.[37]

2.4 *Pliable Professors?*

Both powers shared the aim of creating the so-called pliable professor. This new type of professor implied that he or she would esteem either the American or Soviet model of higher education, either the American or the Soviet approach to research and teaching and, most importantly, would be ready to deliver lectures for newly introduced courses and contribute to the implementation of all the reforms proposed by either the American or Soviet government.

The intention of the American authorities was therefore to make German professors less aristocratic, to insert a special representative board made up of persons from outside the universities in order to establish a general assembly of teaching staff and reduce the power of the senior professoriate, to introduce student body representation into university administrative bodies, to make academic programs and university curricula more suitable for the real world, to introduce general education and political science in every university, and to introduce "classes" and seminars instead of lectures. A new type of professor implied that such a professor would esteem the American model of higher education and the American approach to research and teaching and, more importantly, would be ready to deliver lectures for newly introduced courses

---

36 Reports on the Implementation of the Orders Given to the Educational Division by the SMAD in Germany, 1949, file 14, entry 54, records group P–7317, GARF, p. 10, 12.

37 Report on the Activities Relative to Democratization of the People Education in the Soviet Zone of Occupation in Germany, 1948, file 37, entry 10, records group P–7317, GARF, p. 197.

EUROPE

in the field of political science, American studies, general education, and other subjects. The government believed that professors engaged in giving lectures in these disciplines would have their value system transformed, which would in turn make them more loyal to the United States. But the most important question raised by the military administration was how to achieve these goals and how to encourage the German professoriate to deliver lectures in these new disciplines.

These intentions were to be carried out by means of sending visiting American professors to Germany, and training young German university instructors in the U.S. Soviet plans for creating a new loyal professor to make a Soviet revision of the curricula referred to the training of young lecturers within the newly established pedagogical departments and new system of postgraduate studies. Beginning their transformations in West German universities, American experts and Dr. J. Taylor believed that the old professoriate would follow the new ideology, methods, theories, and knowledge if they were "surrounded" by professors from the U.S. who would bring about new ways of study and scholarship. The Department of State flooded German universities with American lecturers and scientists. These professors transformed German universities on a day-by-day basis, and it was they who are depicted in documents as the primary mechanism for the implementation of reforms and the establishment of grassroots contacts with the German professoriate.

Washington carefully considered the opinion of these American experts. Having analyzed their recommendations, officials of the State Department authorized the plan to send brilliant American and European specialists on an assignment to establish and give an impetus to developing a partnership with German teaching staff.[38] The first visiting professors filled positions that had remained vacant after denazification. This replacement, called the reconstruction of the teaching staff, is illustrated by the following figures for the University of Erlangen: "there were 112 teachers previous to the second denazification investigation; 29 of those were dismissed; 13 were late reinstated; 55 *new people* were added, and the total number as of today [1948] is 151," that is, the number of the university academic staff was increased after denazification.[39] The "new people," mentioned in this document, came from universities in the United

---

38 Review of 1951 Program. HICOG Frankfurt, September 6, 1950, box 2447, records group 59, Decimal Files; Policy Action. Office of Director. HICOG Frankfurt 2742 n/d, [1952], box 2437, records group 59, International Information Administration. Field Program for Germany 1945–1953, NARA; The Exchange Program. HICOG Frankfurt, January 19, 1951, box 5, records group 59, NARA.

39 U.S. Experts to Germany. Memorandum from Civil Administration, OMGUS, 17 January 1949, box 128, records group 260, NARA.

States and Europe. In 1948, the contingent of 90 visiting professors from the U.S. filled positions in German universities. Later, the Department of State sent 100–175 new faculty each year from American universities to German higher education establishments. The official purpose of this program is fairly well described in the following passage: "visiting professors, as it has long been demonstrated by the large number that the United States has sent to Latin America, can be very helpful. The best contribution of such persons is by their example, and they can be helpful by bringing fresh point of view [*sic*], new subject-matter, new methods, and expert advice. Visiting professors should be brought to facilitate the development of new fields and new methods. A few examples of fields in which American visiting professors might be valuable are: social science, general science, education and educational research, political science, American history, international relations, and cultural history."[40] According to this citation, the Department of State intended to exploit American professors to bring new disciplines and methods of research to Germany.

The visiting professors were mostly responsible for introducing such disciplines as political science and American studies. The introduction of political science was considered an effective way to change the political culture and to promote American-style democracy from the American model in Germany. American experts believed that the introduction of new academic disciplines in the field of political science would lead to a fundamental change in the ideology of German society, which was the value, weight, and the role of abstract and philosophical subjects being decreased, and the weight of practical knowledge becoming a central to component in all formal curricula.[41]

Insofar as a segment of the older professors demonstrated their apathy in this regard, the main target of this policy became the younger generation of German teaching staff. The emphasis on the younger generation was also determined by the belief that

> there is a difference between the attitudes of the older and young university teachers, the latter being much more ready [sic] to recognize the need for changes. The latter need to be assisted by outside resources, or it will inevitably imitate their elders. The prestige, seniority, and fellowship of the older men is bound in time to influence the younger to the same

---

40   Report prepared by Robert D. Howard to Dr. Robert T. Ittner. University Education Section. Education and Cultural Relations Division. OMGUS. Nurnberg [sic], 1 October 1948, box 915, records group 260, NARA.

41   Report on Tour of Duty with University Branch, Bureau of German Affairs. Department of State, January 18, 1950, box 2449, records group 59, Decimal Files, NARA.

points of view. The most hopeful solution is for as many as possible of the younger teachers to be sent abroad in the environments of universities such as ours. This is furthermore the best hope for providing successful programs of Social Sciences and of General Education in the German university curricula.[42]

In 1949, "The General Project for the Interchange [*sic*] of University Instructors"[43] was officially initiated by the Department of State. This program provided for short-term visits by the junior faculty staff of German universities to American universities and to institutions of the American government. The program was clearly designed to achieve aims such as conveying to German university instructors information concerning the results of recent developments in the social sciences, political sciences, and American studies, as well as in American teaching methods in higher educational establishments, along with encouraging German university instructors to investigate and teach a range of disciplines in these three areas back in Germany.

However, no visible reforms were actually started by the universities, a fact which was noted by American university curators in the early 1950s.[44] The senior professoriate sabotaged the introduction of political science by stating that this field of knowledge was a quasi-science because of its multidisciplinary approach. These professors pointed out that the subjects studied in political science were related to the curriculum of both the history and law faculties, and this made the discipline a non-independent one. In addition, during the 1950s and 1960s, the experts of the Department of State observed that the position of political studies at the universities was far from satisfactory as universities regularly had vacant chairs in their political science departments. To resolve this problem, the American government sent American professors to occupy these chairs in order to accelerate the development of the prestige of political science; however, this policy did not change the situation, and political science did not attain a strong position vis-à-vis the traditional German disciplines such as history or philosophy until the early 1960s.

In contrast to this policy, the Soviet Union did not send its specialists to German universities until the 1960s. In the opinion of the Soviet authorities,

---

42 German Specialists to the United States: Higher Education Section, n/d, [1948 or 1949]; Personal Data on German Experts Proposed to Study and Observe in the United States, n/d [1948 or 1949], box 916, records group 260, NARA.

43 General Project for the Interchange of University Instructors Purpose of Project [sic], 27 January 1949, box 916, records group 260, NARA.

44 Citizenship Participation Program, 1951, box 1, records group 59, International Information Administration. Field Program for Germany 1945–1953, NARA.

58   CHAPTER 1

the fastest way to create this new type of professor was to convince the German professoriate to deliver lectures on Marxism at German universities. The Soviets, from their side, attempted to instill the universities of East Germany with the special ideology known as Marxism.

Soviet policy implied the fostering and the reproduction of political allegiance on the part of the professoriate. Moreover, this policy was aimed at making the professoriate not only formally acknowledge Soviet ideology, but believe deeply and sincerely in it and, hence, deliver lectures from a Soviet materialist point of view. Creating a favorable community among the professoriate was at the center of Soviet educational policy in Germany. In documents of the Education Division, it was repeatedly emphasized that "German intelligentsia and professors of universities in particular, were the real force whose use would considerably facilitate the implementation of serious objectives relative to reforms in German society."[45]

While the American Military Administration used a two-pronged approach of sending hundreds of visiting professors to win over the German professoriate by means of grassroot contacts and of fostering new pro-American professors through the training of hundreds of young lecturers in American universities, the Soviets created a new professor through the training of young lecturers within the newly established pedagogical departments and within a new system of postgraduate studies. The Soviets did not send Soviet visiting specialists to German universities and did not train German professors in the Soviet Union in the great numbers the Americans were able to do.

In 1947, a program of two-year postgraduate study of the Soviet type was established in all the higher educational institutions and universities of the zone in order to foster a new favorable faculty. By the end of 1948, out of 200 positions available, only 89 were filled. German professors viewed these new methods for preparing new assistant professors for the universities with suspicion and tried to curtail them. For example, the president of the Academy of Sciences in Saxony, and a well-known scholar of German studies, Professor Frings, wrote to the Soviet authorities that the current method [*of postgraduate studies – N. T.*] hampered progress in the training of new and capable scientists more than it helped and that it damaged the traditional German system for fostering scientists. However, he as well as other professors finally yielded to the Soviets and took positions as supervisors in *Aspirantura* studies. The establishment of pedagogical faculties in the six universities in the zone which, as was discussed previously, had a profound effect on the production

---

45   Report on the State and the Use [*sic*] of German Intelligentsia, 1949, file 107, entry 4, records group P–7317, GARF, p. 118–119.

of new loyal university faculty. Each department annually accepted 150 to 300 students who mainly originated in the lower social groups, thereby demonstrating the egalitarian approach of the Soviets to higher education.[46] Never before had there been pedagogical education at the university level in Germany; previously all school teachers had been taught in special Higher Schools of Education.

The ultimate split of Germany, its capital, and the University of Berlin, and the unilateral U.S. policy to create the Free University in West Berlin in particular, inflamed the Soviet administration's actions at the universities of its zone. Courses on Marxist theory became a tool to exert ideas about socialism and the Soviet model of political system on German universities. The most well-known courses in the field were *Fundamentals of Scientific Socialism, Historical Materialism,* and *Dialectical Materialism.* These courses were designed to have an impact not only on the value system of the students, but also to change the research methodology and perception of branches such as philosophy, history, sociology, pedagogy, literature, and music. In addition, these courses transferred the basic foundation for any research, particularly in the social sciences and historical studies, in such a way that, for example, world history and the history of all civilizations would be studied in terms of the movement of the proletariat. However, until the 1950s, Soviet experts had not even considered the introduction of these disciplines because they believed they could never take root in Germany. Growing opposition in the universities to Soviet policy accelerated the introduction of such courses as *Historical Materialism* and *Dialectical Materialism.*[47]

However, it turned out that the professors did not in fact introduce the new disciplines and did not deliver any of the lectures on the imposed disciplines. The disciplines existed on paper but were never taught as such. This situation was similar to that the U.S. faced when introducing the discipline of political science: the professoriate approved the American decision, but the disciplines were never actually offered. The staff of the Education Division was shocked by such behavior on the part of the professoriate, and Pr. P. Zolotukhin reported to Moscow that

> most disciplines are still being taught from the standpoint of a bourgeois world outlook. The history of philosophy is taught by old professors –

---

46 Reports on the Educational Division at the SMAD, 1946, file 2, entry 55, records group P–7317, GARF, p. 98.

47 Reports on the Results of the Inspection of German Universities, 1949, file 11, records group P–7317, GARF, p. 86–87.

followers of various idealistic schools – such as Professor Leisegang[48] in Jena and Professor Jakobi[49] in Greifswald. Among the faction of reactionary professors, there is a tendency to limit and isolate Marxist disciplines, to not allow the penetration of Marxism into the teaching of any of the scientific disciplines, and into history, biology, the history of law, and philosophy in particular. A number of professors excoriate Marxism. For example, Professor Leisegang sharply opposes dialectical materialism not only in the lectures he delivers, but also in a number of papers published in the Western Zones. Leisegang states that 'Marx's dialectics is a step backwards with respect to Hegel's dialectics' in his article 'Hegel, Marx and Kierkegaard's ideas of dialectical materialism and dialectical theology.' The views of this professor are typical to some extent of the majority of the professors who give lectures in the field of the history of philosophy in German universities.[50]

Marxism aroused denial and division in the university community. As one Soviet advisor noted, "there was a tendency on the part of reactionary professors to restrict and isolate Marxist disciplines, to prevent the introduction of the theory to all disciplines, including history, biology, law, and philosophy."[51]

These fragments demonstrate that the professoriate restricted the introduction of Marxism by stating that its tenets could not constitute a new theoretical foundation for philosophical, historical, and other studies. This opposition on the part of the old professoriate served to limit the expansion of Marxism in German universities. As should be remembered, visiting American scholars who attempted to introduce political science in German universities also mentioned that the old professoriate disregarded the disciplines of political science due to the absence of any scientific and philosophical character.

Consequently, courses in Marxism-Leninism were not taught in German universities until the early 1960s. One of the Soviet professors sent to Germany to deliver courses at the universities reported that "the professors have still not introduced courses on Marxism-Leninism because of the lack of appropriate

---

48   Leisegang, a philosopher and professor at the University of Jena, fled East Berlin in 1948 and became a professor at the Free University.

49   Jakobi, a philosopher and professor at Greifswald University, remained in the Soviet Zone.

50   Reports on the Examination of the Activities of German Higher Educational Institutions, 1949 file 12, records group P–7317, GARF, p. 60.

51   Reports on the Opening of the Long–Term Courses to Prepare a New University Teaching Staff in the Field of Philosophy, Political Economy, and others by the SMAD, 1952–1955, file 90, entry 137, records group 17, Central Committee of the Communist Party, Russian State Archive of Social–Political History (hereafter RGASPI), p. 22.

EUROPE

lecturers, and lectures on Marxism were attended by students much less frequently than lectures on Idealism."[52] Another Soviet professor mentioned that

> the curriculum and disciplines in the field of Marxism-Leninism are wrongly compiled; the course on Marxism-Leninism is just entitled 'Philosophy.' Part of the course on Marxism has been substituted by a theme devoted to dialectics. Jena and Berlin Universities are the most oppositional. The courses on dialectical materialism and historical materialism are not taught due to a lack of experienced lecturers.[53]

2.5 U.S. and Soviet Institutions in German Universities

The reluctance of the professoriate to introduce these new disciplines forced the Education Division at the American Military Administration to propose the idea of establishing new academic departments, institutes, or even universities in which new and American disciplines would be introduced to the universities and the professors would not have any power. Instead of attempting to place political science and other disciplines in the existing traditional curricula, the Department of State decided to create establishments, institutes, departments, and chairs named after the disciplines introduced, in order to form a new curriculum based on the American model.

The Department of State officially declared the following as the main reasons for setting up the new academic departments:

> the older German universities looked too traditional and conservative and the founding of new ones could be more effective for the democratization of the German university system: new institutions and universities might be the theater in which American and other visiting professors could make the most useful contributions, since it will be probable that such new institutions will be less bound to tradition than the older ones and that their teaching staff will be more receptive to changes and improvements. <...> Above all, new higher institutions may provide a special avenue for American policy in Germany to realize in a shorter term of years some of its basic conceptions of the social responsibility and social functions of the universities.[54]

---

52 Reports on the Implementation of the Orders Given to the Educational Division by the SMAD in Germany, 1949, file 14, records group P–7317, GARF, p. 10, 12.

53 Reports on the Opening of the Long–Term Courses, 1952–1955, file 90, records group 17, RGASPI, p. 22.

54 Organizations benefited by Exchange Program, HICOG, A–757–A, Frankfurt, 2/21/51 [sic], box 2451, records group 59, Central Files 1950–54, NARA.

Berlin and Munich became the first cities where new institutes were established in the 1950s. In the early 1960s, the universities of Frankfurt, Marburg, Heidelberg, and Berlin (the Free University) established chairs and institutes of political science. These institutes taught and carried out research in the field. The establishment of new chairs and institutes at German universities also involved the work of visiting American specialists. The Department of State invited American specialists to take positions as the chief of chairs at universities or independent research institutes for a period of three to five years. The main responsibility of these specialists was to develop new chairs and institutes, introduce new fields of research, and establish a new community of German scholars. The life of these research establishments was maintained for an extended period of time by the Americans themselves. For example, at the Free University, only 30 professors out of 350 were German due to the employment of American and European specialists in the mid-1950s.[55] The Institute of Political Science in Munich (*Hochschule für Politische Wissenschaften, München*) would later become a department at the university, and the institute in Berlin will become the Otto Suhr Institute of Political Science at the Free University. However, for a long time, the American advisors complained that there were not enough members of the faculty at political science institutes. German professors had no strong aspiration for the work at the institutes, and the Department of State had to invite some American political scientists to take vacant positions. More than 70 percent of professors at the institutes were Americans.[56]

Furthermore, the Department of State was not satisfied with the minor place in German universities occupied by disciplines about the United States. Similar to political science, the introduction of American Studies was considered an effective way to bring fresh knowledge about American civilization to Germany. English seminars had existed in some universities, and Hamburg University provided a number of courses about the U.S. To improve the situation, in the early 1950s, American experts proposed opening institutes of American Studies at every university despite resistance from the professoriate, thereby putting these disciplines on the examination list, filling the university libraries with literature on the United States, training the junior teaching staff in the U.S. in order to involve them in conducting research in the field, and, finally, developing a center of German-American Studies at one of the universities.

---

55 Letter from Berlin to Department of State, March 4, 1958, box 44, records group 59, Records of the Plans and Development Staff, Evaluation Branch, 1955–1960, NARA.

56 Letter from Assistant Secretary [to] Senator Curtis [about the Otto Suhr Institute], n/d [1958], reel 30, records group 59, NARA.

However, misunderstandings between American and German professors created obstacles to the expansion of the field in German universities: While visiting American professors considered American Studies to be the study of American civilization with a compulsory combination of subjects such as American history, American literature, American education, American government, American architecture and arts, and political and social sciences dealing primarily with the development of institutions in the U.S., the German *Amerikanisten*, however, considered American Studies primarily to be a portion of their English-language studies, English and American literature, and history. This discouraged American specialists who stressed that German professors had not differentiated this discipline concerning the United States from the disciplines of language and literature, and of the courses offered by the various departments, the bulk of them were English-language seminars. The American government suggested consolidating American studies into one integrated university department (a *chair*). The US managed to create 13 chairs at 18 universities by 1962, and American universities opened 31 research centers for American studies in Germany. By 1965, there were 23 chairs for American Studies at these 18 universities, and only three of these chairs were held by Americans.[57]

However, during the mid-1960s and the early 1970s, with the midst of the student movement, the leftists, and anti-American moods in the universities, permanent demonstrations by students and young radical lecturers against American intervention in a divided Vietnam seriously impeded the development of American Studies in West Germany.[58] Anti-American radicals attacked the *Amerika Häuser* and disrupted lectures at the J.F. Kennedy American Institute at the Free University. The work of this Institute was terminated by student radicals at the end of the 1960s and re-established in 1973.[59] Establishing new institutes or a Chair of American Studies at every new university in West Germany presented the American government with a new problem: the low growth of student numbers in these American Studies programs during a period when all other departments at the universities were overcrowded. The shortage of students was especially acute in Marburg, Saarbrücken, and Würzburg, and was determined by the fact that the disciplines involved in the American Studies programs were not recognized as being on an equal footing

---

57   Summary Status Report on American Studies at German Universities, 1965, box 206, records group 59, Office of Educational, Cultural Affairs. Lot 98D 252, NARA.

58   See in details: Martin Klimke, *The Other Alliance. Student Protest in West Germany and the United States in the Global Sixties* (Princeton: Princeton University Press, 2010).

59   Reported Kreibich–Loewenthal [*sic*]. Conflict. Correspondence between US Mission Berlin and the Department of State, March 1975, box 403, records group 59, Culture and Information, 1970–1973, NARA.

with other fields in the humanities. They were not included in the examination list and did not constitute either a major or a minor specialization for which a student could present himself for examination for a degree. At universities where American Studies were offered, a student had to choose English history as a major in order to devote most of his or her time to American subjects.

At the end of the 1970s, the government encouraged American universities to develop private partnerships and affiliations with German universities in order to improve their library holdings, strengthen language departments, develop area studies, establish new departments, and conduct exchanges involving both students and faculty members.[60] However, such projects developed too slowly to have much of a bearing on the German university system. Finally, Ronald Reagan endeavored to improve this situation by proposing that the federal government enhance American-German educational ties by simulating the development of American Studies at German universities and German studies at American universities through the exchange of students and professors. By the end of his administration, Reagan achieved certain successes in terms of numbers of students and researchers coming to the United States to learn more about America culture. American Studies began its recovery in Germany before its reunification.

While the United States created chairs and institutes in the fields of political science and American Studies to avoid opposition, the Soviet Union did not hurry to establish chairs and institutes of Marxism-Leninism at every university. The head of the Education Division, Professor Zolotukhin, considered that the establishment of separate institutes and chairs for Marxism-Leninism at the universities would be very harmful for the promotion of socialist ideas, because it would be perceived by professors and students as clearly coercive. The only institute that was established by the Military Administration was the Institute of Dialectical Materialism at Jena University. This institute subsequently became the center for writing and publishing textbooks on Marxist-Leninist subjects and for doing research in this field. However, the institute did not acquire any influence over university education during the 1950s and the early 1960s.

Contrary to American Studies, doggedly developed by the U.S., Soviet Studies were not purposely promoted by the Soviet government. The branch of science called "Soviet Studies" never existed in the Soviet Union and East Germany, and the Soviet government, as compared to the Americans who introduced "American Studies" into German universities, never made the decision

---

60 The University Affiliation Program, 1978–1979, box 27, records group 59, Records of the U.S. Board of Foreign Scholarships, 1971–1980, NARA.

EUROPE 65

to impose a series of disciplines called, in general terms, "Soviet Studies." The Soviets tried to promote the study of the Russian in Germany. The implantation of the Russian language was considered to be a foundation for further disseminating the Russian literature, history, and pedagogies. However, a special and comprehensive policy of promotion never existed.

German universities had an academic tradition of studying the history and language of the eastern and southern Slavs, the peoples who first settled in the territories of Eastern Europe and Russia. Many German specialists in the field remained in the Eastern zone of occupation and cooperated with the Soviets in initiating the reestablishment of Slavic Studies. In 1951, at Halle University, Edward Winter, its rector, became the first scholar in this field to propose that the occupation authorities create a new Institute of Eastern European History at Berlin University in 1951. This was supported by the occupation authorities. However, the Soviets did not go any further, and they did not impose Slavic Studies everywhere. Only two chairs of Slavic Studies were established—at Leipzig and the Greifswald Universities—and were done so on the initiative of German scholars. In addition, German *Slawisten* in their postwar research tended to emphasize Eastern European countries rather than the Soviet Union.

The introduction of Russian departments was more promising for the Soviets. In 1951, the German regime announced that the study of the Russian language was compulsory for students for two hours per week during their first four years. However, these studies developed very slowly due to a lack of teachers of Russian. This situation improved slightly in the 1960s after new German specialists in Russian were trained in the Soviet Union. However, in the early 1970s, the visiting Soviet professors informed Moscow about the miserable situation in terms of training students in Slavic departments, "contemporary and effective textbooks of Russian are absent and no professor is writing one; students study the language only seven to eight hours per week and extra classes outside the university have never been arranged; students and their professors speak Russian very seldom, and their knowledge is very weak; students do not watch movies in Russian, do not organize parties of Russian culture, and do not prepare a student newspaper in Russian; finally, students are admitted to the Slavic departments without entrance examinations due to the low popularity of the division and the shortage of students."[61]

During the 1970s and the early 1980s, the Soviet government attempted to improve this situation by increasing the number of hours allocated for Russian

---

61   Reports on Cooperation between Pedagogical Institutes of the USSR and the GDR [German Democratic Republic], 1984–85, file 4974, entry 1, records group 9563, The Ministry of Education of the USSR, 1966–1988, GARF, p. 1–60.

in both the humanities and the applied science departments of the universities. The visiting Soviet professors, selected by the government among university staff, introduced new curriculum models that were composed in the Soviet Union. Soviet experts prepared and published new textbooks for German students and developed extra-curricular activities to make German students speak Russian. Between 1976–1979, 100 Soviet teachers arrived annually at seven German universities to improve the situation. However, in 1986, the program aimed at developing Slavic and Russian Studies in the universities of East Germany was terminated due to a lack of financial resources.

Nevertheless, in creating a new professor and in introducing new disciplines, both powers encountered resistance from the old German professoriate that undermined the efficiency of all the structural reforms in German universities proposed by either the United States or the Soviet Union. Despite this pressure, these professors followed German traditions in research and teaching, as well as in their understanding of the role of the university in public life.

3   Opposition of "Conservative Professors" to U.S. and Soviet Reforms

As U.S. and Soviet reforms and purges affected the academic and personal lives of German professors and students, the academic community faced a choice: to accept the reforms imposed by the United States or the Soviet Union and continue in comfortable submission at their universities or to deny the reforms at the risk of their academic careers and future lives. Despite that seeming dichotomy, German professors found a third way that allowed them to maintain their positions at their universities along with the traditions of German university education. Their tactic was to demonstrate tacit agreement with the reforms but at once covertly sabotage them. Without careers at stake, students could act more openly, and although some of them immediately supported the foreign authorities, others plainly resisted occupation and suffered expulsion or even arrest as a consequence.

3.1   *U.S. Advisors and Opposed Professors*

American military officers and visiting professors often informed Washington that the conservative professoriate (the *Old Professors*) segment would never agree to the imposed reforms. These traditional German professors believed that the coming reforms would undermine the elite status of German university education. While formally proclaiming their acquiescence to the American reforms to the curriculum, the professoriate neglected to offer lectures in political science and American studies. This position contributed to the mixed results of the reforms instigated by the U.S. government. In the circumstances

EUROPE

when the reforms were actually carried out, the modification of the universities according to the American model proceeded slowly.

In the 1950s and in the mid-1960s, the Department of State indicated that the conservative nature of German universities did not disappear. The German universities remained traditional and elitist, reserving an exalted status and power for full professors, and admitting only a small number of students. University life and studies were organized around small seminars with close personal association between professors and students, all of whom came from the aristocracy. The experts pointed out that the positions of leadership in the universities had been assumed by the survivors of the pre-Nazi era, and for 20 years they had not comprehended their own obsolescence. This segment of professors was defined as *German conservatism* that maintained obsolete norms of teaching methods and behavior.[62]

In the mid-1960s, U.S. advisors began discussing a new round of reforms to eradicate the conservative nature of German universities, which the U.S. government had attempted to eliminate for the previous two decades. Just as they had twenty years earlier, American diplomats reported to the government that the German university remained traditional and elitist, reserving an exalted status and power for full professors, and admitting only a small number of students. University life and study were organized around small seminars, with close personal association between professors and students, all of whom came from the aristocracy. the conservative structure has broken down in the twentieth century; as the old social coherence of the university was disturbed by an influx of students from the middle class and—to a lesser extent—from lower social groups, and as the numerical growth of the student body rendered impracticable a close professor-student relationship the old professors could no longer lead their students. The diplomats especially pointed out that the leadership in the universities had been assumed by the survivors of the pre-nazi era and for twenty years they had not comprehended their own obsolescence. This conservatism was unacceptable to the students and, hence, they were demonstrating primarily against this.[63]

At the end of the 1960s, universities in West Germany underwent another phase of reforms, largely because the university infrastructure could not accommodate all students seeking to enter German universities. Whereas the country had only 18 universities in 1965, by 1975 another 25 institutions had

---

62   Natalia Tsvetkova, "Making a New and Pliable Professor: American and Soviet Transformations in German Universities, 1945–1990," *Minerva,* no. 52 (2014): 161–185.

63   Education Reform—'On Center Stage, Please.' The Focus is on Higher Education. Report from Amembassy Bonn to Department of State, 3 February [*sic*] 1970, box 392, records group 59, NARA.

opened, and the number of students had reached 300,000—more than in any other European country. According to U.S. documents, the student movement and the popularity of Marxism, due to efforts of Marxification, convinced Washington that a new intervention in the life of German universities was necessary. The U.S. government was particularly concerned with the radicalization of students and had little interest in the behavior of professors, who largely aspired to rid the universities of both Americans and radical students.

At the end of 1960s and into the early 1970s, the U.S. faced more severe opposition from this segment of German conservative professors. They disliked both the radical student movement and the interference of the United States in German university education. In 1969 when Washington encouraged the West German government to introduce a new package of reforms for the German universities in order to answer the demands of moderates and to appease radicals, German professors mobilized their opposition against American inference in the universities. In addition to the numerous provisions, the reforms of 1969 increased the power of students and teaching assistants in the university's policy-making councils and in turn decreased the power of old professors.[64] These proposals were met with disappointment and reluctance by German professors. The Chancellor of Germany, Willy Brandt, proclaimed important notions as the democratization of the decision-making process at all levels, and a sharing of power by three or four groups: professors, middle-level academic staff, students, and in some cases nonacademic employees of the university; replacement of the rector serving a one-year term by a president elected for a term of five to seven years, and the establishment of departments to take the place of the large faculties.[65]

If students had earlier demanded improvements in infrastructure, then in the mid-1960s the student movement had learned ways to oppose U.S. revisions of traditional disciplines as well as to facilitate the introduction of Marxism. In response, the tone of reports from U.S. diplomats in Germany became extremely emotional and alarmed. Above all, the United States was concerned that radical students had gained power in the administrations at German universities and demanded the revision of academic disciplines in favor of Marxism–Leninism.[66] A particular problem arose at the Free University, where

---

64 West Berlin's University Law—Two Months Later. Letter from US Mission Berlin to Department of State, September 15, 1969, box 345, records group 59, Central Files, 1967–1969, NARA.

65 Review of Current Exchange Programs. Report from Amembassy Bonn to Department of State, February 18, 1971, box 392, records group 59, NARA.

66 Student Unrest and Right-Wing Extremists. Memorandum of Conversation. April 2, 1969, box 345, records group 59, NARA.

EUROPE

students controlled the curriculum committee and had revamped courses in political science, sociology, and philosophy. At the Otto Suhr Institute of Political Sciences, students even accomplished the overhaul of all academic disciplines; instead of political science and American Studies, courses on Marxism and the history of socialist countries were introduced.[67] Soon after, radicals in the student body, in a new coalition with young faculty members, achieved a plurality in the university senate. Consequently, the senate replaced a rector with 30-year-old Marxist Rolf Kreibich, who officially announced the expansion of the teaching of Marxist disciplines.[68] The Free University thus became a model for other universities in Germany, and by 1967, according to U.S. diplomats, Marxists had gained influence at universities in Frankfurt, Heidelberg, Marburg, and other German cities. In time, criticizing U.S. involvement in the Vietnam War and advocating the New Left, students would begin hosting anti-U.S. demonstrations and boycotting U.S. institutes and departments, thereby effecting the closure of centers such as the Department of Political Science in Munich and the John F. Kennedy Institute for North American Studies in Berlin until 1973.[69]

To counter the radicals, the United States expanded the power of moderate students and young faculty in the administrations of German universities. Washington encouraged Willy Brandt to enact a law that guaranteed the power of young faculty and students in the administrative bodies at universities as long as the influence of the so-called "pre-war generation" of professors was reduced. The number of participants in the decision-making bodies at universities was therefore expanded, as professors, young faculty, students, and representatives of non-academic organizations became allowed to manage the life of German universities, which limited the power of both radicals and professors. In addition, a new Ministry of Education and Science was established, presidents and departments replaced rectors and faculties as new titles, respectively.[70] According to the documents, the German professoriate was extremely unhappy with the turn of events. In order support reforms

---

67   University Crisis Postponed—Bigger One Brewing. Report from US Mission Berlin to Department of State. December 20, 1972, box 392, records group 59, NARA.

68   Reaction to Free University Election. Letter from Berlin to Department of State. December 3, 1969, box 345, records group 59, NARA.

69   Information on American Studies in German Universities. Joint USIA [United States Information Agency]/State Message to USIA, Washington. December 14, 1967, box 345, records group 59, NARA.

70   Proposed Amendment of the Berlin University Law of 1969: "Reform within the Reform" or a "New Structural Crisis"? [sic]. Report from US Mission Berlin to Department of State. March 28, 1973, box 392, NARA.

against the radicalization, W. Brandt offered additional financial assistance to expand the university infrastructure, and numerous former participants in U.S. exchange programs were mobilized to promote the reforms within the academic community.

An important consequence of the 1969 reform was the resignation of old and traditionally minded professors from universities. Some of them left for research institutes, preferring the quiet life of a scientist than the wild life of a professor at a university; some of them were offered retirement by the rectors; and some of them left for the US. The American experts reported to Washington that

> teaching and research activities at several universities, such as Berlin, Frankfurt, Heidelberg, Hamburg, and others, have been seriously impeded, that an increasing number of scholars have either moved to universities less affected by the unrest or looked for jobs outside the universities, and that to an increasing extent [*sic*] research tasks are being transferred to non-teaching research institutions, such as the various institutes of the Max Planck Society.[71]

The professors at the Free University were the first to leave the university circle. As a protest against the enactment of the reform laws, some professors resigned from the staff of the university. In a letter addressed to the Senate of the Free University, Professor G. Knauer, a scholar with a strong international reputation, explained the main reasons for his resignation:

> I have been a member of the Free University for 20 years, but as a result of the university laws of 1969, it has become a travesty of a university. <...> I am leaving Berlin because the university law has destroyed the basis on which the academic profession can function. In a university invaded by politics, everyone is forced to take sides. The distraction is attributable only to the erroneous and deceptive ideas of "reform" as laid down in the university law. In the long run, this is incompatible with the duties of a university teacher.[72]

---

71 Trouble in Berlin's Universities. Letter from US Mission Berlin to Department of State, February, 28, 1972, box 403, records group 59, NARA.

72 Georg Knauer, "Professor Knauer's Resignation from the Free University of Berlin," *Minerva* 12, no. 4, (1974): 510–514.

Following this development, the conservative segment of West German professors united around the idea of revising and rolling back these reforms. The professors established the two most famous and influential groups of the time, *The Emergency Committee for a Free University* and *The Alliance for Freedom and Science*. They declared that the 1969 University Law had become the root of the current politicization of university affairs and the source of the institutional power of extremist forces. They declared that a revision of that law was urgently needed in order to restore authority over academic matters to faculty members and administrators with experience and the proper qualifications.

These professors were able to begin the counteroffensive and successfully lobbied a rollback policy through German government channels. The government of West Germany reviewed the amendments to the university reform law instituted in 1969. The amendment bill promoted by the professoriate demanded that administrative structure be tightened by reducing the number of elected councils, increasing the power of the senate, and recasting the student tutorial program. The leader of this segment of the professoriate was Richard Löwenthal, an internationally renowned political scientist and the director of the Otto Suhr Institute. The mobilized professoriate was attempting to return to their previous all-powerful position in the universities. The amendment bill promoted by the professoriate in 1973 demanded that the administrative structure be tightened by reducing the number of elected councils and increasing the power of the senate. In March 1974, American diplomats finally informed Washington that the prospects for enactment of this bill had become "favorable for professors and unfavorable for us."[73] The 1975 Framework Act on Higher Education enacted by both federal and state governments was the product of these conservative efforts. Such institutions, and the participation of students in the work of the curriculum committees, senate, and other important administrative bodies, were nullified and everything reverted to the traditional university system.

The professors eventually regained their powerful influence in terms of the essence of education and training, and their freedom to make decisions over academic programs and curriculum despite the desire and intention of the student body. They also once again instilled the idea of the isolation of academic life from politics.

After this victory by the conservative professoriate, cooperation between the U.S. and the Federal Republic of Germany in the area of education seriously

---

73 Proposed Amendment of the Berlin University Law of 1969, March 28, 1973, box 392, records group, 59, NARA.

72 CHAPTER 1

cooled until the end of the Cold War. Beginning in 1976, both governments reduced financial support for bilateral educational contacts. German professors were publicly skeptical about any real need to cooperate with American universities in the social sciences because of the belief that the reality of the academic landscape of two nations (such as the wide difference in qualitative terms between American and German universities, the lack of real equivalencies between the universities of both countries in terms of degrees and credits, and the lack of guarantees that students returning to Germany would be admitted to German universities) was too different to develop any cooperative relationships.[74]

As a result of the cooled relations, by the early 1980s the American government concluded that its policy aimed at transforming German universities had failed. This appraisal occurred during the most depressed period of American-West German bilateral relations, a time when power in Germany was assumed by the "Sixties" generation. These former anti-American radicals, the very ones who had attacked the *Amerika Häuser* and disrupted lectures, had become politicians, successful businessmen, professors, and editors. American diplomats found that the continuously negative German television coverage of the U.S. reflects "the ascendency of '60's-generation Germans to editorial positions as German TV networks. This creates 'an ever increasing gap' between Germany, NATO allies, and the negative American on German TV."[75]

During the 1980s, the positive image of the United States in West Germany began to decline, as well as the positive image of West Germany across the Atlantic. American experts again stated that this poor state of affairs was due to a lack of understanding and knowledge resulting from the quality of teaching about each other in both countries. The professors boycotted the American programs: about 20 German professors participated in the American programs in 1988 as opposed to 80 in 1970.[76] As a result, despite a special military and political relationship between the United States and West Germany, the latter sank to last place in terms of statistics of professors invited by the American government relative to other West European countries.

---

74 Educational and Cultural Exchange: Annual Report for Germany, 1976–1977. Airgram from Amembassy, Bonn, to Department of State. September, 1977, folder 17, Germany, box 317, Special Collections. Bureau of Educational and Cultural Affairs Historical Collection, manuscript Collection 468, University of Arkansas Library.

75 French TV Correspondent Examines German TV Coverage of the U.S. Report from USIA Bonn to USIA Washington, April 7, 1982, box 206, records group 59, Office of Educational, Cultural Affairs. Lot 98D 252, NARA.

76 Department of State. *International Exchange and Training Programs of the U.S. Government. Annual Reports* (Wash., D.C.: Bureau of Educational and Cultural Affairs, United States Information Agency, 1988 and 1989).

3.2   *Soviet Advisors and Opposed Professors*

The Soviets also recognized the fact that most of the old professors were predisposed against Soviet reforms and the ideology of Marxism. In addition, in as much as many of these professors were of advanced age, Soviet experts admitted that "it would be difficult to change the minds and views of this segment of the German professoriate."[77] In contrast to the American authorities, who decided to avoid direct confrontation with this old and conservative segment of the professoriate by establishing new institutes independent of the influence of the old professoriate, the Soviets decided to take up the struggle against this segment of the university teaching staff and make Marxists of them. The professoriate agreed to the imposed reforms, but only a few of them ever delivered lectures in accordance with the Soviet plans. The professors in fact did not introduce the new disciplines and did not deliver any of the lectures on the imposed disciplines. The disciplines existed on paper but were not delivered in fact. This was similar to the situation the U.S. faced when introducing the discipline of political science: the professoriate approved the American decision but the disciplines were never actually offered.

The Soviet Union wanted to enhance the activity of Marxist professors and cleanse the university teaching staff of active reactionary elements. However, the Soviet experts in Germany clearly understood that this proposed policy could not be applied with regard to the old German professoriate whose intention was to revive and maintain liberal and autonomous processes in the higher schools. In order to implement Moscow's order and not to undermine the fragile liaison established with the universities, the Soviet Military Administration elaborated a system of formal consultations on the problems of new curricula, disciplines, textbooks, etc., with the German university faculty, fully recognizing that "the syllabi should not be offered to German universities from above, but that they should be discussed, elaborated and finally approved at meetings held by the university teaching staff."[78] This approach, in the opinion of the Soviet officers, would contribute to winning the confidence of German professors that was necessary.

The other challenge for the Soviet occupation authorities and consequently the political regime of the German Democratic Republic became the so-called "escape of professors to the West," the term used in the Soviet political vocabulary. According to the documents, ideological motives were the primary reason for leaving the Eastern part of Germany. These motives were perfectly stated

---

77   Reports on the Implementation of the Plans by the Educational Division at the SMAD, 1947, file 3, records group P–7317, GARF, p. 95.

78   Materials relative to the Control over the Activities of the German Agencies in the Field of People Education, 1948, file 11, entry 55, records group P–7317, GARF, p. 22.

74 CHAPTER 1

in a letter of resignation from Professor Wanstrat of the University of Jena addressed to his rector. It was entitled "The letter of resignation for ideological reasons," and the professor wrote that

> I must inform you that I have decided to leave the teaching staff <...> The reasons which have forced me to resettle concern the [following] events. The Soviet delegates as well as the German communists emphasized at the pedagogical congress in Leipzig in July 1949 that all lecturers who do not wish or cannot be advocates of the Marxist-Leninist outlook should be "removed" little by little. <...> My serious and objective work with Marxism and Leninism has shown me that this was a speech not about science, but about having a class-coherent outlook. According to my specialty – sociology – I cannot become a supporter of this outlook in a German university because I consider this outlook, on the basis of my scientific conscience, to be wrong.[79]

The opposition against the Marxism-Leninism disciplines and research methodology existed at the German universities. The Soviet advisors noted that

> The distinctive frame of mind of the reactionary professoriate is demonstrated by the statement quoted below from the dean of the philosophy department at University of Halle. The offer of a curator [a Soviet supervising officer at universities] to distribute two vacant positions of heads of chairs among two rival representatives of idealistic and materialistic philosophies was objected to by the dean as follows: "I do not understand what you want with your materialism and Marxism. This, in fact, was a concern [in science] until some- time in the 60s of the last century. It became a relic long ago. Nowadays, Marxism is a superstition or something like a scarecrow for children."[80]

The tradition of delivering lectures according to intentions and desires of professors without any programs stunned the Soviets: "in as much as the syllabi are not regulated, they created a loophole for the reactionary professoriate to build a course of lectures any way they like and to deliver lectures whichever way they prefer."[81]

---

79 Ibid, p. 139.
80 Report on Political Attitudes of Intelligentsia [in Germany], 1946, file 273, records group P–7133, p. 311.
81 Reports on the Inspection of Higher Educational Institutions, n/d, file 27, entry, 10, records group P–7317, GARF, p. 205.

EUROPE

And elsewhere one reads:

> The introduction of Marxist disciplines in higher education schools proceeds extremely slowly and encounters great difficulties. The main difficulty in this regard is the absence of qualified personnel. None of the leading figures of the German Communist Party possesses the theoretical knowledge necessary to give lectures in universities. The compulsory course for all students, 'Contemporary political and social problems,' called upon to play a significant role in the political education of students, was not provided with qualified manuals in sufficient quantity. Moreover, the lectures of professors supporting Marxism are attended by students to a lesser degree than those that state the facts from the position of idealism.[82]

Resistance from the German university faculty and the shortage of staff forced the Soviet authorities to initiate a new program of financial support and a new pension system for the German professoriate. The improvement of the financial position and welfare standards of the university teaching staff became a key step in implementing Soviet policy. From January 1947 onwards, the basic and hourly wages for all categories of teaching staff, along with payments to rectors and deans in particular, increased tenfold, with the income tax being lowered. Special pensions for scientists and national prizes in the field of pedagogy were introduced. All members of the university faculty were provided with extra food and extra firewood during the initial years of the Occupation.

When Marxism was more or less imposed on the universities, covert, hostile attitudes on the part of a substantial segment of the university teaching staff towards socialism and the USSR became the most pressing problem for the Soviet government. The articulation of this hostile attitude was the specific stance of East German university professors during the entire period of the Cold War. Soviet diplomats accredited in Berlin reported to the Soviet Ministry of Foreign Affairs that

> the significant part of intelligentsia, which consists of a number of scientists and university teachers, adheres to hostile attitudes. The majority of teachers adhere to bourgeois views and this negatively affects the social order of East Germany and the socialist transformations implemented in it.[83]

---

82 Reports on the Examination of the Activities of German Higher Educational Institutions, 1949 file 12, records group P–7317, GARF, p. 62–63.

83 The German Democratic Republic: Notes and Letters, 1965, file 102, entry 35, records group 5, Central Committee of Communist Party. Records of the Education and Science

The Soviet diplomats believed that the grounds for this attitude lay in the weak belief in communism of the professoriate. According to Soviet observations, the members of this opposition were the lecturers who articulated various critical comments about Marxism and who were estimated to be *unconvinced lecturers* on the topic and belief in Marxism-Leninism.

Hostile attitudes on the part of a substantial segment of the university teaching staff toward socialism, East Germany, and the USSR became the main discourse of the reports prepared by the visiting Soviet professors from Moscow University for the Soviet government after their trips to East Germany at the end of the 1970s and in the early 1980s. Soviet professors, on the basis of conversations with German professors, noted the following mood of the intellectual elite of East Germany:

> the work among the intelligentsia faces still greater challenges. The old scientific and technical intelligentsia is starting to change its attitude when there are strong political earthquakes. Its representatives affected young intellectuals. Many oppose the social order by keeping silent. The German intelligentsia is partially incited against the USSR and does not recognize the value of the role of the communication with the USSR.[84]

Professors of Marxism-Leninism led the resistance. Some revisionist ideas flowing from a segment of the professoriate who were members of the Socialist Unity Party of East Germany (SED) and taught Marxism philosophy. Soviet diplomats noted that the grounds for this revisionism lay in the weak belief of the professoriate in communism. The members of this opposition were the lecturers who articulated various critical comments about Marxism. The representatives of the German government also noted that even the professor-members of the SED resisted indoctrination. They complained to the Soviet diplomats:

> We have a rough time working with the professors in the universities. They are constantly dissatisfied with the situation in East Germany and impart to students their negative attitudes about the party and its ide-

---

Commission, 1949–1991, The Russian State Archive of Modern History (hereafter RGANI), p. 8.

84 Notes of Conversations: Politicians and Eminent Persons in the German Democratic Republic. The Correspondence with the Soviet Embassy in the GDR and the Correspondence with the Central Agencies of the USSR relative to Cultural Cooperation, 1983, file 883, entry 1, records group 9518, The Committee on Cultural Ties with Foreign Countries at the Council of Ministers, 1957–1987, GARF, p. 109–10.

EUROPE

ology. The difficulties with our communication with the intelligentsia are defined by the fact that we have become accustomed to pressure the intelligentsia but not to convince them.[85]

Special popularity among the professoriate and student body was attained by a professor of physical chemistry at Humboldt University, Robert Havemann, who was expelled from Humboldt University for his criticism of the SED and for publishing his papers in West Germany in 1966. He was reported to have a strong influence on students because his lectures in the early 1960s became a forum for discussion about revisionism in Marxism. However, he, like some other professors, was a true believer in socialism and communist dogma; he collaborated with the Stasi and heralded the building of the Wall. The SED tolerated him until he published an article in *Der Spiegel* in 1964. He was expelled from the party and dismissed from academic establishments. No protests in the universities ensued, and Havemann was kept under virtual house arrest until his death in 1982.[86]

In a new attempt to convert these hostile attitudes of the German professors, the Soviets encouraged the East German government to introduce a new university law in 1969. In addition to all the well-known provisions (the elimination of the senate and the establishment of sections to take the place of the large faculties, etc.) of the 1969 reform, in East Germany all professors specializing in Marxist-Leninist philosophy, history, and other social disciplines, as well as in mathematics, physics, chemistry, and other applied disciplines, had to expand or introduce additional lectures on Marxism-Leninism. All university curricula and every syllabus, both in the arts and the applied sciences, were revised in 1969 to contain additional information about Marxist-Leninist philosophy. Discussions about reforms and negotiations with the professors lasted for a long time. However, the events in Czechoslovakia in 1968, notably the student demonstrations and arrests at the University of Prague, became a catalyst for accelerating the reforms. By the end of 1968, all discussions were terminated, a government commission was established, and during the following four years the reform plan was formally implemented despite opposition from the universities and part of the professoriate. The traditional German subdivision of the universities was reorganized into a number of more manageable departments (sections). These departments reduced the number of faculties: for example, instead of 167 faculties and institutes, 23 departments

---

85   Reports on Communist Cultural Relationships, November 1965, file 55, entry 55, records group 5, RGANI, p. 21.
86   John Rodden, "The Galileo of the GDR: Robert Havemann," *Debatte* 14, no. 1 (2006): 37–48.

78   CHAPTER 1

were established at Humboldt University. Every university established general departments of Marxism-Leninism, economics, sports, foreign languages, a pedagogical department, and several departments for specializations.

By 1972, the mentioned Soviet reforms were being formally executed with little opposition from professors or students, at least as far as the documents show. Only a few professors refused to introduce additional segments devoted to Marxist–Leninist philosophy into their lectures, just as they had during the period of occupation.[87] On the whole, the government of East Germany was satisfied with how effectively the reforms had been conducted. However, in the early 1970s, Soviet diplomats reported to Moscow that even though the reforms existed on paper, neither professors nor students were teaching or studying Marxist–Leninist philosophy. Indeed, at no university was the curriculum in compliance with the requirements of the reforms in terms of increasing the number of classes on Marxism–Leninism. The most disappointing situation developed in the faculties of pedagogy at universities established before by the Soviet Military Administration, which were responsible for training pliable teachers of the Russian language. However, the Russian language—a core feature of Soviet cultural and political influence in Germany—was dismally taught and highly unpopular among German students.

The Soviet diplomats in Berlin, however, showed displeasure with the reforms. The Soviets, after making their own secret analysis of the reforms, found that the German professoriate did not really implement the mandatory inclusion of Marxist-Leninist philosophy in their courses. The Soviets noted that the professors who did teach students how this philosophy could be applied in mathematics, physics, and other sciences did so without any personal conviction, and often in an ironic manner. They reported that these academics simply did not want to change their beliefs and professions and preferred to maintain the old German traditions of education, such as academic freedom and the isolation of the university from politics, which ran counter to the Marxification policy. Thus, their position vis-à-vis the proposed innovations was known as the *conservatism of German professors*. The professors, in the opinion of the Soviet visiting experts, did not believe in Marxism-Leninism, and this feeling was transmitted to the student body. The Soviet Ministry of Education concluded that "the German professors did not indoctrinate students, and they did not know how to indoctrinate them; moreover, they themselves needed to be indoctrinated in the spirit of socialism."[88]

---

87   Reports on Cooperation between Pedagogical Institutes of the USSR and the GDR, 1984–
      85, file 4974, records group 9563, GARF, p. 36–37.
88   Ibid.

EUROPE 79

Scientific collaboration in the field of history demonstrated how the German professoriate restrained the concepts of Marxism in historical studies. The aim of this cooperation was to convince professors at last to apply Marxist-Leninist philosophy in their investigations. Such controls were determined by the fact that a part of the German professoriate continued doing research on irrelevant topics (in the opinion of Soviet ideologists), such as a study on the "Development of a German National Language from the 16th to 18th Centuries." Instead of this and other irrelevant topics, the Soviets in the early 1970s proposed "Modern Bourgeois Historiography and its Critique," "The Role of the People at Different Stages of History," etc. However, the Soviet government, evaluating the results of the scientific collaboration with German historians, stated that "the historians in German universities were not yet true Marxists, the implantation of the Marxist-Leninist philosophy had not succeeded, and the German professoriate still resisted carrying out collaborative research projects on such topics as revolution, people's movements and others of a similar nature."[89]

Similar to the U.S. advisors, who had labelled German professors as "conservatives," Soviet experts in the 1970s identified the part of the professoriate who opposed conversion into pliable Marxists as "conservative," "bourgeois," and "traditionalist." That so-called "conservative" German professoriate resisted the introduction of additional courses and disciplines within Marxist–Leninist studies and persisted in upholding their own philosophy and beliefs about German education. Soviet diplomats noted that

> the significant part of intelligentsia, which consists of a number of scientists and university professors, adheres to hostile attitudes. The majority of teachers adhere to bourgeois views and this negatively affects the social order of the German Democratic Republic (GDR) and the socialist transformations implemented in it.[90]

In response to this, the Soviet Government elaborated its own plan of reforms to overcome this strong conservatism on the part of the German professoriate. Visiting Soviet professors became the primary means for reform at German

---

89 Transcripts of Meetings of the Standing Committee at the Ministry of Education of the USSR and at the Ministry of People Education of the GDR, 1972, file 2032, entry 1, records group 9563, GARF, p. 116–22.

90 About the Problems with the German Intelligentsia, Letter from Soviet Ambassador in the German Democratic Republic Pervukhin, 1978, file 102, entry 35, records group 5, RGANI, p. n/n.

universities. These visiting professors were selected among the Soviet university teaching staff by the Ministry of Education. According to the plan, they were to visit every university and through collaboration and personal contacts convince every professor to honestly revise the syllabi along the lines of Marxist-Leninist philosophy. In addition, these Soviet professors were to urge their East German colleagues to insert changes into the curriculum at universities where the professoriate had yet to weaken the content of their ideological courses.

Russian was chosen as the discipline that could unite Soviet and German professors. Moscow realized that it had no leverage to further pressure the academic community, because only 5–8 percent of professors were members of the Communist Party, and very few of them believed in Soviet ideology. A soft power policy to persuade the professors was suggested in order to make "Marxism their personal belief and philosophy, and the Russian language would be popular among them."[91] Such a utopian change of mind among the German professors was to be accomplished by hundreds of visiting Soviet professors sent to German universities in a push to establish contacts with German professors. The new Soviet invasion into the life of German universities began in the 1973 academic year, when the Soviet professors were instructed to make the warmest, friendliest contact possible with their German counterparts and, in that way, convince them about Marxist ideology.

The visiting Soviet professors managed to gain a considerable foothold at universities in East Germany. In particular, they revised curricula such that the number of classes about Marxism–Leninism and courses in Russian increased. Study plans in Departments of Pedagogy soon required 10 percent of each student's academic load to be dedicated to Marxism–Leninism. To further strengthen the ideological education, the Soviet visitors published new textbooks in German such as *Dialectical Materialism and Its Ideological Enemies*, *Criticism of Falsifiers of the Philosophy of Philosophy*, and *History of the USSR for Students of the German Democratic Republic*.[92] Courses on the Russian language were also increased twofold. The visiting professors prepared drafts of new textbooks, and by 1979, approximately 100 German teachers of Russian were being sent to the Soviet Union each year for further training in the language.

---

91   Reports on Cooperation between Pedagogical Institutes of the USSR and the GDR, 1984–85, file 4974, records group 9563, GARF, p. 36–37.

92   Report on the Participation of the Soviet Delegation at the Conference of Scholars–Pegagogues [*sic*] from Socialistic Countries: "Fostering the Marxist–Leninist Outlook of a Student," 1981, file 4150, records group 9563, GARF, p. 15.

Similar to the American visiting professors who reported to the Department of State, the Soviet professors reported to the Soviet government upon their return. Their numerous reports showed that they attempted to establish contacts based on trust with their partners, to organize a friendly environment, and to convince the Germans to become Marxists according to the Soviet model. There is no doubt that this was pure fantastical utopian thinking on their part, but this plan remained the priority of the Soviet cultural offensive in East Germany until the mid-1980s. The project was finally terminated in 1986 due to its failure and a lack of financial resources in the Soviet budget.

From 1973–1986, the number of Soviet professors and specialists in the domain of higher education continued to increase from year to year. Every year 100 Soviet professors, on average, were sent to seven universities.[93] Every department at an East German university included a number of Soviet experts who worked with the teaching staff. However, in their numerous reports, visiting Soviet professors noted the negative attitude of the German professoriate toward both the Soviet Union and East Germany, "many professors oppose the social order but kept silence. The German intelligentsia is partially incited against the USSR and does not recognize the role of our relations with the GDR [German Democratic Republic]."[94] Elsewhere one stated, "many representatives of intelligentsia declare a disappointment in the public system of the GDR and professional dissatisfaction and, therefore, aspire to flee to the Federal Republic of Germany."[95]

However, the situation surrounding the teaching of Russian was tragic. The advisors reported back about the miserable situation in terms of training of students in the Slavic departments:

Contemporary and effective textbooks of Russian are absent and no professor is writing one; students study the language only seven to eight hours per week and extra classes outside the university have never been arranged; students and their professors speak Russian very seldom, and their knowledge is very weak; students do not watch movies in Russian, do not organize parties of Russian culture, and do not prepare a student newspaper in Russian; finally, students are admitted to the Slavic division

---

93   Reports on Cooperation with Socialistic Countries in the Field of Higher Education, file 301, entry 1, records group 9606, The Ministry of Higher and Vocational Education of the USSR, GARF, p. 2–28.

94   Notes of Conversations: Politicians and Eminent Persons in the German Democratic Republic, 1983, file 883, records group 9518, GARF, p. 109.

95   Information Letters. The Embassy of the Soviet Union in the German Democratic Republic, 26 September 1982, file 208, entry 88, records group 5, RGANI, p. 1.

of the pedagogical departments without entrance examinations due to the low popularity of the division and the shortage of students.[96]

Moscow was shocked by this state of affairs. The Soviets, in comparison to the Americans, who imposed American Studies and maintained the viability of this field in West Germany, had neglected this area. Moscow had established chairs of Russian language and Slavic Studies during the Occupation and then let them take their own course. In 1975, the Soviet government decided to correct this mistake by sending a number of Soviet specialists to change the situation by revising the curriculum and writing new textbooks for students. This group of Soviet specialists in the fields of education, philosophy, pedagogy, and the teaching of Russian for foreigners elaborated a detailed plan for cultivating love for Russian in German universities. Initially, they moved from university to university where they delivered special seminars for professors about the Soviet approach of preparing a teacher of Russian for a socialist school. The Soviet specialists demonstrated curriculum models composed in the Soviet Union, proposing that German colleagues apply them in their universities. According to the documents, the Soviet experts spent one year convincing the German professoriate to revise the academic curriculum of the Slavic divisions. Consequently, they managed to increase the hours allocated for Russian classes. During the next four years, these Soviet experts prepared and published new textbooks for Russian for German students in Slavic Studies in East Germany; they made students speak Russian outside the universities, involving them in parties, concerts, etc. They sent about twenty German teachers who taught Russian to the Soviet universities annually, and distributed the Soviet teachers who arrived among various universities and schools; this latter number reached 100 per year in 1976–79.

Although the cultural offensive was thought to have some effect, the reports of Soviet advisors prepared for the Ministry of Education and the Committee on Higher Education and Science at the Central Committee of the Communist Party indicate otherwise. The advisors stated that the Marxist–Leninist ideology had not entered the heart of the university community, while German professors had not altered their views. The most critical situation concerned the teaching of Russian. Despite all efforts, attitudes toward the language remained extremely negative, and "teachers of the Russian language themselves were poorly trained, and so the requirements for students remained at the lowest level; students and teachers did not communicate in Russian while

---

96   Reports on Cooperation between Pedagogical Institutes of the USSR and the GDR, 1984–85, file 4974, records group 9563, GARF, p. 1–60.

EUROPE

in class, and there were no additional resources and materials in terms of films to improve the quality of knowledge."[97]

Moreover, the influence of Soviet ideology at universities was downgraded by cultural programs and contacts with relatives visiting from West Germany:

> The impact of West Germany on university teachers is not limited by two radio stations. The main thing is family relations between teachers from West Germany and the GDR that comprise millions of letters, parcels, and phone calls. Influence through these channels is much stronger than that of radio propaganda.[98]

Some agreements were signed between West and East Germany during the 1970s that spurred German propagandists to complain to the Soviet ambassadors that "the cultural projects of West Germany have increased in East Germany and could contribute to the ideological defeat of [the] East."[99]

The Soviet government then made its final attempt to secure the loyalty of the German youth. A new exchange program was initiated to train German students at Soviet institutions, and East Germany was given priority of place among all other participating countries in terms of the number of students invited to the Soviet Union during the 1970s and 1980s.[100] In 1979, the number of East German students studying in Soviet universities—an astonishing 4,000—even became the largest in the entire history of student exchanges between two countries. Even though their numbers began to fall thereafter, in 1989, among other socialist countries, the German Democratic Republic sent the most students of all foreign students who studied in the Soviet Union: 2,300 out of 115,300.[101] In 1985, the Soviet government again attempted to reinforce ideological indoctrination by proposing a compulsory final examination on Marxist–Leninist disciplines. After a long debate, the government introduced the examination in 1988, in the belief that it would make students

---

97 Ibid, p. 36–37.

98 Excerpts from the Diary by P. Abrasimov, n/d, file 55, entry 55, records group 5, RGANI, p. 18–19.

99 Letter from Soviet Ambassador in the German Democratic Republic Mr. Tarasov, 1982, file 208, entry 88, records group 5, RGANI, p. 1–18.

100 The Training of Foreign Students at Soviet Higher Educational Institutions. Information Letter for the Central Committee of the Communist Party, no date, file 180, entry 35, records group 5, RGANI, p. 82.

101 Cumulative Report on Admission, Graduation, and Contingent of Foreign Citizens Studied in the USSR, 1989, file 589, entry 1, records group 9661, State Committee on People's Education, 1988–1991, p. 12.

become passionate believers in communism. However, the prospect of the test failed to shift the attitudes of students toward the ideology. None of them took the course seriously, classes were not attended, the exams became a formal procedure, and students ultimately protested.

Evaluating the results of its reforms in 1986, the Soviet government recognized the fact that all the efforts to make the professoriate believe in the communist ideology had failed. The ideology of Marxism never became a personal and deep belief for German professors. All Soviet projects were seen to be implemented only on paper.[102] The reports of the Soviet Ministry of Higher Education openly recognized that cooperation between Soviet and German university professors in Marxist–Leninist studies and the Russian language had failed, and the Soviet government blamed its visiting professors for the failure.[103] Of course, the reasons for the failure were clearly different. Above all, covert resistance and the reluctance of the most influential group in the university community—professors—to surrender to Soviet reforms spelled the failure of Sovietization in German universities. The German faculty won the unspoken war with the Soviets, and as the end of the Cold War approached, the more often the documents mentioned that Marxism–Leninism and the Soviet Union were losing ground, that the university professors were oriented toward the West, and that the United States and the Federal Republic of Germany were exercising an effective influence on German intelligentsia via television, radio, and both cultural and educational exchange.

4 Conclusion

Our analysis has revealed the special and exceptional role played by professors in the fate of both the American and Soviet transformations of German universities.

Both American and Soviet governments considered that fostering a favorable professorship was the way to transform German universities. In order to create a loyal professoriate, the American government introduced the system of visiting professors who established contacts with German faculty members and urged the latter to transform their universities. These visiting professors

---

102   Materials of the Seminar: "Increasing Efficiency of the International Cooperation in the Field of Higher Education and Improving Quality of Soviet Specialists to Be Sent in Foreign Educational Institutions: Challenges and Objectives, 1986, file 5186, entry 1, records group 9563, GARF, p. 1–44.

103   Ibid.

shouldered all the reforms, established new institutes and chairs in the universities, introduced new themes and methods of research, wrote textbooks, and filled the libraries with new books. The Soviet authorities created a new professoriate by persuading the German professoriate to revise courses and academic programs according to Soviet ideology.

The professoriate, while formally demonstrating its loyalty to both American and Soviet reforms, nonetheless remained dissatisfied with the values, disciplines, and ideas that had been imposed. In addition, they sabotaged and restrained the proposed transformations. Consequently, in the mid-1970s, the conservative professoriate protested against both the Americanization and Marxification of the universities in both parts of Germany. In the universities of West Germany, the traditional power of the professoriate was re-established in 1975. The American advisors were unable to overcome this strong opposition and were forced to admit that American influence was undermined in German universities. The further reluctance of the professoriate to participate in American university projects during the mid-1970s and 1980s demonstrated this failure. In East Germany, the Soviet reforms were blocked by the stubborn disobedience of a segment of the professoriate whom the Soviet Union also labeled as the conservative professors. The Soviet government attempted to eliminate the conservatism of the professors by sending Soviet professors to Germany, as well as by encouraging the professors to believe sincerely in Marxist philosophy. This rather utopian program failed in 1986 when the Central Committee of the Communist Party finally admitted that the German professoriate was not and never would become true Marxists.

Hence, both superpowers encountered either open or masked forms of opposition from professors who admired the old traditions of the German universities such as academic freedom, isolation from politics, repudiation of imposed ideologies, and a powerful position for the senior staff. This opposition on the part of the professoriate in both parts of Germany condemned external influences. Both the West German and East German professoriate believed that both American democracy and Soviet Marxism undermined the concept of academic freedom and the other traditions of German university life. Consequently, both governments acknowledged the failure of their policies in Germany, and the academic community of both parts of Germany was able to retain certain traditional features of the German university system throughout the entire period of the Cold War.

CHAPTER 2

Middle East and Central Asia

Americanization, Sovietization, and Resistance in Afghanistan

1 Introduction

The United States and the Soviet Union pursued a profound and sometimes harsh transformation of local traditions at universities and higher educational institutes located in the Middle East and Central Asia along with the patterns of their rival educational systems. The wide-scoped transformations were determined by the political rivalry of both countries in the context of the Cold War, when each power aspired for allegiant friends and cooperation, and, more importantly, by the aspirations of the powers that the development and modernization brought by either American or Soviet universities would uproot foundations and sources for religious clashes.[1]

The transformations and Americanization and Sovietization that accompanied them, like nowhere else, were associated with the aspirations of both superpowers to make universities in the Middle East more effective, modernized, and capable of contributing to local development. For both powers, there was no space and time to keep some outdated (as considered by them) local traditions in education. In addition, when introducing innovations, both Washington and Moscow advisors could not adapt and sometimes could not understand the localisms that referred to family clans, tribalism, and to the slowness in decision making that was completely integrated within the space of local universities. This fact pushed the advisors to pursue the Americanization and Sovietization at universities more rigorously than in other parts of the world in order to get accustomed to the academic world. Moreover, the legacy of European colonization profoundly imprinted in universities—the large autonomy of departments and various educational units, the absence of united university campuses and of strong central management—slowed down the modernization and made both Washington and Moscow revise the traditions of local education more severely. Finally, the realities of the Cold War in the regions, notably, the clash of the superpowers' political interests, encouraged them to accelerate the disseminating and rooting of their opposing ideologies

---

1 Geraint Hughes, "The Cold War and Counter-Insurgency," *Diplomacy & Statecraft* 22, no. 1 (March 2011): 142–63.

© NATALIA TSVETKOVA, 2021 | DOI:10.1163/9789004471788_004

MIDDLE EAST AND CENTRAL ASIA 87

into the universities of the Middle East in order to foster a more pliable elite and society.[2]

The universities of the Middle East and Central Asia, and of Afghanistan in particular, demonstrated the most unusual resistance against Americanization and Sovietization. The superpowers and their advisors, who worked at the universities of the Middle East, called for the ongoing transformations as the Americanization and Sovietization progressed, and were uncomfortable with the resistance from the local academic community. This struggle rarely happened elsewhere in such a thoroughgoing manner, as revealed in the documents about the reforms in other regions. Consequently, the Middle East turned out to be the region that made the superpowers to argue that it was not possible to build an American- or Soviet-modeled university.

Hence, this chapter is used the concepts of Americanization and Sovietization despite the fact that the superpowers' transformations in universities of other regions might be reviewed in terms of Americanization and Sovietization. In the Middle Eastern and Central Asian countries the transformations of local universities provoked strong open as well as hidden resistance on the part of academic community and allow us to apply these two concepts to the story of U.S. and Soviet university policy in the region.

The case of American and Soviet cultural diplomacy at Kabul University illustrates that the concepts of Americanization and Sovietization have more shared features than divergent ones. Both superpowers imposed new departments, study plans, disciplines, and pliable professors in order to undermine local traditions. The only different point in their transformations was an ideology. The case of Afghanistan and Kabul University and the new corps of archival documents allow us to demonstrate how the policies of Americanization and Sovietization were conducted and finally failed in Kabul and hence to redefine the concepts of Americanization and Sovietization.[3]

---

2   Thomas Barfield, *Afghanistan: A Cultural and Political History* (Princeton: Princeton University Press, 2010).

3   Despite the interest of scholars – historians, political scientists, and experts in the field of international relations; specialists of foreign assistance and development; and researchers in comparative education – in what has happened in Afghanistan and in its university system, the scholarship on the question is still scarce. The questions that are more or less investigated by the scholarship concern modernization of Afghanistan, political and religious movements among students of Kabul University, a situation in Afghanistan under the Soviet regime, the development of Islamic education, etc. See, Nick Cullather, "Damming Afghanistan: Modernization in a Buffer State," *The Journal of American History* 89, no. 2 (September 2002): 512–37; Jenifer Van Vleck, "An Airline at the Crossroads of the World: Ariana Afghan Airlines, Modernization, and the Global Cold War," *History & Technology* 25, no. 1 (March 2009): 3–24; Tahir Amin, "Afghan Resistance: Past, Present, and Future," *Asian Survey*

Afghanistan, considered as a strategic territory in the foreign policy of both the United States and the Soviet Union, occupied a primary place in their cultural diplomacy. Afghan education, its schools, and Kabul University in particular, became the powerful agencies through which both superpowers implanted their rival political cultures. Kabul University turned out to be a reflection of Afghanistan's unusual condition in terms of various cultural influences, which have come from Great Britain, the United States, Saudi Arabia, India, Iran, and the Soviet Union, in different periods of modern history. Established in 1933, but built and renovated by the United States, Kabul University turned out to be an epicenter of American reforms and influence during the 1960s and 1970s. It was a peaceful period in Afghan history. The king, Mohammed Zahir Shah, the Royal Government, and the Parliament closely cooperated with the United States and European countries. In 1973, after the monarchy was overthrown, the political and cultural influence of the United States quickly faded. A new republican government reluctantly interacted with the West, giving preference to cooperation with Saudi Arabia, Iran, China, and the Soviet Union. The political influences of Islamic groups, communists, and nationalists intensified in Afghanistan, in its education, and in Kabul University in particular. The Saur (April) revolution of 1978 brought the pro-communist People's Democratic Party to the power. In 1979, Afghanistan and Kabul were occupied by the Soviet Union when a new leader of the party, Babrak Karmal, "invited" Soviet troops to maintain his political regime after a plot to kill Hafizullah Amin, who was his party rival and opponent. Kabul University remained in the hands of the Soviet Union until 1989, when its troops left the country. Both the United States and the Soviet Union tried to transform Kabul University in order to make it more suitable for instilling their political culture in different periods of the

---

24, no. 4 (April 1984): 373–99; Hafizullah Emadi, "Radical Political Movements in Afghanistan and Their Politics of Peoples' Empowerment and Liberation," *Central Asian Survey* 20, no. 4 (December 2001): 427–50; K. Wafadar, "Afghanistan in 1981: The Struggle Intensifies," *Asian Survey* 22, no. 2, A Survey of Asia in 1981: Part II (April 1982): 147–54; Lee O. Coldren, "Afghanistan in 1984: The Fifth Year of the Russo-Afghan War," *Asian Survey* 25, no. 2, A Survey of Asia in 1984: Part II (February 1985): 169–79; Anthony Hyman, "The Struggle for Afghanistan," *The World Today* 40, no. 7 (July 1984): 276–84; David B. Edwards, *Before Taliban: Genealogies of the Afghan Jihad* (Berkeley, CA: University of California Press, 2002): 177–286; Abdul Satar Sirat, "Sharia and Islamic Education in Modern Afghanistan," *Middle East Journal* 23, no. 2 (Spring 1969): 217–19; Donald N. Wilber, "The Structure and Position of Islam in Afghanistan," *Middle East Journal* 6, no. 1 (Winter 1952): 41–48; Geoffrey Swenson, and Eli Sugerman, "Building the Rule of Law in Afghanistan: The Importance of Legal Education," *Hague Journal of The Rule of Law* 3, no. 1 (March 2011): 130–46; Natalia Tsvetkova, "Americanisation, Sovietisation, and Resistance at Kabul University: Limits of the Educational Reforms," *History of Education* 46, no. 3 (May 2017): 336–43.

MIDDLE EAST AND CENTRAL ASIA 89

Cold War. However, in contrast to their policies in the universities of Europe, Latin America, and the Asian-Pacific area, Kabul University strongly resisted both American and Soviet reforms that finally undermined their policies at Kabul University and in the Afghan educational system as a whole.[4]

The chapter compares American and Soviet attempts to transform Kabul University during the Cold War. The chapter is divided into three sections. The first section reviews the policy of the United States at Kabul University. The second section of the chapter depicts the policy of the Soviet Union there. Transformations in the organizational structure of the university, the introduction of new disciplines, the policies towards professorship and students are reviewed. Finally, the third section examines the resistance on the part of the university community to both American and Soviet reforms that contributed to the failure of Americanization and Sovietization of the structure, study plans, disciplines, and local traditions at the university. The chapter concludes by discussing some successes and failures of both superpowers' policies at Kabul University and the limits of Americanization and Sovietization as well.

2 Kabul University under the Control of the United States

2.1 *Promoting the Faculty of Engineering*
Establishment of diplomatic relations between the United States and Afghanistan during the 1920s and 1930s opened Kabul University for American assistance, professors, and influence. Kabul University, founded in 1933 and comprised of twelve faculties and 2,700 students by the early 1960s[5] was a leading institution in Afghanistan. Under the administration of Harry Truman's Point Four Program, Kabul University and other educational institutions of Afghanistan were provided with modest financial aid in the early 1950s.[6] The huge development policy of the Soviet Union, unfold in the middle 1950s, and the aspirations of both superpowers to establish and maintain friendly political regimes in the context of the Cold War boosted American assistance to

---

4 Katya Drozdova, and Joseph H. Felter, "Leaving Afghanistan: Enduring Lessons from the Soviet Politburo," *Journal of Cold War Studies* 21, no. 4 (2019): 31–70; Rodric Braithwaite, "The Russians in Afghanistan," *Asian Affairs* 42, no. 2 (2011): 213–29.

5 Letter from O. P. Bergelin, Director of United States Engineering Team, to S. B. Hamblen, Chief, Education Division, U.S. Agency for International Development Record, [1963], box 1, records group 286, Agency for International Development, entry 66, USAID Mission to Afghanistan, Education Division, National Archive Records Administration (hereafter NARA).

6 Jim Turner, *United States Foreign Assistance to Afghanistan. A History by Sector, 1952–1979* (Washington, D.C., 1988).

educational institutions in Afghanistan. The Agency for International Development (USAID), set up by President Kennedy in 1961, increased funding for foreign educational projects, and, soon, Afghanistan and Kabul University took priority among other targets in American development policy.[7]

However, the diplomats of the American mission in Kabul spent much time trying to convince the Afghan government to acquiesce to American reforms and to the arrival of American visiting consultants at Kabul University. They mentioned in a report for Washington "to the Mission's surprise, the program [proposed for Kabul University] was not immediately accepted as we had been lead to believe it would be."[8] The difficult and long negotiations demonstrated to American diplomats such features of an Afghan national character as slowness, passivity, and apathy: "After final approval, the Afghans move too slowly and the education program is still not able to move freely forward."[9] Later, it became clear that the passivity, apathy, and ignorance of American suggestions, reforms, papers, and plans demonstrated by the Afghan university community were the manifestation of its resistance.

In 1962, the first eleven visiting professors and advisors from Teachers College, Columbia University, and the University of Wyoming arrived in Kabul in order to formulate a plan for reforms. American visiting professors were full of enthusiasm to improve the university structure, students' affairs, and the academic life for the professorate.[10] However, what they saw at Kabul University stunned them. The buildings of Kabul University were so structurally unsound as to be hazardous; toilet and washroom facilities were nonexistent, lighting was poor, and there was no heat.[11] It was the outmoded university to be modernized. The first plan of the reforms was, therefore, aimed at constructing new buildings, dormitories, laboratories, toilets, etc., in order to make Kabul University look like a modern institution of higher education and research.[12] The most significant contribution of the American assistance was the establishment of a

---

7   Report from Educational Service Incorporated to Mr. Harold E. Schwartz, Director, USAID/Afghanistan, Kabul, November 9, 1962, box 2, records group 286, NARA.

8   Long-Range Plans for U.S. Assistance for Afghanistan, Report. February 17, box 6, records group 286, NARA.

9   Ibid.

10 Education Activities USAID/Afghanistan, [1962], box 6, records group 286, NARA.

11 Grant Project Paper. Afghanistan. Department of State. Agency for International Development, [1962], box 4, records group 286, NARA; Use of the New Kabul University Campus. Office Memorandum from Kent Hawley, Student personnel Advisor, Teachers College at Columbia University, to Dr. Harold See, Education Division, USAID, November 13, 1963, box 5, NARA.

12 Letter from Chief, Education Division, USAID, Kabul to Dr. Ali Ahmed Popal, Minister of Education, Royal Afghan Ministry of Education, December 21, box 1, NARA.

MIDDLE EAST AND CENTRAL ASIA 91

unified university campus. The central campus was built in 1964 at Aliabad, in the western section of Kabul, largely with U.S. funds.[13] Before it, the completely autonomous faculties and schools had been scattered throughout the city of Kabul. The American government provided funds to build and equip five new university buildings, including an administration and classroom buildings, a library, an engineering building, and student dormitory.

Besides these building projects, the specialists of both the American universities and the USAID elaborated a long-term program of transformation for Kabul University. They intended to revise the management of Kabul University, promoting a new constitution, effective and modernized administration; to introduce a master's-level of education at the university; to establish, develop, and supervise the Faculty of Engineering; and to make English a primary language for teaching at Kabul University. In addition, the plan included administrative reforms, improvements to students' lives, and a revision of general curriculum. However, only the Faculty of Engineering and English unexpectedly became a priority in American educational policy.[14] The Chief of Education, Division of the U.S. Agency for International Development, Dr. Harold See, submitted this plan to both an Afghan Minister of Education and the President of Kabul University, Dr. Anwary. The Afghans expressed concerns, but finally agreed to it. As soon as the Afghans agreed to the proposal, the president of Kabul University turned out to be under the supervision of his principal advisor, Dr. See.[15]

The Faculty of Engineering at Kabul University became the principal target for the Americanization of higher education in Afghanistan during the Cold War.[16] The decision to develop and aid the Faculty of Engineering was primarily based on U.S. aspirations that the department would become the country's only source of engineers broadly trained in four major fields of engineering: civil, electrical, mechanical, and agricultural.[17] During the 20–25 years

---

13   U.S. Agency for International Development, "Examination of USAID Assistance to the Afghanistan Education Sector. Audit Report, September 30, 1972," accessed July 08, 2020, www.usaid.gov; U.S. Agency for International Development, "Kabul University Administration Improvement. Airgram, from AID/W to Kabul, November 11, 1969," accessed July 08, 2020, www.usaid.gov, p. 3.

14   Congressional Inquiry—Education Program. Department of State Telegram from Kabul to AID/Washington, July 8, 1963, box 6, records group 286, NARA.

15   Assistance to Kabul University General Administration. Minutes of Meeting: Members of Ministry of Education, Afghanistan, and Education Division, USAID, May 20, box 1, records group 286, NARA; Tsvetkova, "Americanisation, Sovietisation," 336–43.

16   Grant Project Paper. Afghanistan, 1962, box 4, records group 286, NARA.

17   U.S. Agency for International Development, "The Technical Education Project. Airgram from USAID/Kabul, 1969," accessed July 08, 2020, www.usaid.gov, p. 3.

that followed, assistance provided by several U.S. universities contributed to its development. On top of that, contracts with the University of Wyoming, Southern Illinois University, Indiana University, Nebraska University, and 11 U.S. engineering schools were aimed at making the Faculty one of the most successful institutions in the world.[18]

The attention of American advisors to the Faculty of Engineering was also warmed by a Soviet educational policy in Afghanistan. In 1962, after the arrival of American visiting professors to Kabul, the Soviet diplomats convinced the Afghan government to build the Polytechnic Institute at Soviet expense in order to teach engineers according to a Soviet pattern. Initially, the American advisors did not perceive the Soviet rival proposals as a threat for an American-sponsored Faculty of Engineering, suggesting that the Soviet project would not be successful:

> The Polytechnic will compete with Kabul University for faculty and students. By the time the first graduates from the Polytechnic, the Faculty of Engineering will have been well established as the prime Afghan engineering school.[19]

These aspirations were not realized, however. The rise of the Faculty of Engineering was blockaded by the low qualifications of both professors and students:

> The level of teaching in the Faculty has been low for a number of reasons. The staff has been small and inexperienced, the laboratories have lacked equipment and utilities, and the entering students have been poorly prepared.[20]

Initially, there were a united Faculty of Agriculture and Engineering opened to students. In 1962, the university separated the two branches of this faculty, thus creating a separate Faculty of Engineering.[21] When the Polytechnic, in contrast to the Faculty of Engineering, formally introduced the master's level of

---

18   U.S. Agency for International Development, "Retrospective Review of US Assistance to Afghanistan: 1950–1979. Report by USAID, 1988," accessed July 08, 2020, www.usaid.gov, p. 20.

19   Grant Project Paper. Afghanistan, 1962, box 4, records group 286, NARA.

20   The Kabul Program of Educational Services, Inc. Situation Report by O. P. Bergelin, Program Director, United States Engineering Team, May 10, box 2, records group 286, NARA.

21   U.S. Agency for International Development, "The Technical Education Project. Airgram from USAID/Kabul, 1969," p. 3.

education,[22] American diplomats recognized that "with this U.S.S.R. [sic] venture into previously exclusive U.S. sphere of activity in Afghanistan, the Mission considers that a successful program at the University of Kabul Engineering Faculty is now even more in the U.S. national interest."[23]

The Russian Polytechnic Institute received frequent mention in the reports of members of the U.S. engineering team at Kabul University. Compared with the Faculty, the Institute was built for a large number of students—approximately 1,500—with on-campus residential facilities to accommodate about 1,200 of them. Its average annual enrollment was slightly greater than 1,000.[24] The Institute had narrower training options, however: only nine courses of study from approximately 150 possibilities in the Soviet system of technical and engineering training. Without doubt, the Soviet-assisted Polytechnic Institute aroused some concern among Afghan and U.S. partners alike, chiefly about attracting an adequate number of qualified student candidates for both of the new schools. The United States encouraged graduates of vocational schools to enter the Faculty of Engineering as well as recruited students in Afghan provinces by offering them an intensive pre-engineering course to improve their skills in studying.[25] Needless to say, the Faculty of Engineering and the Polytechnic Institute competed fiercely for students, the best instructors, and engineers.

Unlike reports by U.S. experts who had worked in other countries, reports from the team at Kabul University often emphasized possible cooperation with Soviets and the Polytechnic Institute, considering calculations about the funding and human resources that developing Afghanistan would require. U.S. consultants who visited the Polytechnic Institute sought to pave the way for U.S.-Soviet cooperation never before seen in other countries during the Cold War. The US advisors noted the Moscow's activities while communicating with the Soviets:

> Several Russian team members were met and talked to during the tour [sic]. For the most part, these were fairly young, apparently well-educated [sic] and enthusiastic people interested in their laboratories and in showing what was possible with their equipment. The buildings

---

22 Weekly Report to the Director, Education Division, USAID, 1967, box 1, records group 286, NARA.

23 Report from Educational Service, November 9, 1962, box 2, records group 286, NARA.

24 U.S. Agency for International Development, "Examination of USAID Assistance."

25 U.S. Agency for International Development, "The Technical Education Project. Airgram from USAID/Kabul, 1969," p. 4.

and laboratories are well-equipped and well [*sic*] laid out, on the whole, considerably more extensive than the Faculty of Engineering's [*sic*]. The Polytechnic is on its own compound [*sic*] with its own dormitories, cafeterias, and faculty housing apartment buildings [*sic*]. There are some 130 participants in Russia who go a six-year period but are able to return to Afghanistan [*sic*] each summer, thus renewing their home ties and maintaining their contacts within the country.[26] Increasingly enough, both deans [Faculty of Engineering at Kabul University and Polytechnic Institute] and the Minister of Education, spoke in terms of the long-run cooperation of these two institutions [*sic*] referring to possible common first and second year programs [*sic*].[27]

However, such cooperation was not further developed, as Moscow and Washington repeatedly voiced their desires to have their institutions dominate engineering education in Afghanistan. The Cultural Cold War and the rivalry of the powers in any sphere strictly prohibited their advisors from cooperating and thereby contributing to the development of education and the nation of Afghanistan. Both countries had limited resources, including labs and equipment, and their cooperation likely would have generated more positive results.

The Russian Polytechnic Institute inspired the U.S. team to pursue new reforms and achievements. In order to compete with the Institute effectively, U.S. advisors attempted to improve the qualifications of professors by offering special training programs in the United States and by introducing stricter requirements for the admission of students.[28] The experience of the Soviet Union in training foreign specialists for five or six years also impacted the duration of education at Kabul University. The United States expanded the institution's undergraduate program extending its duration from four to five years.[29] However, U.S. advisors never introduced master's programs, which limited the

---

26   There is the visible mistake made by an author of in the original report. It could be written as follows: "There are some 130 participants in *Afghanistan* who go a six-year period but are able to return to *Russia* each summer, thus renewing their home ties and maintaining their contacts within the country."

27   U.S. Agency for International Development, "Report of Visit to the United States Engineering Team (USET) Kabul, Afghanistan by R.G. Carson, Chairman, Kabul Afghan-American Program Steering Committee, March 12–28,1970," accessed July 08, 2020, www.usaid. gov, pp. 13–14.

28   Relationship to Russian Polytechnic. Report. USAID, Department of State, 1962, box 4, records group 286, NARA.

29   U.S. Agency for International Development, "Report of Visit to the United States Engineering Team, 1970," p. 2.

MIDDLE EAST AND CENTRAL ASIA

production of qualified professionals and justified the Afghan government in officially stating that the Polytechnic Institute's graduates received more recognition than graduates of the Faculty of Engineering.[30]

Later, U.S. advisors aimed to improve the curricula at the Faculty of Engineering in order to raise the qualifications of its graduates. The team from the University of Nebraska especially sought to facilitate and strengthen the Faculty's capacity to reform its curriculum, establish new courses, and introduce program offerings through the 1970s.[31] However, Afghan traditionalism and tribalism undermined the project, and the courses were introduced too slowly. At the same time, other courses were instituted but lacked sufficient Afghan instructors to teach them.[32] The problem of faculty shortages was never resolved, and by 1979, the excessive number of students required approximately 170 teachers, whereas only 60 were on the staff.[33] The United States tried to solve the problem by hiring former graduates, but that strategy dramatically affected the quality of teaching. As a result, before the invasion of Soviet troops, U.S. experts reported that chronic program failures and inefficiencies at Kabul University were directly attributable to the dismal outcome of the reforms.

2.2 *English as the Language of Instruction*

Critical damage to the Faculty's development came from the flawed calculations of U.S. advisors. The advisors briefly intended to hire staff qualified to deliver classes in English, which was supposed to be the primary language of instruction in the Faculty and at Kabul University in general. In the 1960s and 1970s, the advisors believed that they could effectively Americanize Kabul University largely by introducing English as the primary language at the institution. After all, the United States and the whole world was witnessing the rising popularity of English among citizens of the countries in the Middle East. Indeed, in the 1960s, English turned out to be very popular among nations of

---

30 Bi-Weekly 'Alert' Report to The Director, Education Division, USAID, October 19, 1968, box 1, records group 286, NARA; USAID 6-Month Review, 1971, box 2, records group 286, NARA.

31 U.S. Agency for International Development, "Retrospective Review of US Assistance to Afghanistan," p. 126.

32 U.S. Agency for International Development, "Higher Education/Kabul University. Project Appraisal Report. University of Nebraska at Omaha, 1973–1976," accessed July 08, 2020, www.usaid.gov.

33 U.S. Agency for International Development, "Higher Education/Kabul University. Project Appraisal Report. University of Nebraska at Omaha, 1973–1976," accessed July 08, 2020, www.usaid.gov.

the Near and Middle East. American University in Beirut, American University in Cairo, and other institutions established in the countries of the region developed educational programs that demanded students know English. Numerous clippings witnessed that "many Arab parents want their sons and daughters to learn English as their major foreign language despite current diplomatic strains."[34] This situation enabled the United States to introduce English as a language for teaching and research at Kabul University. In order to achieve this goal, the United Stated planned to foster a new generation of teachers for secondary schools through their training at the Faculty of Education.[35] This new generation of teachers was reported to know not only linguistics, but to have knowledge about American civilization, history, political institutions, and cultural values.[36] American advisors suggested that these newly qualified teachers at secondary schools would provide qualified prospective students for Kabul University who could read American textbooks, understand American professors, and write papers in English that consequently could raise the educational standards of the university. In 1967, the Agency for International Development convinced the king to approve *The National English Language Program*[37] that implied introduction of English to each secondary and vocational school, to each department of higher education in institutes and universities. In 1971, nine faculties out of twelve at Kabul University announced English as the language of teaching.[38] It seemed to be a success.

However, the use of English as the language of instruction at the Faculty of Engineering produced numerous problems for the American advisors. This was a policy that was not unanimously accepted by Afghan staff and no doubt there were profound lapses. Afghans recommended to their American colleagues that they give up this idea and teach the classes in local languages,

---

34   Letter from American University of Beirut to Department of State, March 8, 1968, box 11, records group 286, entry 549, Bureau for Food for Peace and Voluntary Assistance. Office of Food for Peace, American University in Cairo Grant AID and American University of Beirut—English Language Training, NARA.

35   Special Teacher Education Program, 1963, box 2, records group 286, NARA.

36   English Department, Kabul University. A Joint Project of the Teachers College, Columbia University Team and Institute of Education, Kabul University, Afghanistan, 1963, box 1, records group 286, NARA.

37   English Language Program. A Proposal for a Structure within the Royal Afghan Ministry of Education which will Eventually Assume Full Independence Responsibility for the Direction of the national English Language Program. USAID, May 29, 1963, box 2, records group 286, NARA.

38   Letter from Antony Lanza, Chief, Education Division, USAID to Minister of Education, Afghanistan, 1971, box 4, records group 286, NARA; Tsvetkova, "Americanisation, Sovietisation," 336–43.

MIDDLE EAST AND CENTRAL ASIA

but the team of American experts stubbornly promoted the thesis that English should be the language of teaching for the Faculty of Engineering and other departments at Kabul University. English became the principal question in the American policy and the advisors did not want to step back. Soon, it became clear that the students were not well enough equipped by their high school training to understand lectures in English and therefore English was taught in the Faculty of Engineering as a supplementary subject, with the instruction being provided by Peace Corps volunteers. It took time and postponed the classes in professional disciplines. However, weak knowledge of school graduates and the unwillingness of many faculty members to give lectures in English led to a final compromise between the advisors and faculty leaders: the language of instruction was superficially made easier and different from the normal English instruction including technical report writing and technical language.[39] However, the teaching and studies in English produced the a permanent crisis in personal communication and confidence between the Americans and Afghans at the University. Later, the Ministry of Education, which had resisted the National Program since its inception, undermined all the efforts of the United States to disseminate American textbooks and qualified teachers throughout Afghan schools. American specialists noted that

> the National English Language Program lacks the essential coordination and support of the Ministry of Education, which has not adequately supported the Royal Government of Afghanistan's decision to adopt English as the principal language of Afghanistan. The low priority given to this policy has led to ineffective teacher training programs and has adversely affected the morale of teachers and the motivation of students. Some programs are being curtailed and discontinued.[40]

After the 1973 coup d'état, the English project was terminated and the staff at the Faculty of Engineering delivered class in Pushto and Dari. The harsh promotion of English, when qualifications of both Afghan professors and students were low can be evaluated as the mistake in the cultural diplomacy that damaged the American project and compelled the advisors leave the university.

---

39   U.S. Agency for International Development, "Report of Visit to the United States Engineering Team, 1970," pp. 7–9.

40   Annual Report of the United States Educational Commission in Afghanistan, 1970, box 4, records group 286, NARA; Coordinating U.S. Support to English Teaching in Afghanistan. A Summary Report by Ad Hoc Mission Committee on Coordinating English Teaching. American Embassy, May 22, 1971, box 4, records group 286, NARA.

2.3 _Turmoil and Termination of Projects_

Moreover, new factors made an impact on the American policy. As in other countries, the university faced students' strikes in the early 1970s. The strikes were a reflection of a national sense of frustration and Kabul University had become the focus for expression of political unrest.[41] And the university had the same problems faced by other institutions in other countries. The university had more students than the staff was prepared to deal with; the budgets were inadequate; the relatively traditional character of the staff coupled with the poor secondary education preparation of students resulted in overall low quality of graduates and there was recurrent student unrest that made further progress in the work of American advisors problematic. The academic year at Kabul University for 1970 was somewhat foreshortened due to problems originating from the closing of the University as a result of student unrest.[42] The University was closed from December 1971 to May 1972 due to the long student strike.[43] In the early 1970s, the most of technical education's projects and faculty development at Kabul University were almost phased out. The American experts reported a threat to their projects stemming from the political instability. On the eve of the revolution (July 1973), many projects at the Faculty of Engineering were terminated that June.[44]

The failure of projects referred to the Faculty of Engineering and English and the period of turmoil gave the American advisors a chance to promote a constitution that could make the central administration and Kabul University more adapted to the civilized world. The university constitution promoted the unification of all the departments because each department was strongly influenced by various foreign countries, notably France, Germany, the United States, Saudi Arabia, and other donors who, according to American advisors, damaged American intentions to make the university more manageable. Kabul University remained a collection of separate and somewhat autonomous faculties and the U.S. Mission believed that a strong central administration was needed for the University to be effective.[45] In such circumstances, the system

---

41   U.S. Agency for International Development, "Higher Education—Kabul University."

42   U.S. Agency for International Development, "Report of Visit to the United States Engineering Team, 1970," p. 3.

43   U.S. Agency for International Development, "Examination of USAID Assistance;" U.S. Agency for International Development, "Higher Education—Kabul University. Revised PROP. Airgram from USAID/Kabul to AID/W, March 1, 1973," accessed July 08, 2020, www .usaid.gov.

44   U.S. Agency for International Development, "Examination of USAID Assistance.

45   Ibid.

MIDDLE EAST AND CENTRAL ASIA 99

of voting and elections of deans but not the appointment by the administration was criticized by the American advisors: "A good illustration is that Faculty Deans are not appointment by the University president, or his staff, but instead, elected for a two-year period by the University Senate."[46]

The constitution suggested the establishment of a board of trustees and non-political leadership of the university. The Americans believed that the adoption of the constitution would move the university toward an administrative pattern more like that of an American state university and would provide greater stability in the leadership.[47] Moreover, the adoption of a new constitution of the university was seen by the American experts as the first and essential liberation of the university from obsolete and ineffective governance, tribalism, and permanent sabotage of modernization. When a new rector was elected due to the student strikes at the end of the 1960s, the United States hoped for success. The rector (president) was popular and respected. He promised to make Kabul University more Americanized, and having earned a university MA degree in the U.S., he was familiar with the structure of a large American university that allowed him to take steps.[48] However the parliament did not ratify the constitution and the rector and the American advisors were handicapped by the nebulous situation with respect to the new university constitution.[49]

Therefore, the United States hoped for the promotion of capable and pliable administrative officials who could endorse the constitution. The advisors elaborated a project to revise staff in the administration of the university finding those employees who could continue the modernization of the university. Having known the slowness and the sabotage of the Afghan faculty in the past, the United States chose the tactics of persuasion: "Since officials, deans, and professors are persons of some status and responsibility, the advisory and on-the-job training approach used with tact and vigor was been chosen."[50]

However, Secretary of State Rogers, who observed this sensitive project, acknowledged that its goals could not be achieved because of Afghan

---

46 Ibid.
47 U.S. Agency for International Development, "Report of Visit to the United States Engineering Team, 1970," p. 7–8.
48 U.S. Agency for International Development, "Kabul University Administration Improvement," p. 5.
49 Ibid.
50 U.S. Agency for International Development, "Technical Education. Faculty of Engineering. Kabul University. Project Appraisal Report, 1970–72," accessed July 08, 2020, www.usaid.gov, p. 2.

traditionalism and tribalism.[51] Rogers then wrote a letter to the USAID office in Kabul stating that "another difficulty <...> is the use of American educational institutions as a model for Kabul University. <...> The objective of this project to develop an institution which meets the needs of Afghanistan and not to transplant an American-type university."[52]

And only after the understanding at the highest level that it would be better to slow down the Americanization, the advisors treated the university smoothly and depicted the traditions of management and training in Afghanistan in more sensitive terms. Offering assistance, the experts stipulated that the experienced U.S. staff was wise and able to adapt and not attempt to transplant American administrative know-how to Afghanistan.[53] However, this project, like others, was terminated in 1972.

Before their departure, the American advisors summed up their previous activities. They noted the growth of the faculty and the university as the positive results of their projects. By early 1970s, the Faculty of Engineering consisted of 52 teaching staff and 500 students.[54] Kabul University embraced nine faculties, and its 1971 enrollment was 5,719 students. This total represents a 55 percent increase over 1956 when the student enrollment was 3,136.[55] However, the advisors mentioned in a negative tone uncoordinated planning and a rigid administrative system. Funds devoted to education were too limited and Afghanistan remained in the bottom among developing countries. Budgets were inadequate to provide practical training in laboratories. Despite the staff supported by the United States and its vigorous efforts to improve administration, the university possessed inadequate capacity to plan, administer, and integrate programs, to coordinate among faculties and to bring the university's resources to bear on the problems of the development of the nation. Moreover, there was inadequate preparation of students at each level of education for entry into the next level. But the Afghan traditionalism remained the most intolerable and grave problem. Traditional attitudes toward change had a negative impact on the quality of education, and the political strife within the university reflected tensions and dissatisfaction in the larger community. These problems hampered effective educational activity and undermined the environment for further delivery of technical assistance.[56]

---

51   U.S. Agency for International Development, "Kabul University Administration Improvement," p. 1.

52   Ibid.

53   Ibid, p. 3.

54   U.S. Agency for International Development, "Examination of USAID Assistance."

55   Ibid.

56   U.S. Agency for International Development, "Retrospective Review of US Assistance to Afghanistan," p. 123–125.

MIDDLE EAST AND CENTRAL ASIA 101

2.4 Aftermath...

When a new government of Afghanistan was formed in 1973, the Chief of Education Division at the USAID, Anthony R. Lanza, reported to Washington that American diplomats and visiting advisors established friendly relationships with the new leaders of Afghanistan.[57] However, despite this report, further reforms were reported to be terminated by a new rector of Kabul University.

According to documents, the Rector S. Baha blocked both the work of American advisors at the university and further negotiations between Afghans and USAID.[58] Instead, he promoted the development of Islamic education at the university. The Faculty of Islamic Law, which previously had enrolled only five students each year, increased the number of students admitted and became enormously developed due to funds coming from Saudi Arabia. After several unsuccessful attempts by American specialists to convince the rector to enact further reforms, the Agency for International Development reported to Washington that there were no conditions under which the work of the Agency could continue.[59] The advisors from Columbia University and the University Wyoming left Kabul. The Indiana University contract team was reported to continue advising the university administration with four professional advisors and supporting clerical staff.[60]

A year later, however, the government led by President Dauod and the new rector, Ghulam Siddiq Mohibbi, were aware of the need to restore U.S. participation in the development of Kabul University. In March 1974, a round of negotiations was held between representatives of the U.S. Embassy and the Afghan government, the latter of which expressed a desire for the wide participation of the United States in developing the institution and for a huge investment to that purpose. However, the United States rejected any fullscale funding of the entire university and instead offered assistance only in improving the management of the Faculty of Engineering and executing some projects there. Although the Afghan government agreed, they needed to wait several months for the consent of the university's Academic Council to restore relations between USAID and Kabul University.[61] Advisors from the University of Nebraska worked with senior administrators to create systems

---

57 Relations with new Government in Afghanistan—for Ambassador's Information. Education Division, USAID, 1973, box 2, records group 286, NARA.

58 *Kabul Times*, March 26, 1970, 1.

59 Higher Education Program for Kabul University—Afghanistan. Memorandum. USAID, 1976, box 2, records group 286, NARA.

60 Letter from Edwin Martin, Chief, Education Division, USAID to Hamidullah Seraj, First Deputy Minister of Education, 1968, box 1, records group 286, NARA.

61 U.S. Agency for International Development, "Contacts with Government of Afghanistan. Report. USAID/Kabul, April-May 1974," accessed July 08, 2020, www.usaid.gov.

102   CHAPTER 2

for curriculum development and administrative management procedures. However, when no visible results were achieved, the projects were terminated in 1977 and 1978, and, later, a few education projects functioned in Afghanistan, albeit at primary schools, during the Soviet occupation. The Education Sector Support Project, implemented through a contract with the University of Nebraska-Omaha, began in 1986 with the objective of meeting educational needs by supporting primary schools inside Afghanistan, by providing literacy training for Afghan Freedom Fighters while in Pakistan, and by assisting political groups in Pakistan with developing capabilities in administering educational programs. A non-degree university scholarship was added in 1987, and a two-year degree program followed in 1989.[62]

In sum, the U.S. government managed to introduce some structural transformations to Kabul University, and U.S. specialists launched new faculties, laboratories, and libraries, among other facilities. The buildings of Kabul University were also renovated with funding from USAID, and U.S. architects, engineers, and builders, among other personnel, were employed to modernize the institution. However, U.S. advisors were unable to introduce master's-level studies due to both the inadequate qualifications of the teaching staff and the limited knowledge base of the student body, despite numerous exchange and training programs. Kabul University continued to produce graduates with BA diplomas; however, low salaries and local traditions in promotion based on family and tribal connections, not merit, weakened the potential of qualified staff. English as the language of instruction, the introduction of a new constitution, and other projects met with limited enthusiasm on the part of the academic community.[63] Ultimately, traditionalism weighed most heavily in the scale that did not tip in favor of U.S. reforms in higher education in Afghanistan.

3   Kabul University under Soviet Control

3.1   *Purging Everything "American"*
The Russian Polytechnic Institute provided the new owners of Kabul University an opportunity to shift focus from producing specialists in engineering to eradicating everything that could be called "American" from the institution after the beginning of the Soviet military intervention in 1979. Several

---

62   U.S. Agency for International Development, "Education Sector Support Project, AID Evaluation, 1986–1990," accessed July 08, 2020, www.usaid.gov.

63   U.S. Agency for International Development, "Retrospective Review of US Assistance to Afghanistan."

MIDDLE EAST AND CENTRAL ASIA

other client polytechnic and technological institutes built and supported by the Soviet Union throughout the Middle East, most notably in Egypt, Syria, and Yemen, contributed to the training of specialists needed by Afghanistan. Indeed, many Afghan students enrolled at Soviet institutes in those countries, including at the Tabbin Institute for Metallurgical Studies in Egypt and in the Department of Chemistry at Damascus University in Syria. Both of those institutions were equipped with Soviet laboratories considered to be the chief centers for training specialists for Afghanistan who could not learn a profession at the Polytechnic Institute in Kabul. In current terminology, the universities formed a "network" of educational establishments at which Afghans studied. Soviet specialists contributed enormously to the development of advanced technical education in those countries, especially by constructing the Faculty of Chemistry and opening an isotope laboratory at Damascus University. The Soviets also worked and delivered classes in vocational education at institutes in Lebanon, Kuwait, Libya, Iraq, Kuwait, Morocco, Jordan, and other places that guaranteed Afghanistan specialists and freed Moscow to pursue a special policy at Kabul University, one geared more toward an ideological purge than development, as had been the case before the occupation. As another result, the U.S. Faculty of Engineering at Kabul University was to be closed.[64]

The first 27 Soviet advisors arrived at Kabul University in 1980. They were professors and associate professors in the fields of Russian language, philosophy, history, education, and of various disciplines of natural science from different Soviet universities.[65] It was not the first contact between Soviet educationalists and the Afghan university community. Some Soviet professors in the fields of physics and chemistry came to Kabul University to deliver lectures within the framework of UNESCO's agreements in the 1950s. In addition, the building and the development of the Polytechnic Institute in the 1960s created a community of Soviet advisors in Kabul. However, they rarely visited Kabul University before the April revolution of 1979 because the university was the American sphere of influence in Afghanistan.

---

64   Report on the Work of Soviet Professors and Specialists at the Tabbin Institute for Metallurgical Studies, 1973–1974, folder 65, Reports about the Work of Soviet Professors and Specialists at the Tabbin Institute for Metallurgical Studies, Egypt during the period of 1973–1974, entry 11, records group 9606, Soviet Ministry for Higher Education, State Archive of Russian Federation (hereafter GARF), p. 1.

65   Report. Beginnings of the Work of Soviet Specialists at Kabul University, [1984–1987], folder 353, Reports on the Work of Soviet Specialists at Educational Institutions of Afghanistan, 1984–1987, vol. 1, entry 11, records group 9606, Soviet Ministry for Higher Education, GARF.

104   CHAPTER 2

The coup d'état of 1979 made it possible for the Soviets to occupy Kabul University. At that time, the university embraced 11 faculties, 7,500 students, and 600 members of the teaching staff.[66] However, the number of both students and professors soon diminished: in 1980. About 2,000 students and 230 qualified professors left Kabul University and Afghanistan to find shelter in Pakistan.[67] Despite the fact that the number of students and teachers would increase to 7,000 and to 500 in 1987–1988, respectively, the Soviets would never be able to reproduce the qualified part of the teaching staff that was exiled to Pakistan.

Only in 1983, three years or so after their arrival in Kabul, did the Soviet advisors elaborate on a plan of reforms for the university. The Soviet government was going to eliminate so-called western influence from the curricular and structural organization of the university, to introduce compulsory ideological disciplines like Marxism, political economics, Soviet history, and the History of the Communist Party of Afghanistan, etc., to establish a master's level of studies, to translate into Dari and publish a lot of textbooks for new courses, to train about 100–120 new lecturers in the Soviet Union, to enhance the admission of lower social groups, to increase the number of students with majors in the Russian language up to 40–50 percent of total enrolment, and to make the professoriate be loyal to Soviet values and ideology. This plan definitely sounded more ambitious than the previous American one and identified clearly the intention of Moscow to transform Kabul University to the Soviet model that implied its Sovietization.[68]

The plan demanded sending more Soviet advisors to Kabul University. During the period of 1984–1987, about 50 Soviet specialists worked at Kabul University, which was twice as many as the number of former American advisors.[69] The group of Soviet specialists was led by one of the professors who had a position as the rector's advisor. This Soviet professor was placed in the university's room near the office of the rector. During the crucial period of reforms in the 1980s, a famous professor in the field of geology from Kazan University, Alexey Dedkov, led the Soviet advisors.

Before beginning the implementation of the plan, the Soviets replaced the rector. A poet, a specialist in the Russian language, graduate from a Soviet

---

66   Ibid.
67   Kabul University. Brief Information Letter by the Professor A. S. Moskvin, Chief of Soviet Specialists Group at Kabul University, Advisor of the Rector, 1987, folder 353, records group 9606, GARF.
68   Development of Kabul University, 1983, folder 353, records group 9606, GARF.
69   Report on the Work of Soviet Specialists at Kabul University, 1984, folder 353, records group 9606, GARF.

higher educational institute, and member of the pro-Soviet party, Asadullah Habib, became the new rector of Kabul University.[70] However, he had the reputation of being anything but a puppet of the Soviet advisors. Documents and memories of some Soviet advisors witnessed that the rector conducted policies similar to those of former rectors who were compelled to cooperate with American advisors. Asadullah Habib complied with many proposals made by the Soviets, but later skillfully slowed down the implementation of proposals through long discussions. Over several years, the rector and the administration were able to limit the activities of the Soviet advisors by forbidding them to be set themselves up in the Faculties of Engineering, Letters, and Islamic Law. In order to overcome this resistance, the Soviets reorganized these faculties and changed deans.[71] Later, as mentioned before, the Faculty of Engineering, established by American advisors, was closed due "its anti-Soviet activities."[72] Instead of the Faculty of Letters created by the United States in the 1960s, a Historical-Philosophical Department was set up. Finally, such new Faculties as the Worker-Peasant Department and the Military Department were soon established. The former was established to help prospective students who had no strong knowledge but were loyal to the new political regime to enter the university. The latter provided all the male students with an additional military education. Both departments were patterned on the Soviet model of university education.

Among these first organizational reforms, the introduction of master's studies at Kabul University took priority. As noted above, the American advisors, did not introduce master's studies because of the teaching staff's and students' low qualifications.[73] The Soviet specialists recognized the fact that the teaching staff that remained at Kabul University was too academically weak to teach at the master's level. According to the Soviet statistics, 50 percent of the total members of the teaching staff had only BA diplomas, 35 percent were graduates from MA foreign programs, and 15 percent earned PhD degrees, mainly at

---

70   Kabul University. Brief Information Letter by the Professor A. S. Moskvin, 1987, folder 353, records group 9606, GARF; Report on the Trip Abroad in the Framework of International Scientific Cooperation by the Professor A. P. Dedkov, Chief of Soviet Specialists Group at Kabul University, 1986, folder 354, Reports on the Work of Soviet Specialists at Educational Institutions in Afghanistan, 1984–1987, records group 9606, GARF.

71   Report on the Work of Soviet Specialists at Kabul University, 1984, folder 353, records group 9606, GARF.

72   Kabul University. Brief Information Letter by the Professor A. S. Moskvin, 1987, folder 353, records group 9606, GARF.

73   Report on the Work of Soviet Specialists at Kabul University, 1984, folder 353, records group 9606, GARF.

universities in the United States, Germany, and France.[74] The Soviet advisors reported honestly to the Soviet Ministry of Education and Ministry of Foreign Affairs that "Kabul University had a teaching staff of very low qualifications that made it impossible to start teaching master's students."[75] Moreover, the students of Kabul University demonstrated a weak knowledge that hindered them from being involved in master's studies. However, the establishment of master's studies at Kabul University became a question of prestige and supremacy in the ideological competition between the United States and the Soviet Union. In order to improve the qualifications of the teaching staff necessary for the establishment of master's studies, the Soviet government set up a specific department at Kabul University called the Institute for Professional Development. In 1984, the first 26 young Afghan lecturers earned master's degrees in the fields of History, Philosophy, and Russian.[76]

This project likely increased the qualifications of the university community and, consequently, in 1987, master's studies were formally set up at eight out of the fourteen faculties, and at 18 out of the 52 chairs at Kabul University. Before the withdrawal of the Soviet army from Afghanistan in 1989, more than 140 students were engaged in master's studies in the fields of history, philosophy, political economics, and Russian.[77] It seemed to be a success; however, numerous memories of Soviet advisors published later, and an interview between the author and one of the Soviet advisors gave evidence that the master's studies existed on paper only. In reality, most of students could not graduate due to weak knowledge.

Despite the war, failures, and constant resistance to Soviet transformations, the advisors were able to revise the curriculum and to introduce new disciplines in each department. In 1980, the Soviet advisors stated in their first reports that all the disciplines in the social sciences were Americanized, the textbooks and practical seminars were absent, the students had only notes from lectures, and they learned only English as a foreign language.[78] The learning and teaching at Kabul University were assessed by Soviet advisors as

---

74 Ibid.

75 Kabul University. Brief Information Letter by the Professor A. S. Moskvin, 1987, folder 353, records group 9606, GARF.

76 Report on Information-Propagandistic Activities Accomplished by Soviet Specialists at Kabul University, 1984, folder 353, records group 9606, GARF.

77 Information on Institute for Professional Development for Teaching Staff in the Field of Social Sciences at Kabul University by the Professor A. P. Dedkov, Chief of Soviet Specialists Group at Kabul University, no date, folder 353, records group 9606, GARF.

78 Report. Beginnings of the Work of Soviet Specialists at Kabul University, [1984–1987], folder 353, records group 9606, GARF.

MIDDLE EAST AND CENTRAL ASIA

unsatisfactory. The revision included, therefore, the content of disciplines and the methods of teaching in order to eliminate the previous influence of American virtues. Instead of the American ideas, the ideology of Marxism-Leninism was formally imposed on all the social sciences.[79] In order to guarantee the formal availability of this ideological component, the teaching staff was assigned to prepare new syllabi. However, it was not possible for Soviet advisors to control the real content of lectures delivered in accordance with the formal syllabi. Recognizing this fact, the disciplines of Marxism, Philosophy, Modern History of Afghanistan, Soviet History, Political Economics, Soviet Sociology, etc. were delivered by Soviet professors themselves through interpreters. However, the Soviet advisors failed to make students attend classes on these new ideological disciplines. The classes were often cancelled due to the absence of students. One of the Soviet advisors reported to Moscow: "The students disrupt classes, are often late to classes, and demand to cancel them."[80]

Finally, Russian classes were imposed on each faculty. The teaching of the Russian language was said to be the most effective project. The number of students who wanted to study Russian rose every day due to cultural and social extracurricular activities set up by Soviet specialists.[81] However, in the conditions of war, violence, and the killing of those Afghan students who cooperated with *shuravi*,[82] the Soviet advisors could attract only 18 to 26% of the total student enrollment to study the Russian language.[83] The percentage was less than the Soviet government had planned.

In 1988, on the eve of the withdrawal of Soviet troops, the advisors noted the most visible shortcomings of the Soviet policy at Kabul University. First, the setting up of the master's studies was entirely stalled.[84] Second, the ideological disciplines did not embrace the student body, who effectively restrained their expansion at Kabul University. Third, the war against Soviet troops undermined all the efforts of the Soviet advisors to shape a pro-Soviet Kabul University.

---

79   Letter from the Professor A. P. Dedkov, Chief of Soviet Specialists Group at Kabul University, to the Soviet Embassy in Kabul, Afghanistan, no date, folder 353, records group 9606, GARF.

80   Political Situation in Kabul University. Report by the Professor B. A. Shiriaev, Soviet Advisor at Kabul University, 1983–1987, folder 354, records group 9606, GARF.

81   Boris Shiriaev, *Soviet Advisor at Kabul University, 1983–1987*, Interviewed by Natalia Tsvetkova, September 25, 2013.

82   *Shuravi* means 'soviet' by the Persian language. Both Afghan people and Soviet advisors used this name for all the Soviets who occupied Afghanistan during the 1980s.

83   Report on the Work of Soviet Specialists at Kabul University, 1984, folder 353, records group 9606, GARF; Tsvetkova, "Americanisation, Sovietisation," 336–43.

84   Main Directions of the Work by the Soviet Consultants at the Afghan Ministry of Education for 1986–1990. [A Plan], no date, folder 353, records group 9606, GARF.

108   CHAPTER 2

4   **Professors and Students at Kabul University: Resistance to Americanization and Sovietization**

4.1   *Professors against U.S. and Soviet Advisors*

U.S. advisors, similar to their Soviet counterparts, recognized that the success of all of their reforms depended upon the loyalty of Afghans who occupied positions as professors, associate professors, assistant professors, and lecturers at Kabul University. However, while dealing with the professoriate there, U.S. and Soviet advisors faced problems that undermined Americanization and Sovietization and reinforced traditional approaches to higher education in Afghanistan.

The primary problem was the teaching staff's lack of qualifications, coupled with their reluctance to change local academic life. The first U.S. visiting professors were shocked by the wholly inadequate training of instructors and demanded a policy of staff re-education and professional development at U.S. universities.[85] Until the beginning of the 1970s, more than 200 members of the teaching staff, who comprised half of the total lecturers at Kabul University, earned American degrees at U.S. universities.[86] Although professors did participate in U.S. exchange programs, they only reluctantly supported U.S. proposals to change local teaching practices, introduce more practical classes, and make students read more specialized textbooks. Moreover, the administration and students at Kabul University resisted the introduction of new rules for admission that would mean the matriculation of more highly skilled students. Consequently, Olaf Bergelin, the Program Director of the United States Engineering Team, stated in his final report to the Department of States in 1968 that

> For five years I've been trying to promote engineering research here, haven't had much success. Physical conditions are much better now than they were in 1963 as we have new laboratories. We have been able to do a little work in our Faculty when we had some special funds and found we could get the teachers to work if they were paid in addition, but if not, they will do nothing.[87]

The weak qualifications of the teaching staff and its reluctance to cooperate with Americans became the main obstacle on the way to improving standards of education at the Faculty of Engineering and at Kabul University as a whole.

---

85   The Kabul Program. Situation Report. USAID, 1963, box 2, records group 286, NARA.
86   Letter from Edwin Martin, 1968, box 1, records group 286, NARA.
87   Letter from O. P. Bergelin [1963], box 1, records group 286, NARA.

MIDDLE EAST AND CENTRAL ASIA 109

The most serious problem of all, however, was potential defections by those same participants, some of whom failed to return to Kabul after finishing training in the United States. Initially, the United States considered such cases to be isolated, but later on, new members of the university's teaching staff exhibited considerable reluctance to leave the United States. The same situation plagued the Fulbright Program's participants, when 11 of 42 Afghans did not return home for various reasons, including the desire to continue studying at their own expense in the United States or immigration to Canada.[88] Such problems were viewed by the U.S. team at Kabul University as symptoms of general unrest. However, the top reason for defection was reported to be the low salaries paid at Kabul University. Indeed, the paltry salary of $40 to $60 per month made it nearly impossible for a faculty member to finance the lifestyle enjoyed by the average professor in Europe or the United States. Some potential faculty members even considered taking a quite attractive scholarship abroad compared to the situation offered by the Faculty of Engineering. The U.S. government could not increase the salaries for the teaching staff against the budget policy of the Ministry of Education, however, nor could it allow decreasing the number of qualified teaching staff in the Faculty. To put a stop to the defections, the project to train teaching faculty in the United States was terminated in July 1973, which critically damaged the aspirations of U.S. advisors to shape a modern professoriate in Afghanistan.[89]

The reluctant behavior of professors and their sabotage of the reforms seemed to be common experiences faced in implementing U.S. and Soviet policies. For their part, the Soviets mentioned in their reports on Afghanistan that the teaching staff utterly lacked qualified Arab specialists and that staff were in no hurry to earn the meager salaries offered at the universities and institutes built by Moscow.[90] Describing the situation in its ally Egypt, Soviet professors stated that it was difficult to replace the Soviet teaching staff with Arab colleagues, because salaries were unattractive, and Moscow had to send more specialists so as to not interrupt students' coursework. Moreover, Arab colleagues working with the Soviets sabotaged the rising number of classes and worked extremely little, at least according to Soviet reports; for example, only 11.5 percent of classes were delivered by Egyptians at the Tabbin Institute

---

88   U.S. Agency for International Development, "Technical Education. Faculty of Engineering. Kabul University Project Appraisal Report, 1970–72."

89   U.S. Agency for International Development, "Report of Visit to the United States Engineering Team, 1970," p. 4–5.

90   Report about the Work of Soviet Professors and Specialists at the Tabbin Institute for Metallurgical Studies, 1973–1974, folder 65, records group 9606, GARF, p. 4.

110   CHAPTER 2

for Metallurgical Studies from 1973 to 1974.[91] Another problem was staff turn-over, especially of laboratory assistants, which led to a regular lack of continuity in scientific research. Soviet advisors, similar to their U.S. counterparts, complained that the Arabs did not teach and did not conduct research: "The participation of Egyptian professors leads to the impediment of the studies and teaching."[92] At Cairo University, for example, visiting Soviet professors attempted to reform the engineering curriculum; however, the local academic staff stymied the introduction of new classes and disciplines because they were Soviet and required larger course loads from the local teaching staff. The Egyptians did not intend to expand the number of hours for the Soviet curriculum, even in the field of vocational education.[93] The visiting Soviet specialists, as the U.S. ones had, supported academic life at universities: revising curricula and disciplines, publishing manuals, and teaching and supervising students. However, all of their efforts and reforms were meaningless without the help of local professors, who alone could maintain the continuity of Americanization or Sovietization and, in turn, the modernization of local universities.

On the flipside of U.S. and Soviet projects aimed at training the teaching staff abroad was the impossibility for educated Afghans to secure decent employment, not even at Kabul University, to say nothing of a position in the Afghan economy that remained less developed and technologically backward despite the enormous investments of many countries, including the United States and the Soviet Union. That underlying problem was first brought to light by U.S. advisor Olaf Bergelin, head of the first U.S. team at Kabul University, who returned to Afghanistan in 1970 to examine the successes and failures of past reforms at the university made by his colleagues. He noted:

> The majority of the staff members <...> showed a feeling of restlessness and an undefined dissatisfaction with their situation [sic]. These men had an early background in an undeveloped society where they were exposed to poverty and archaic social conditions. They then attended middle and secondary schools [sic] that were based on foreign concepts and represented a sharp cultural break with their childhood. From these

---

91   Report about the Work of the Foreign Affairs Department at the Ministry for Higher Education, 1977, folder 128, Reports of the Foreign Affairs Department at the Ministry for Higher Education on the Cooperation between the Soviet Union and the Countries of the Middle East, Africa, and Latin America, records group 9606, GARF, p. 7.

92   Report on the Work Accomplished in Syria, 1961–1964, folder 1942, reports on Visits Abroad by Professors to the Developing Countries – Iraq, Cambodia, United Arabic Republic, Ethiopia, 1964, records group 9606, GARF, p. 50.

93   Ibid.

schools they were sent for study in the United States which [*sic*] has an advanced economy that offers great opportunities to scientists and engineers. After two to four years in this advanced culture, [*sic*] where their fellow students were heading for professionally attractive and highly paid positions, these men returned to Kabul and to much less attractive professional positions. The teaching assignments are at a relatively low level, the pay is very low, there is little encouragement to do research, and there is little evidence that the situation will change appreciably for many years. It is no wonder that these highly trained men are restless. They feel that [they] have knowledge, skills, and technique that can be used outside the University, and if the situation in the University is not attractive to them, they will use every means possible to move to where the rewards are greater. The returned participants are the key in the success or failure of the Faculty and something must be done to keep them [*sic*] growing professionally within the Faculty.[94]

However, such problems could not be overcome with the help of grants and assistance from the United States, especially not to the degree to sustain the educated, professional, qualified faculty required for a developed economy or their salaries, which Afghanistan could not provide either. Most U.S. reforms in Afghanistan and at Kabul University therefore failed to achieve their goals. Moreover, negative reactions were common among the university administration and the other part of the professoriate to U.S. protégés—that is, young Afghan lecturers who received American degrees and returned to Kabul University to continue their careers. The nominations promoted by U.S. advisors were too often blocked by the administration, which strained political relations between the advisors and the government. Soviet documents indicate the same problem raised by Olaf Bergelin; many faculty members went to complete internships in the Soviet Union, where they received doctoral degrees, and the qualification of returnees did not match Kabul University's outdated infrastructure, its lack of equipment, and its distaste for research. Consequently, those "highly educated faculty lost their qualifications and remain general teachers."[95]

The second problem concerned the negative reaction of the professoriate to American or Soviet reforms. The Afghan professoriate demonstrated passivity,

---

94   U.S. Agency for International Development, "Letter by Olaf Bergelin to Education Office. USAID/Washington, November 05, 1970," accessed July 08, 2020, www.usaid.gov, pp. 1–2.

95   Report on the Work at the Damascus University, 1964, folder 1942, records group 9606, GARF, pp. 70–73.

112   CHAPTER 2

slowness, and restraint to American proposals, projects, etc. They agreed to all the ideas proposed by the Americans, but then nothing happened: professors postponed follow-up meetings, did not implement agreements, and did not introduce revisions into curricula, disciplines, and methods of teaching.[96] Olaf Bergelin mentioned this mode of behavior in one of his reports:

> My first meeting with President [of Kabul University] Osman Anwary was pleasant. [Anwary] suggested that I call him at any time for assistance. Later, however, when I wanted to see him about a new staff member, it took me over a week to get an appointment with him.[97]

In addition, the administration of Kabul University always assured the Afghan public of its unenthusiastic attitudes towards American reforms, which damaged the relationship between Afghans and Americans. One of the American advisors mentioned the following observation in his report about the president's public speech:

> Anwary indicated some dissatisfaction with the Afghans' association with Americans in education in general and with American efforts in teacher education in particular. The tone of speech might best be described as 'I love you, but....[98]

These attitudes and reactions of the teaching staff towards the American transformations at the university became the primary reason for their failure.

All countries in the Middle East, their local academic communities, and their political elite frequently alternated their political orientation to the Soviet Union and the United States. For example, Egypt, an ally of Moscow until the mid-1970s, reprioritized its friendship with the United States, which immediately affected the behavior of the Arab teaching staff and the number of advisors sent from Moscow. If, in 1973, 114 Soviet professors had worked at the Institute, then in 1977 their ranks were thinned to 50 and, by 1978, only 35.[99] Moreover, Egypt stopped propaganda promoting the Soviet way of life

---

96   Letter from Antony Lanza, 1971, box 4, records group 286, NARA.

97   The Kabul Program, May 10, 1963, box 2, records group 286, NARA.

98   For Discussion with the Ambassador. Review of the Developments in Teacher Education. [By] Stewart S. Hamblen, Chief, Education Division, USAID, January 24, 1963, box 2, records group 286, NARA.

99   Report about the Tabbin Institute for Metallurgical Studies, 1977–78, folder 147, Reports about the Work of Soviet Professors and Specialists at the Tabbin Institute for Metallurgical Studies, Egypt during the period of 1977–1978, records group 9606, GARF, p. 15; Report

MIDDLE EAST AND CENTRAL ASIA

at educational institutions. The traditional so-called *Friendship Days*, for instance, previously held for both students and the teaching staff to familiarize them with Soviet life, were renamed "Recreation and Sports Days" when Egypt was involved in negotiations with the U.S. administration.[100]

The Soviet advisors introducing their reforms, also recognized the fact that the most difficult problem was the unfriendly, hostile attitude of the professoriate towards the Soviet occupation, reforms, and policy at Kabul University. It was clear that the success of Soviet reforms depended on the favorable position of the professoriate. Being an influential professional group in Afghanistan, professors could enormously influence the final effects of Soviet transformations. The Soviet advisors needed to win the hearts of the teaching staff and to attract them to their side.

After the first wave of exiles in 1980, the university professors continued seeking shelter in Pakistan in subsequent years.[101] This emigration created a constant problem for the Soviets in finding new staff with any possible degrees and diplomas. In addition, the silent resistance of so-called neutral lecturers, those who remained in the university but did not support the political regime of Babrak Karmal and the Soviet reforms, also became an everyday problem for the Soviets. This part of the teaching staff committed covert sabotage or demonstrated apathy and ignorance. They did not cooperate with the Soviet advisors and at the same time did not protest openly.[102] The Soviets stated that

> the future of Kabul University would depend on our ability to attract and to win the confidence of the neutral part of the teaching staff. They are indecisive and follow the policy of wait-and-see. Our alliance with the part of the teaching staff can crush down the anti-Soviet resistance movement.[103]

To attract them, the Soviet advisors raised salaries and assigned the neutral lecturers to higher positions. However, the alliance with the frustrating part of the teaching staff was undermined by the hard policy of the Afghan communists.

---

about the Work of the Foreign Affairs Department at the Ministry for Higher Education, 1977, folder 128, records group 9606, GARF, p. 2.

100   Report about the Work, 1977, folder 128, records group 9606, GARF, p. 9.

101   Kabul University. Brief Information Letter by the Professor A. S. Moskvin, 1987, folder 353, records group 9606, GARF.

102   Report. Beginnings of the Work of Soviet Specialists at Kabul University, [1984–1987], folder 353, records group 9606, GARF.

103   Evaluation of a Political Situation in Kabul University, 1985, folder 353, records group 9606, GARF.

114   CHAPTER 2

They pressured and terrorized the neutral lecturers, making them declare their political position, enter the leading party, and play a more active role in university life. This part of the academic community was consequently frightened, took the opposition's side, or left Kabul University.

Despite this fiasco, the Soviets tried to foster a new pliable teaching staff through reeducating some of the lecturers at Soviet universities. This part of the university community was reported to be the future academic elite of Kabul University. About 100 members out of 500 that comprised about 20 percent of the total teaching staff were reeducated and trained in the Soviet Union during the period of the Soviet occupation. The scope of this Soviet educational policy was less than that of the American one. The Americans were able to reeducate about 50% of the total teaching staff. Even in 1987 to 1988, most of the lecturers were reported to be graduates of American universities.[104] Furthermore, the factor of time was not on the Soviet side: the American reforms lasted more than fifteen years, while the Soviet ones lasted about seven years and were unexpectedly disrupted by the withdrawal of troops in 1989. In addition, another factor did not give Moscow a chance to Sovietize the Afghan teaching staff. The lecturers trained in the Soviet Union did not gain influence and power after their return to Kabul University. The advisors reported to Moscow that "a new generation of the teaching staff trained at Soviet institutions took a subordinated position and some of them were engaged in anti-Soviet activities or did not cooperate with the Soviets upon return to Afghanistan."[105] Mistakes and failures in the policy towards the professorate crucially undermined the Soviet plans to transform Kabul University.

4.2   *Students against U.S. and Soviet Advisors*
If the professoriate gained the attention of American advisors, then the student body was somehow neglected by them. Students produced too many problems to deal with effectively. The most urgent problem was the loss of students because they could not pass exams at different departments. The university lost about 50 percent of its students every year due to low admission standards and, speaking more precisely, due to the absence of any admission exams.[106] American advisors insisted on a revision of admission rules in order

---

104   Political Situation in Kabul University, 1983–1987, folder 354, records group 9606, GARF.

105   Information on Institute for Professional Development for Teaching Staff in the Field of Social Sciences at Kabul University, no date, folder 353, records group 9606, GARF; Kabul University. Brief Information Letter by the Professor A. S. Moskvin, 1987, folder 353, records group 9606, GARF.

106   Enrollment of Kabul University, 1963; Bi-Weekly 'Alert' Report to The Director, Education Division, USAID, August 14, 1967, box 1, records group 286, NARA.

MIDDLE EAST AND CENTRAL ASIA 115

to impose entrance examinations. They put pressure on the government, the king, the Ministry of Education, and the rector. However, the government of Afghanistan approved a law against introducing admission exams, and, consequently, the American advisors were not able to limit the enrollment.[107] The lack of entrance exams increased the student enrollment year by year, which turned out to be dangerous for the weak infrastructure of the university. Dormitories, laboratories, libraries, canteens, and classrooms were overcrowded, which paved the way for an Afghan student movement. Initially, students protested against the conditions of life and studies at Kabul University; however, as happened in other countries, the student movement was quickly politicized by local communists, nationalists, Maoists, and Islamists. Moreover, tribalism provoked additional conflicts between students. American democratic policy to admit students from different tribes and different Afghan provinces to the university caused an unfriendly environment in the dormitories.[108]

In 1967–68, the administration finally introduced admission tests as American advisors had suggested; however, 2,000 high school students who failed admission examinations went on strike, exacerbating the situation in the spring of 1968.[109] On the first day of May 1968, students disrupted classes at the most Americanized department, the Faculty of Education. They demanded cancellation of the entrance examinations, revisions of the Faculty's curriculum, improvements in their conditions of life, and development of social programs from the administration of the university. The demonstration paralyzed the work of Kabul University, which was soon closed. One of professors recalled:

> To contain the spread of social unrest in the future the state closed down the Kabul University for 160 days hoping that students would return home; however, students continued their struggle until their demands were met. Student strikes also inspired a segment of the tribal communities to oppose the state policy of eliminating local participation and initiatives in the decision-making process regarding local development.[110]

Since 1968, American advisors and diplomats have perceived the student movement as something dangerous for their reforms. New consultants in the field of student affairs were sent to Kabul University. Visiting professors from

---

107   Weekly Report to the Director, USAID, 1968, box 1, records group 286, NARA.
108   Tsvetkova, "Americanisation, Sovietisation," 336–43.
109   Emadi, "Radical Political Movements," 435.
110   Ibid, 435.

116   CHAPTER 2

Indiana University were assigned to reorganize university administration, admission rules, and deal with students. Herman Wells, a famous scholar in the field of international education, the president of Indiana University, and a contributor to American transformations in German universities during the occupational period of 1945–1952,[111] proposed strengthening the authority of the central administration of the university over the entire university in order to deal more effectively with opposing students and academic staff of different departments. However, student riots escalated into violence and compelled the advisors to close their project. Moreover, American advisors did not seek to neutralize radicals and extremists, and, finally, did not make any attempt to establish pro-democratic, liberal student organizations in order to manage the student body, as American specialists had effectively done in other countries.[112]

In 1971–72, the student protest movement embraced all the Afghan educational institutions and was mixed with a general wave of anti-government strikes. The students now protested against the king, the government, its corruption, and the monarchy itself. They became a political power opposing the pro-American government and the king. Now, it was clear to American advisors that they had lost sight of students who supported the revolution of 1973. After the overthrow of the king, the student protests were ended and Kabul University resumed its academic life.[113] However, as said above, in 1976, all American advisors and the Agency for International Development left Kabul University, where Islamic education was rapidly developed.

The Soviet advisors, like their American counterparts, could not effectively deal with students and their open resistance. Despite a wide-ranging exchange program that embraced annually about 150 university students to be trained at Soviet institutions, the programs' body demonstrated hostile attitudes, established anti-Soviet organizations, and induced terrorist attacks at Kabul University. To stop the hostile attitudes, the Soviet advisors tried to revise the social composition of the student body by giving admission priority to the children of workers and peasants. They intended to admit 40–50 percent of the students originating from lower social groups, who could be much more loyal to the

---

111   Herman Wells was the primary advisor for the education and religious affairs office at the American military occupational government in Germany. He elaborated new criteria and procedures of selection, notably, that young and loyal German students with leadership potential should be selected and then sent to Washington. See Henry J. Kellermann, *Cultural Relations as an Instrument of US Foreign Policy: The Educational Exchange Program between the United States and Germany, 1945–1954* (Washington, D.C., 1978), 3–39; Lucius Clay, *Decision in Germany* (London: Doubleday & Company, 1950), 298–305.

112   Tsvetkova, *Failure of American and Soviet Cultural Imperialism.*

113   Kabul University—Development During Dr. Javid's Tenure, 1973, box 2, records group 286, NARA.

MIDDLE EAST AND CENTRAL ASIA

existing political regime and Soviet occupation. However, in 1987 only about 10 percent of the total student body was comprised of students from lower social groups.[114] In addition, the policy to attract students to the pro-Soviet *Democratic Union of Afghan Youth*, established by the advisors at Kabul University, did not come to fruition. According to Soviet documents, this student union was comprised of 3 percent to 12 percent of the student body.[115] The Soviet specialists stated that "the influence of this organization was very weak, its leaders took a passive position and did not organize mass events to attract students."[116] In addition, the violence against those students who cooperated with *shuravi* diminished any efforts of the Soviet advisors to win the hearts and minds of the student body. Kabul University remained a university that mostly accommodated the anti-Soviet students. It was dangerous for Afghan students to study at the university patterned on the shuravi's model. Some of the students were killed by mujahedeen for their cooperation with a Soviet power.[117]

Consequently, in their reports, the Soviet advisors recognized the fact that "Kabul University exists in the conditions of a permanent war against Soviet reforms. This war varies from a covert propaganda to an open terror."[118] In 1983–1984, Kabul University sheltered various Islamic organizations, which opposed the Soviet activities. The most popular were *Islamic Society, The Union of Professors and Students,*[119] and *The Independent Union of Afghan Students*. According to the Soviet reports, they were initiators of demonstrations, disorders, sabotage, and terror actions. Bomb explosions that killed students, teachers, and Soviet advisors were often heard in the buildings of the university.[120] In 1985, the Soviet Union was able to temporarily diminish the terror activity when fourteen students and some leaders of Islamic organizations were executed.[121] The advisors assured Moscow that "the Islamic underground exists,

---

114   Kabul University. Brief Information Letter by the Professor A. S. Moskvin, 1987, folder 353, records group 9606, GARF.

115   Report on the Work of Soviet Specialists at Kabul University, 1984, folder 353, records group 9606, GARF.

116   Political Situation in Kabul University, 1983–1987, folder 354, records group 9606, GARF.

117   Brief Information Letter by the Professor A. S. Moskvin, Chief of Soviet Specialists Group at Kabul University and Advisor of the Rector, 1987, folder 353, records group 9606, GARF; Political Situation in Kabul University, 1983–1987, folder 354, records group 9606, GARF; Shiriaev, *Soviet Advisor at Kabul University, 1983–1987.*

118   Report on the Trip Abroad, 1986, folder 354, records group 9606, GARF.

119   Barnett Rubin, "Post-Cold War State Disintegration: The Failure of International Conflict Resolution in Afghanistan," *Journal of International Affairs* 46, no. 2 (January 1993): 475.

120   Concerning our knowledge, three Soviet advisors who worked at Kabul University were perished during the Soviet occupation: Shiriaev, *Soviet Advisor at Kabul University, 1983–1987.*

121   Evaluation of a Political Situation in Kabul University, 1985, folder 353, records group 9606, GARF; Report on the Trip Abroad, 1986, folder 354, records group 9606, GARF.

but it is not too active, and it embraces 250 students and professors that is comparably little."[122] However, in 1986 to 1988, Kabul University was quickly transformed into the center of Islamic resistance to the Soviet occupation, and the Soviet advisors were compelled to report to Moscow that "there was considerable diversity in clandestine student organizations: radicals, leftists, extremists, and Islamic conservative ones. They act against the Soviet Union."[123] Both the Soviet government and Soviet advisors had no ideas on how to deal with influential, oppositional Islamic organizations at Kabul University, which quickly radicalized the student body. The Soviet advisors, like the American ones, missed the development of a radical student movement. If the Americans overlooked students who participated in the coup d'état of 1973, then the Soviets were not able to engage university students, some of whom would soon participate in Islamic radical movements in Afghanistan.[124]

Both Washington and Moscow encountered resistance to their reforms on the part of the students and professors. The introduction of new and non-Afghan disciplines and study plans, the transformation of Kabul University on the models of American and Soviet educational systems, and the attempts to re-educate the teaching staff provoked sabotage, protest, and dissident movements at Kabul University. Neither American nor Soviet advisors could overcome the resistance. The students were more active in their offensive against reforms participating in the overthrow of the monarchy that undermined the further Americanization of Kabul University in the early 1970s and participating in radical Islamic movements against the Soviets in the early 1980s. The professorship demonstrated slowness, passivity, and ignorance to the advisors of both states and undermined both Americanization and Sovietization of study plans, disciplines, and values imposed by either the United States or the Soviet Union.

5   Conclusion

We now know that the development of Kabul University went along with the imposing of American or Soviet values, English or Russian languages,

---

122   Evaluation of a Political Situation in Kabul University, 1985, folder 353, records group 9606, GARF; Report on the Trip Abroad, 1986, folder 354, records group 9606, GARF; Report on the Work of Soviet Specialists at Kabul University, 1984, folder 323, records group 9606, GARF.

123   Political Situation in Kabul University, 1983–1987, folder 354, records group 9606, GARF.

124   Tsvetkova, "Americanisation, Sovietisation," 336–43.

American or Soviet disciplines, etc., with local traditions being neglected by the superpowers. Primary documents have allowed us to state that the policies of Americanization and Sovietization were resisted by the university community. The resistance contributed to the failure of transformations and to further Islamization of Kabul University.

When comparing the American and Soviet transformations at Kabul University, it is observed that both powers attempted to impose their rival models of university education by pressuring the university community and by working to attract this community to their divergent political cultures. It is evident that their reforms were stimulated by ideological confrontation; both the United States and the Soviet Union exploited Kabul University in order to transform Afghan society, to disseminate their rival political cultures, and, generally, to win over the minds of Afghans in the Cultural Cold War. It turns out that the policies of both of Americanization and Sovietization of Kabul University pursued similar political goals and moved in very similar directions, despite divergent political systems, values, and state ideology. However, both American and Soviet transformations of the university were limited due to the resistance of the academic community.

The concepts of Americanization and Sovietization broadly contrasted as the soft and hard notions in the historiography can therefore be redefined in terms of their resemblance and limitation. First, there is no difference between the concepts of Americanization and Sovietization. This conclusion of our research challenges the literature that argued that Americanization makes reference to the soft and even mutual cultural transfer, while Sovietization is relative to hard policies. The case of Kabul University demonstrates the similarities of both phenomena. The policies of both Americanization and Sovietization had the same political aims and exploited the same methods in order to deal with the university. Second, in order to understand the limitation of Americanization and Sovietization, it is necessary to take into consideration both the successes and failures of the policies accomplished by both American and Soviet advisors. The advisors of both countries were able to change university structures, to introduce new management, and to develop a new infrastructure for students and teaching staff. However, they were not able to transform the traditional Afghan way of teaching, to make the professoriate give new courses, to make students study new subjects, etc. Both silent and open resistance on the part of the Afghan university undermined American and later Soviet cultural influences, and thus their policies of reform eventually failed. Both superpowers recognized the fact that the university had only formally acquiesced to the imposed revisions while a part of the university community did not believe in the ideas brought either by the American or the

Soviet powers. Communism provoked more opposition activities on the part of both professors and students than did American liberal democracy because of the association of communist ideology with the real occupation of Afghanistan. However, neither power was able to engage students. The students supported the revolution of 1973 that interrupted American reforms at Kabul University and, later, the student body supported the Islamist movement that undermined Soviet reforms.

The cases of both Americanization and Sovietization at universities of Afghanistan have also illustrated that professors and students were the main obstacles to the American or Soviet transformations. The assistance in the development of Kabul University provided by both American or Soviet governments was welcomed by the local public, but the indoctrination of students or the introduction of new ideological disciplines were restrained.[125]

In Afghanistan, both superpowers could not subdue the localism and conservatism of Kabul University that undermined both American and Soviet cultural pressure and, according to our analysis, saved some traditional, local features peculiar to Afghan universities. Kabul University's professors and students resisted this subordination silently and openly with their resistance being shaped in different forms—notably sabotage, student strikes, and Islamic movement. All of these forms of resistance successfully rolled back the impact of both Americanization and Sovietization of Afghanistan on education.

The case of Kabul University demonstrates the inability of superpowers to encourage the formation of pliable, friendly, and loyal students and professors. Despite crucial Americanization and Sovietization of the structure, administration apparatus, and content of disciplines, both superpowers were not able to change the traditions and values of professors and students. The university community restrained both Americanization and Sovietization of its Kabul University and, speaking more widely, professors and students have proved to be the main causes for the success or failure of any reforms brought to a university by external power.

---

125   Natalia Tsvetkova, "International Education during the Cold War: Soviet Social Transformation and American Social Reproduction," *Comparative Education Review* 52, no. 2 (2008): 199–217.

CHAPTER 3

Africa

When Development and Professors Erased U.S. and Soviet Transformations in Universities of Ethiopia

1 Introduction

Throughout the Cold War in general and the Cultural Cold War in particular Ethiopia occupied a pivotal place in policies developed by Washington and Moscow towards Africa. Viewed as providing a bridge to the nations of the Middle East and a frontline in the security of North Africa, Ethiopia's strategic location encouraged the United States and the Soviet Union to increasingly funnel development aid to the country in a bid to attract local elites and ensure their loyalty. Unlike in Europe, Asia, and Latin America, the processes of transformation did not commence in Africa until the 1960s, namely when U.S. policy became relevant in African countries following a spike in funding due to the newly established U.S. Agency for International Development (USAID) and special divisions for foreign aid at educational institutions abroad at the Soviet Ministry for Higher Education. In Ethiopia in particular, Americanization lasted until the early 1970s, after which Soviet policy gained traction before plateauing and eventually declining in the mid-1980s.[1]

Even prior to the Cold War, the power of the Ethiopian emperor, Haile Selassie I, who heralded Ethiopia's modernization, had ensured that the United States would participate, assist, and provide expertise in that endeavor. Later, when Egypt quit cooperating with the United States in the early 1950s, Ethiopia emerged as a channel by which Washington sought to promote American influence in the Middle East. Seizing the opportunity, the United States began directing financial and military resources to Ethiopia for use in establishing educational institutions as well as a military base. Between the 1950s and the early 1970s, U.S. efforts resulted in the construction and significant expansion of Haile Selassie I University in Addis Ababa, an institution that soon became the chief target of U.S. education policy in Ethiopia. Close cooperation between

---

1 Getachew Metaferia, *Ethiopia and the United States: History, Diplomacy, and Analysis* (New York: Algora Publishing, 2008); Harry Brind, "Soviet Policy in the Horn of Africa," *International Affairs* 60, no. 1 (1983): 75–95.

© NATALIA TSVETKOVA, 2021 | DOI:10.1163/9789004471788_005

the United States and Ethiopia in education and modernization continued until the 1974 Ethiopian revolution, when a follower of Marxism, Mengistu Haile Mariam, took control of Ethiopia and, as a result, reduced the flow of U.S. aid to the country's universities and schools. Just as Ethiopia's government had once worked closely with Washington, the new regime began to cooperate intensely with Moscow in further developing projects for education set in motion long before the Marxists came to power. Chief among those efforts, the Soviet Union established the Polytechnic Institute in Bahar Dar in the 1960s,[2] which remained the principal target of Sovietization in Ethiopia once the Americans left and until the Cold War ended, even despite Soviet attempts to develop various other educational institutions.[3]

Unlike in Afghanistan, both Germanys, and other countries where the transformation of universities engineered by Washington and Moscow followed a policy of ideological purge and containment, in Ethiopia and other African countries the United States and the Soviet Union were compelled to pay more attention to establishing local systems of higher education and constructing facilities for educational institutions. From their outset, those and other development projects eroded all policy aimed at propagating American or Soviet ways of life and political culture at African universities. As in other countries on the continent, decolonization and the rapid growth of the education system in Ethiopia demanded that the United States and the Soviet Union plan and build dormitories, libraries, and other university infrastructure. As a consequence, such efforts left neither time nor opportunities for any profound transformations of Ethiopian educational institutions that would have been possible, for example, by introducing political science or Marxism, English, or Russian, or American or Soviet Studies into the curriculum. In parallel, the strong legacy of colonists in education in Africa, the visits of U.S. and Soviet specialists cut short by regime changes or security threats, and the active work of various international donors, including the World Bank and private foundations, somehow managed to dissipate the influence of the superpowers in Ethiopia. Washington and Moscow emerged as not the only actors in African

---

2   Both U.S. and Soviet documents followed spelling the town's name *Bahar Dar* instead of *Bahir Dar*.

3   Edward Kissi, "Paradoxes of American Development Diplomacy in the Early Cold War Period," *Past & Present* 215, No. 1 (2012): 269–95; Piero Gleijeses, "Moscow's Proxy? Cuba and Africa 1975–1988," *Journal of Cold War Studies* 8, no. 2 (2006): 3–51; Gregory Sanjian, "Promoting Stability or Instability? Arms Transfers and Regional Rivalries, 1950–1991," *International Studies Quarterly* 43, no. 4 (1999): 641–70.

AFRICA 123

education and had not wielded their power widely in order to stifle their rival's political values in local systems of education.

Against the best-laid plans of the United States and the Soviet Union there was also opposition, to one degree or another, from academic communities in Africa that wanted to maintain local traditions and did not always admire the transformations of their national universities. Of course, at universities in Europe, Asia, Africa, and Latin America, all divided by the Cold War, so-called "unfriendly" academic communities, typically referred to as the conservative professoriate in both U.S. and Soviet documents, resisted the implementation of U.S. or Soviet models of education and, in turn, thwarted the cultural diplomacy of both superpowers. However, in the international education policies of the superpowers, Ethiopia became a unique case. Above all, the Ethiopian academic body, including professors and students alike, reacted to the reforms proposed for their educational institutions by both powers in ways unlike their counterparts at Afghan, German, and Vietnamese universities, where the superpowers had imposed their models of education and sought to politicize schooling.

Ethiopia is the case that shows how professors at Ethiopian universities interacted with advisors from the United States or the Soviet Union and were triggers for the success and failure of the education policies of the superpowers. In addition, the case of Ethiopia stirs debates on a range of concepts from sociology, history, the history of education, and international relations through which the relationships between local academic communities and either U.S. or Soviet reformers can be understood. The most incisive conclusions on that topic, which can be discussed in terms of poststructuralist theories, have been formulated with reference to critical theories and concepts in educational sociology, if not also by constructivism as developed by political scientists. Indeed, the ideas of Antonio Gramsci, Pierre Bourdieu, and other thinkers holding that values, culture, and ideology are essential for legitimizing political power through education, along with the ideas of constructivist Alexander Wendt—namely, that any intentions of a power in the system of international relations can be limited by interests and traditions of local communities and groups—can partly explain the conduct of the academic community in Ethiopia toward U.S. and Soviet education policy during the Cold War. In particular, the theories can shed light on how the professoriate behaved under the pressure of and in dialogue with the bearers of alien ideology, values, and models of education and, in turn, critically shaped the effects of both superpowers' policies in Ethiopia.[4]

---

4 Alexander Wendt, "Constructing International Politics," *International Security* 20, no. 1 (1995): 71–81; Antonio Gramsci, *Selections from the Prison Notebooks* (New York: International

124 CHAPTER 3

From another angle, U.S. and Soviet education policies in Ethiopia during the Cold War have passed under the radar of scholars conducting empirical studies.[5]

Comprising reports, letters, memoranda, and other formal and informal documents prepared by U.S. and Soviet advisors working at Ethiopian institutions can help to answer questions about the essence of U.S. and Soviet reforms at top institutional targets in the country, including Haile Selassie I University and the Polytechnic Institute in Bahar Dar, as well as about the reactions and influence of the local academic community, especially professors, in relation to the outcomes of both Americanization and Sovietization in Ethiopia.

This chapter has two sections. The first section describes U.S. projects conducted at Haile Selassie I University and examines the reactions of local academics to those projects as well as to certain proposals. For comparison, the second section describes Soviet projects at the Ethiopian Polytechnic Institute and examines the reactions of faculty and students there to Soviet policy. In conclusion, the chapter discusses the impact of the professors on the transformations in Ethiopian higher education.

Publishers, 1971); Pierre Bourdieu, "Cultural Reproduction and Social Reproduction," In *Power and Ideology in Education*, ed. Jerome Karabel and A. H. Halsey (New York: Oxford University Press, 1977); Natalia Tsvetkova, "International Education during the Cold War: Soviet Social Transformation and American Social Reproduction," *Comparative Education Review* 52, no. 2 (2008): 199–217.

5   Of course, Ethiopian institutions of education are touched upon in the vast amount of literature on development, assistance, and modernization during the Cold War, and studies especially addressing the Cultural Cold War have addressed questions about the everyday lives, identities, and racial discrimination of African students while attending U.S. and Soviet universities. However, Ethiopian students, who represented a significant number of those international students, have received only superficial attention. Researchers have not raised any questions about how the Ethiopian academic community reacted to U.S. and Soviet policies at their universities, especially not any about what U.S. and Soviet experts did at Ethiopian universities, about the categories of U.S. advisors, Soviet advisors, and professors, or about how students endured the transformations that occurred in education in Ethiopia in the context of the Cold War. See, Amanda McVety, "Pursuing Progress: Point Four in Ethiopia," *Diplomatic History* 32, no. 3 (June 2008): 371–403; Lemma Legesse, "The Ethiopian Student Movement 1960–1974: A Challenge to the Monarchy and Imperialism in Ethiopia," *Northeast African Studies* 1, no. 2 (1979): 31–46; Roger Kanet, "Soviet and American Behaviour Toward the Developing Countries—A Comparison," *Canadian Slavonic Papers/Revue Canadienne Des Slavistes* 15, no. 4 (1973): 439–61; Tobias Broich, "U.S. And Soviet Foreign Aid During the Cold War: A Case Study of Ethiopia," *Working Papers*, No. 10 (2017) accessed March 10, 2020, https://www.merit.unu.edu/publications/working-papers/abstract/?id=6367.

AFRICA   125

2   U.S. Advisors at Haile Selassie I University: Under the Pressure of Ethiopianization

2.1   *Building a University Scattered across the City*

Higher education in Ethiopia was formally established when Emperor Haile Selassie I founded the University College of Addis Ababa in March 1950.[6] In the years that followed, six additional public colleges were opened under contracts with various U.S. universities, although the administration and coordination among them were flawed, according to U.S. sources. In 1959, when the Ethiopian government requested U.S. assistance with examining possible courses of corrective action, a program for joint U.S.–Ethiopian cooperation in education was established.[7] However, the United States was not the sole benefactor of education in Ethiopia but ranked among several other Western states and organizations, including Sweden, France, the United Kingdom, West Germany, the United Nations Development Program, the Ford Foundation, the Soviet Union, and other nations in the Eastern Bloc also provided assistance for higher education in Ethiopia.[8]

Nevertheless, the United States not only provided the most funding for the construction of the university college's buildings and dormitories but also contributed enormously to unifying all of the other colleges under its auspices. In 1960, following an invitation from USAID, a team from the University of Utah offered recommendations for integrating the several institutions into one university, while USAID itself offered to assist with organizing it. After accepting the offer, Ethiopia's government issued an imperial charter in February 1961 for the autonomous institution of Haile Selassie I University, abbreviated as "HSIU" in U.S. government documents and thus referred to as such in the remainder of this chapter. Emperor Selassie was so excited about the assistance furnished by the United States that he donated his personal residence in Addis Ababa, the Guenete Leul Palace, to be converted into the new university's main campus.[9]

From then until 1974, three major U.S. agencies dealt with HSIU: USAID, the Peace Corps, and the U.S. Information Service. Whereas USAID provided grants

---

6 Contract between the USAID and Haile Selassie I University, 1973, box 4, records group 286, Agency for International Development, entry 254, USAID Mission to Ethiopia. Education Division, National Archives Records Administration (hereafter NARA).

7 Historical Summary of Haile Selassie I University, 1967, box 2, records group 286, NARA.

8 Report on Examination of the Education Sector Projects of the AID Program in Ethiopia, 1971, box 2, records group 286, NARA.

9 Contract between the USAID and Haile Selassie I University, 1973, box 4, records group 286, NARA.

126 CHAPTER 3

for construction projects in education and training programs for students and teachers, the Peace Corps sent more than 300 volunteers each year to work at the university as well as other educational institutions in Ethiopia. For its part, the U.S. Information Service selected Ethiopian students to study in the United States, distributed books among the university public, and supported two libraries and six reading rooms in Ethiopia, including the John F. Kennedy Memorial Library, that had been constructed by the U.S. government.[10]

Of the three agencies, USAID and its education division managed by the Chief Education Advisor, USAID Ethiopia, became central reformers of higher education in Ethiopia. Among other accomplishments, USAID coordinated the work of experts recruited from universities in the United States, especially the University of Utah. Throughout the period of U.S.-led reforms in Ethiopian higher education from the early 1960s to the early 1970s, HSIU was governed by President Aklilu Habte, a graduate of The Ohio State University, from which he earned both master's and doctoral degrees in education. A passionate admirer of reforms and transformations, Habte worked closely with USAID via two U.S. advisors assigned to serve as academic vice president and associate academic vice president. However, their cooperation began deteriorating in the late 1960s when Habte's bid to replace U.S. and other foreign professors with local ones sparked conflicts between the U.S. experts and HSIU's faculty.[11]

To develop higher education in Ethiopia, the U.S. government had to develop, implement, and sustain a range of ambitious projects.[12] After all, education in Africa was supposed to contribute to the rapid development of human resources required by local and national economies, and to that end in Ethiopia, as well as for the purpose of modernization, HSIU needed to train professionals in agriculture, education, business, and administration. However, despite the crucial goals of United States set to contain Soviet ideology during the Cold War, Washington failed to elaborate projects in Ethiopia that would promote the same American values, culture, and ideology typically pursued in other projects of education in other countries. Indeed, not until the early 1970s did U.S. documents begin to address the development of social disciplines or American Studies in Ethiopia that was commonplace in other nations during the confrontation between Moscow and Washington. Instead, because both

---

10 Historical Summary of Haile Selassie I University, 1967, box 2, records group 286, NARA.

11 Memorandum of Conversation. Haile Selassie I University—Development, 1970, box 4, records group 286, NARA; Report on Examination of the Education Sector Projects of the AID Program in Ethiopia, 1971, box 2, records group 286, NARA.

12 Report on Examination of the Education Sector Projects of the AID Program in Ethiopia, 1971, box 2, records group 286, NARA.

AFRICA

the U.S. and Ethiopian governments were keenly interested in nurturing specialists for Ethiopia's economy, faculties of agriculture, education, and business administration were developed first. Shortly after, the unexpected growth of the student body required the construction of new dormitories, the expansion of classrooms, and, more ungently, the training of Ethiopian instructors amid the denial of foreign ones by the local academic community. On the whole, such endeavors wholly absorbed the attention of U.S. advisors in Ethiopia at the expense of other projects geared toward inculcating American values and ideology.

By 1967, it had become clear that the Guenete Leul Palace, donated by Emperor Selassie for HSIU, could not accommodate all of the students matriculating into the university. As experts at USAID described the problem, HSIU's

> physical facilities in general leave much to be desired. The main Addis Ababa campus is the former Palace of the Emperor. It consists of a hodge podge of halls [*sic*], residences, servants' quarters, stables, etc. The situation will be relieved somewhat if the Emperor moves his horses out of the stables which will make it possible to occupy these premises.[13]

However, the lack of space for studying was not the sole problem, for dormitories were also in short supply, and the living conditions in the ones on hand were far from what modernization demanded:

> There is a severe shortage of dormitory space on the Addis campus. Four temporary pre-fabricated barrack type dormitories are being erected on the Addis campus to accommodate app. 356 males. These structures are austere in the extreme and probably do not meet reasonable minimum space requirements. Similar structures house app. 100 female students.[14]

As the student body increasingly exceeded the capacity of HSIU's buildings and the university required new, expensive building projects, the American advisors decided to distribute the campus across Addis Ababa in places where buildings were already available and more or less appropriate for students.

Despite the plan's successes, the scattering of the campus in different parts of the city also created tremendous problems for transportation. Moreover, year-over-rise increases in the number of students highlighted another, particularly painful problem—namely, the shortage of teachers on staff—that prompted

---

13   Historical Summary of Haile Selassie I University, 1967, box 2, records group 286, NARA.
14   Ibid.

128   CHAPTER 3

U.S. experts to set new priorities for HSIU's development. Ultimately, they concluded that because the success of Ethiopia's modernization and Americanization depended primarily on the availability of qualified instructors who could teach at both the university and secondary schools, a faculty of education needed to be developed.

2.2   *Faculty of Education: Between Success and Failure*

The development of HSIU's Faculty of Education, established in 1961 to train both secondary school teachers and academic staff for the university, became the most prominent as well as controversial project of the U.S. government in Ethiopia during the Cold War. Despite the urgent need to overcome the shortage of teachers, the Faculty grew slowly and was not fully operational until 1968. Moreover, as a project, the Faculty of Education became one of the most expensive at HSIU. By early 1970, when the influence of U.S. policy at the university began to wane, Washington had spent more than $4 million on building, developing, and maintaining academic life at the Faculty.[15]

To become modernized, Ethiopia's economy in the 1960s required qualified teachers in vocational fields who could instruct future specialists in managing complicated, technologically advanced equipment.[16] The need for new vocational teachers was so great that USAID introduced the position of technical teacher education advisor in its Ethiopian affiliates in order to assist with developing polytechnic education for faculty. Consequently, in the mid-1960s, the Faculty of Education restructured its curricula and began offering teachers vocational training, instead of encouraging graduates to continue their education with the promise of being recruited for HSIU's teaching staff.[17]

Each year from 1961 to 1972, approximately 15 professors from the University of Utah and Oklahoma State University served as faculty advisors in the Faculty, designed the curriculum, taught the first generation of students, and, as such, shaped academic practices within the Faculty of Education. Tasked with initiating and developing warm relations with their Ethiopian counterparts, the U.S. professors established the Faculty's management and faculty chairs, selected young Ethiopians to study at various universities in the United States, prepared teaching manuals, and supplied textbooks for teacher training.[18]

---

15   Report on Examination of the Education Sector Projects of the AID Program in Ethiopia, 1971, box 2, records group 286, NARA.
16   Historical Summary of Haile Selassie I University, 1967, box 2, records group 286, NARA.
17   Ethiopian Education Sector Review, 1971–72 box 3, records group 286, NARA.
18   Report on Examination of the Education Sector Projects of the AID Program in Ethiopia, 1971, box 2, records group 286, NARA.

AFRICA

Although able to establish a four-year degree program as well as courses in psychology, social sciences, and English, they failed to accomplish their principal task of developing a graduate program in education, which undermined HSIU's prospects for fostering local teaching staff for the university.

Numerous problems, particularly ones related to transport and the use of technology, hampered the work of the U.S. specialists. One documented complaint was that

> staff loads increased to an average of 15 class contact periods per week. Each staff member carried out an average of 8 visits per week to supervise student teachers. The transportation time involved easily doubled this time.[19]

By the early 1970s, the Faculty had not accomplished most of the objectives set for the process of Americanization, and half of its students had failed to earn diplomas due to their lack of knowledge and their dismal grades. The U.S. specialists especially noted the Faculty's failure to generate vocational teachers: "Only four students had received diplomas in technical subjects by 1970."[20] By 1972, despite the goal of having 40 students graduate with diplomas in technical fields, no students had earned such credentials, and the projected quantitative outputs concerning objectives originally set for the Faculty of Education exhibited substantial shortcomings. Among them, by 1972, instead of producing 200 teachers with degrees in secondary school subjects, the Faculty had produced only 120.[21]

In short, the Faculty had failed to realize its chief goal of creating a pool of new vocational teachers for secondary schools who could also serve as faculty at HSIU or as administrators in Ethiopia's developing education system. To overcome the setback and provide Ethiopia's schools with new teachers, U.S. experts reduced the length of study in the Faculty and began issuing diplomas to students after two instead of four years of study. At the same time, the Faculty of education was renamed the "College of Education," which undoubtedly diminished its status as a university department because it could train teachers only for primary and secondary schools but not for the university itself.[22]

---

19   Memorandum. Haile Selassie I University. Technical Teacher Education Problems, 1970, box 4, records group 286, NARA.

20   Report on Examination of the Education Sector Projects of the AID Program in Ethiopia, 1971, box 2, records group 286, NARA.

21   Ibid.

22   Ibid.

The top reason for the Faculty's dysfunction stemmed from the limited knowledge of students who matriculated into its MA degree program. After all, the formation of HSIU's student body was supported by extremely permissive admissions. Because entrance exams did not exist, any student could enroll at the university, which hampered the quality of education and, in turn, the development of graduate programs.[23] Beyond that, changes in Ethiopia's political climate, especially the rise of anti-Americanism during the late 1960s and the early 1970s, prompted HSIU's rector and professors to revise their stances about the activity of U.S. advisors at the university, which stifled further reforms in the Faculty of Education in particular, and at HSIU in general. As a result of those shifts in attitude, the rector advocated the Ethiopianization of the teaching staff, meaning the replacement of foreign professors with local ones in order to appease local protesters who demanded that foreigners be purged from the country's educational institutions.

2.3   Ethiopianization: A Clash between Local and U.S. Professors

Shortly after HSIU's rector first voiced concerns over the imbalance between the number of foreign professors and local ones in 1966, the call for the mentioned purge and the Ethiopianization of the university's faculty was often heard. Although the number of local cadres had gradually increased since the 1950s, in 1958 HSIU's faculty contained only four Ethiopians, and even more than a decade later, in 1970, the staff of approximately 500 comprised only 200 Ethiopians (40 percent).[24] Further still, though another 180 Ethiopians studying abroad were expected to join the university's staff upon their return, the perpetual growth of students demanded increasingly more professors, and visiting experts from various countries and former expatriates returning home could not meet that demand.[25] After all, to serve the ever-growing student body, HSIU's staff needed to expand by at least a third each academic year. Added to that problem was a lack of continuity within the faculty. Only one of every seven instructors at HSIU in 1965 remained on the faculty in 1969, for the most talented academics had assumed administrative positions that guaranteed steadily higher salaries.[26] Worse still, Ethiopian citizens who had achieved academic success in U.S. or European universities were not returning

---

23   Memorandum of Conversation. Meeting held December 18, 1969 with USAID and HSIU [Haile Selassie I University] Officials, 1969, box 4, records group 286, NARA.

24   Memorandum of Conversation. Courtesy Call on the Administrator by Dr. Aklilu Habte, President of Haile Selassie I University, Ethiopia, 1969, box 4, records group 286, NARA.

25   Memorandum. Conference with President Aklilu, 1970, box 4, records group 286, NARA.

26   Memorandum. Haile Selassie I University. Technical Teacher Education Problems, 1970, box 4, records group 286, NARA.

AFRICA   131

home. Perhaps worst of all, HSIU had never established any graduate programs
within the Faculty of Education, which presented a persistent obstacle to creating a local pool of prospective faculty.[27]

Recognizing the problems, U.S. advisors sought to contribute to the development of the university and its teaching staff by introducing new programs,
courses, and, more importantly, lab equipment at HSIU. In so doing, they
also seemed able to form and sustain cooperative relationships with not only
the local staff but also foreign professors. In support of HSIU's rector, the
U.S. government additionally sought to create a teaching staff that would be
able to maintain the university's various departments, programs, and laboratory equipment. To accelerate that process, U.S. experts even introduced the
position of technical assistant to be held by graduate students after two years
of study who would assist U.S. professors in the laboratories, among other
assignments.[28]

However, the salaries and statuses of the technical assistants, similar to
those of the Ethiopian staff who generally served as lecturers and assistant
professors, were far less than those offered to Americans. In time, the disparity
in pay sparked major conflicts between the rector, local academic circles, and
U.S. advisors. When Ethiopians demanded equal salaries, opportunities for
career advancement, and, in turn, the displacement of U.S. professors, advisors
from the University of Utah and Oklahoma State University, who had worked
at HSIU for 16 years, informed the rector that they would immediately leave
the university.[29] In response, the demarche provoked new demands from the
Ethiopian staff for all other U.S. advisors from the Oklahoma State University
to resign. A letter from the U.S. team to USAID in Washington perhaps best cap-
tures the tension between U.S. and local professors: "[Staff from] Oklahoma
had been in Ethiopia about 16 years and their relationships with the personnel
at HSIU had deteriorated to such an extent that the Ethiopians could hardly
wait for Oklahoma State University to pull out."[30]

The situation became so critical that the U.S. professors even objected to
continuing the exchange program and to teaching Ethiopian participants at

---

27   Memorandum of Conversation. Meeting held December 18, 1969, box 4, records group
     286, NARA.
28   Memorandum of Conversation. Haile Selassie I University, 1970, box 4; Letter from
     Clifford S. Liddle, Chief, Human Development Group to Dr. Willie A. Whitten, Agency for
     International Development, 1973 box 5, records group 286, NARA.
29   Memorandum. Haile Selassie I University. Technical Teacher Education Problems, 1970,
     box 4, records group 286, NARA.
30   Letter from Roger Ernst, Director-Counselor, USAID, to Mr. Jerry Knoll, Bureau for Africa,
     Agency for International Development, 1970, box 4, records group 286, NARA.

132   CHAPTER 3

Oklahoma State University.[31] Though experts at the Ethiopian affiliation of USAID briefly sought out new U.S. professors, the strategy became completely unfeasible, for it risked not only the continuation of U.S. efforts in Ethiopia but also the preservation of previously achievements. The head of the U.S. team even went so far as to report that phasing out HSIU's contract with Oklahoma State University would mean phasing out HSIU.[32]

The shortage of qualified local academic staff, the failure of U.S. advisors to create a graduate program, and, more importantly, the clash between Ethiopian and U.S. professors contributed to the demise of Americanization in Ethiopia during the Cold War. In his final report to Washington in 1972, Cliff Liddle, Chief Education Advisor at USAID Ethiopia, bitterly wrote about the situation at length:

> I recently received some information concerning the staffing for next year. I was shocked to learn that there many positions were vacated [*sic*]. I was told that the entire HSIU would be staffed by Ethiopians. I think this would be fine, if you can find qualified Ethiopians, but unless circumstances have changed drastically during the past few months, I doubt very much if you will be able to find any who are qualified to continue the program as it is intended to be carried on. I would hope that every effort would be made to maintain a viable program until we have well qualified and trained Ethiopians to take over – which, in my opinion, will not be until last year's and this year's Participant Trainees have obtained their degrees and returned to Ethiopia. I become very discouraged when I receive reports which tend to indicate that the many years of effort put forth to make that program a success may have been spent in vain.[33]

In 1972, Washington attempted to make its final intervention at HSIU against several problems, at least according to U.S. experts, occasioned by the rapid development of the university from a small to a large institution.[34] The experts noted that aside from problems with the faculty, the university's administration was understaffed and its administrative development poorly planned. In particular, plans of study reflecting how founding professors from the United

---

31   Ibid.

32   Memorandum. Dr. Paul J. Manchak's Memorandum on "Technical Teacher Education Problems," 1970, box 4, records group 286, NARA.

33   Letter from S. Elvon Warner, USAID, to Dr. Cliff Liddle, Chief Education Advisor, USAID/Ethiopia, 1972 box 5, records group 286, NARA.

34   Memorandum of Conversation. Faculty of Law, Haile Selassie I University, 1971, box 4, records group 286, NARA.

AFRICA   133

Kingdom, the United States, and other nations viewed the curriculum needed revision, especially in the social sciences, and more importantly, graduate programs needed to be modified in order to eliminate some of the overseas study necessary for the growth of the staff.[35] Above all, the university, which had joined six educational institutions scattered throughout Addis Ababa, had have not achieved academic unity. The new education advisor for USAID Ethiopia, Howard K. Holland, even wrote the following to Washington:

> The admissions and Registrars functions are badly in need of professional help if the University is to develop smoothly and efficiently. Each college and school of the University serves in some ways as its own Registrar: they keep records, make an endemic accounting decisions, schedule their own classes. There is lack of unity and much haphazardness and inefficiency. Invite one mature and experienced Registrar from the United States and one younger man to help him.[36]

In 1972, USAID had sent a new team from Florida State University, none of whose members had worked in Ethiopia and thus lacked any bias toward HSIU.[37] After examining the state of affairs at the university, the team proposed a new plan for HSIU's development to be executed through 1990. The plan suggested doubling the campus's size by building additional dormitories and classrooms, increasing the Ethiopian staff so as to handle anticipated growth in student enrollment, and establishing graduate programs that could help to cultivate local staff for the university. In fact, the plan proposed that all academic positions would be occupied by Ethiopian professors by 1976.[38] To that end, a new agreement was signed between HSIU and USAID in 1973, the latter of which promised to fund the faculty's salaries, the construction of new buildings, the development of curricula, and the purchase of textbooks.[39] However, all of those plans were stopped in their tracks when a student movement in Ethiopia precipitated the abandonment of HSIU's development under the auspices of the U.S. government.

---

35 Memo of Conversation: President Aklilu, Haile Selassie I University, and H. K. Holland, 1970, box 4, records group 286, NARA.
36 Departmental Development Plan. Haile Selassie I University. Department of Economics. Faculty of Arts, 1971, box 4, records group 286, NARA.
37 Letter from Clifford Liddle, Education Officer, USAID/Addis Ababa, Ethiopia, 1972, box 3, records group 286, NARA.
38 A Blueprint for Development: Haile Selassie I University, 1970, box 4, records group 286, NARA.
39 Contract between the USAID and Haile Selassie I University, 1973, box 4, records group 286, NARA.

2.4 Anti-Americanism of Students: Undermining American Transformations

From the early 1960s to the early 1970s, weak admissions criteria and lack of entrance examinations caused HSIU's student body to grow rapidly with each passing year. Whereas approximately 930 students studied at the university in the 1962–1963 academic year, more than 3,100 were enrolled in 1967–1968 and more than 4,600 plus another 2,200 in extension in 1970–1971. By the 1972–1973 academic year, roughly 9,000 students were attending HSIU, with an additional 3,200 in extension. The phrase "in extension" means the "distant studies" in terms of the current educational language.

In general, however, HSIU's students were dissatisfied with aspects of university life. Located in different corners of Addis Ababa, HSIU's campuses and dormitories presented persistently unresolved problems with transport, which along with overcrowded dormitories, canteens, and classrooms as well as poor living conditions embittered the university's students, who lived and studied in the shadow of the luxury of the royal family and Ethiopia's government in the country's capital city. Due to a host of social barriers, graduates rarely found jobs while the nation's elite flourished and grew rich. Another less visible problem derived from the rector's decision to introduce tuition fees in 1970, which triggered student protests across a country whose political and economic situation was deteriorating day by day.[40]

The abundance of students concentrated in Addis Ababa soon provided fertile ground for political turmoil. Inspired by Marxism, communism, other revolutionary ideas, and the 1968 European student movement, various political groups sought to mobilize students in protests against the Ethiopian government. Slogans once calling for HSIU's infrastructure to be improved were rapidly revised to demand the dissolution of Ethiopia's monarchy, along with other changes to the nation's government and the elimination of tuition fees. In particular, students opposed the vastly unequal salaries paid by the Ethiopian government to foreign professors and the luxurious living standards of local elites compared to the rest of the population. At the same time, the United States was accused of not only supporting Ethiopia's corrupt emperor but also spreading values that subverted local traditions. For example, students opposed the dress code permitting women to wear short skirts and demanded the expulsion of some 340 U.S. volunteers, mostly members of the Peace Corps, who worked in Ethiopia's schools and universities, including HSIU.[41] The

---

40 A Blueprint for Development, 1970, box 4, records group 286, NARA.

41 Memorandum. Visit to Ethiopia under the Auspices of the Center for Educational Technology, 1972, box 3, records group 286, NARA.

AFRICA 135

protest against the Peace Corps volunteers especially illustrated the bitterness against U.S. education policy harbored by students, who believed that all U.S. volunteers and professors who supported the emperor only prolonged the life of the regime. In that way, U.S. volunteers, who for better or worse disseminated the seeds of freedom and liberalization among Ethiopia's youth, ended up becoming victims of the protest movement.

In response, HSIU's rector attempted to halt the student protests with threats as well as tactics of persuasion. In February and March 1972, he officially appealed to students participating in the strikes to return to their classrooms by promising that ones who did not would be deprived of dormitory rooms, barred from meals, and eventually expelled from the university: "The University cannot guarantee that students, particularly those in the freshmen program, will be re-admitted to the University to some future date, in view of the large number of students who will be graduating from the secondary schools and seeking University admission."[42]

However, no documents among the sources offer details about the number of students who were ultimately expelled. In a further bid to disband the protest movement, the rector dissolved the University Students Union of Addis Ababa, which

> was actively involved in off-campus activities aimed at inciting secondary school students to boycott classes. The President of the Union and his colleagues who were caught by the police mimeographing and preparing disruptive literature on the university campus for distribution off-campus to secondary school students and others.[43]

Despite the attempt, suspending the student organization only prompted new waves of strikes that led to the fall of Ethiopia's monarchy in 1974 and, in turn, the evacuation of U.S. advisors from HSIU.

All told, though the U.S. government developed HSIU's infrastructure—its academic buildings, library, dormitories, and laboratories, among other facilities—U.S. modernization and reforms also lurked behind the rapid growth of Ethiopia's student body that eventually fueled the monarchy's dissolution. HSIU's limited capacity and lack of professors could not adequately serve Ethiopia's students, and unlike in other countries, the need for development, construction projects, and maintenance in Ethiopia prevented U.S. experts from cultivating a local teaching staff and enhancing the quality of education. In

---

42   Memorandum. Decisions of the Faculty Council, 1972, box 5, records group 286, NARA.
43   Ibid.

136   CHAPTER 3

particular, the utter neglect of HSIU's admissions policy contributed to lowering the standards in education and thus to the peculiar adaptation of some university departments into two-year colleges. Only in the early 1970s did U.S. advisors begin addressing problems concerning the local teaching staff and student admissions; however, by that time, the seeds of political turmoil and revolution against all U.S. reforms in Ethiopia had already been sown.

In a sense, the marginalization of local professors, staff, and students in the U.S. agenda for transforming Ethiopia, largely as a consequence of the need to physically develop HSIU's capacity to perform the tasks of education, undermined the necessary relationships between local professors and U.S. advisors as well as between U.S. professors and HSIU's students. In short, preoccupied with building and developing the university itself, the U.S. government failed to integrate those two groups into its policies for reform, and the values and ideas introduced by U.S. educators turned out to be alien to Ethiopians. When such minor problems as improving the skills of local teachers and furnishing equitable salaries remained unresolved, mounting conflicts between local and foreign professors, values, and traditions ultimately inflamed resistance against U.S. reforms in Ethiopia during the Cold War.

3   **Soviet Advisors at Bahar Dar Polytechnic Institute: Caught between Sabotaged Professors and Loyal Students**

3.1   *The Ethiopian Government versus Soviet Advisors*
Unlike the United States, the Soviet Union approached the development of Ethiopia's education system during the Cold War not by constructing a university in the nation's capital but by founding a polytechnic college in the city of Bahar Dar. Later dubbed the "Polytechnic Institute in Bahar Dar," the college was built and equipped in accordance with the 1960 Soviet–Ethiopian agreement, signed after Emperor Selassie's visit to Moscow, and donated to Ethiopia's government in June 1963. Upon becoming responsible for the institution, Ethiopia's government arranged all visits by Soviet specialists via special invitation. At the opening of the school, representatives of the Soviet government claimed that "the college is the only educational institution in the country that trains highly professional workers at the technical level."[44]

---

44   Report by Soviet Advisor of the Director at the Polytechnic School A. Shumikov, Bahar Dar, Ethiopia, August 01, 1964, folder 1943, Reports on Visits to Ethiopia by Soviet Specialists, 1964, entry 1, records group 9606, Soviet Ministry for Higher Education, State Archive of Russian Federation (hereafter GARF), p. 1.

AFRICA   137

Due to the Soviet involvement in activities related to the school's construction and the training of specialists, the institute soon became nicknamed the "Moscow School" by locals.[45] During a three-year period from 1960 to 1963, the Soviet Union built a new campus for the college that comprised academic buildings, an assembly hall, dining rooms, laboratories, a farm pavilion, a soccer field, jogging tracks, two volleyball courts, and a basketball court. The school was supplied with hot and cold water, an internal telephone network, and a cinema, among several other amenities.[46] Ethiopia's government appraised the scope of the school's construction as a genuine case of modernization, and Emperor Selassie twice visited the college and, later, the institute: first at its grand opening in 1963 and second during student strikes in 1970.

From 1963 to 1968, the college trained 1,000 students into qualified workers in six departments—agriculture, chemistry, energy, industry, textiles, and wood technology. Because nearly all students with secondary school certificates representing 12 years of education were admitted, the vast number of students enrolled made the college comparable to most other technical and polytechnic institutions.[47] Both the college's director, an Ethiopian citizen, and the Ethiopian government suggested rebranding the college as an institute as a means to afford it the status of a higher polytechnic school. Within the school, each of the six departments was supplied with laboratories and technical equipment shipped from the Soviet Union, as well as study plans and textbooks elaborated by Soviet specialists following Soviet models of higher education. Although tuition was not levied by the school, students did not receive scholarships, either. Instead, the Soviets introduced a system that provided all students with room and board, uniforms, stationery, and textbooks, as well as paid for their travel expenses.[48]

Arriving in Bahar Dar after the completion of the campus's construction, the first and most famous team of Soviet advisors transformed the school into the Polytechnic Institute. The team consisted of five instructors for academic teaching, five instructors for vocational and practical training, and four translators. Each year, the 15 to 20 Soviet instructors working at the college were tasked with preparing the college for each new term and with launching all teaching activities. Moscow's detailed plan for the team stipulated steps

---

45   Fantahun Ayele, "A Brief History of Bahir Dar University," accessed March 10, 2020, https://bdu.edu.et/sites/default/folders/A%20Brief%20History%20of%20BDU.pdf, p. 1.

46   Report by Soviet Advisor, folder 1943, records group 9606, GARF, p. n/n.

47   Ibid.

48   Report on the Work at Bahar Dar Polytechnic Institute, 1971–1974, folder 6461, Reports on Visits to Ethiopia, entry 1, records group 9606, Soviet Ministry for Higher Education, GARF, p. 9.

138   CHAPTER 3

to finish equipping and liquidating all of the imperfections in classrooms and labs; to finalize official educational documents and to assist
the Ethiopian side with commencing the first academic year; to produce
the teaching manuals for laboratory work; to assist Ethiopian instructors
in teaching and organizing practical classes applying our syllabuses; to
arrange extracurricular activities with students; to install equipment in
laboratories and workshops; and to train the Ethiopian side to properly
operate the equipment, laboratories, and buildings.[49]

In light of those tasks, the primary duties of the Soviet advisors entailed setting
up the laboratory facilities, supporting the teaching process, and training Ethiopian colleagues to maintain the equipment.

Although the living conditions of Soviet advisors in Ethiopia were not luxurious by any means, compared to the life of their counterparts working in
Vietnam, for example, life in Ethiopia was satisfactory. All Soviet specialists
and their families were placed in houses with heating, cold and hot water,
gas, a shared dining room, and a radio, all surrounded by landscaping. The
apartments of Soviet specialists were built near the institute, which favor-
ably affected their work compared to the situation of U.S. specialists, whose
housing was located far from the various campuses of HSIU in Addis Ababa.[50]
Moreover, the institute paid each Soviet advisor a salary equal to that of Ethiopian instructors—usually, from $275 to $300 per month.[51]

Reports of Soviet advisors who worked in Ethiopia differ starkly from those
of Soviet instructors who worked in other countries. Most of the former reports
describe projects geared toward development and problems with installing
equipment, for example, but rarely mention propaganda activities or ideological concerns. Indeed, all of the time and energy of advisors in Ethiopia became
invested in equipping the college and, later, the institute, to train professionals
who could contribute to modernizing the country. As per their reports, Soviet
specialists spent much of their time fixing or compensating for equipment,
instruments, and machines to ensure the continuity of education, which at
times demanded significant creativity and ingenuity. Unlike in other countries, such demands in Ethiopia left little time for distributing propaganda
among students and local instructors.

Similar to their U.S. counterparts at HSIU, however, Soviet advisors at the
institute developed new curricula, syllabuses for each course, and instruction

---

49   Report by Soviet Advisor, folder 1943, records group 9606, GARF, p. 10–11.
50   Ibid, p. 35.
51   Ibid, p. 15.

AFRICA 139

manuals. They also taught their Ethiopian colleagues how to keep records and organize admissions campaigns:

> The college administration is assisted with elaborating the register of student attendance, grades, achievements, etc. Moreover, measures for organizing admissions to the college have been developed.[52]

All of the study plans elaborated by the Soviets needed approval from the college's director, and as indicated in the reports, negotiations with the college's administration about their approval was the chief duty of the head of the Soviet team.[53]

Similar to U.S. advisors, Soviet instructors faced various problems while attempting to convert the college into an educational institution. A shortage of local instructors, the sabotage of foreign ones on the staff, and a lack of equipment and textbooks prompted the team's specialists to seek additional help from Moscow, as did critical problems with infrastructure. As in Addis Ababa, the dormitories of the Polytechnic Institute were overcrowded and without enough furniture to accommodate all of the students. In their reports, Soviet advisors mention that "the dormitory is not sufficiently equipped; there are almost no chairs, tables and other furniture. From 16 to 18 students stay in each room."[54] To resolve those urgent problems in housing, Moscow built an additional dormitory for 500 students by the end of the 1960s. Nevertheless, other problems with infrastructure continued to plague the Soviets, including leaky roofs, that Ethiopia's government, as the principal owner of the institute, could not overcome:

> As a result of shoddy construction, the roof is leaking, and it even leaks for ten to twelve hours after it rains. We reported the defect to Moscow. But the answer was that the roof was built properly. The rainy seasons remind us again and again about the defect. The institute's administration has repeatedly pointed out to us that the unsatisfactory roof is the responsibility of Moscow and has denied help.[55]

By donating the college to the Ethiopian government, the Soviet specialists had hoped to transfer responsibility for its maintenance; however, because

---

52 Ibid, p. 17.
53 Ibid.
54 Ibid, p. 3.
55 Ibid, p. 26.

140   CHAPTER 3

the government was not prepared to make repairs or invest in construction projects, all of the mentioned problems fell to the Soviet specialists, who were rarely experts in construction or maintenance.

In 1970, the Soviets faced the unexpected switch to two-year courses of study at the Polytechnic Institute, much as their U.S. counterparts had experienced at HSIU.[56] However, if the transformation at the Faculty of Education was provoked by a shortage of qualified instructors, then the change at the Polytechnic Institute stemmed from the prerogatives of Ethiopia's Ministry of Education and the institute's administration to halt the student-led antigovernment movement, which, in the opinion of Ethiopian officials, could have been buoyed by the Soviet team. Citing political imperatives, Ethiopia's government pursued a course of action to reduce the period of study in the hope that the school would accommodate fewer students as a result.

Although Soviet sources remain silent about the Soviet Union's compliance with the Ethiopian government's decision, the transition to two-year courses of study significantly altered the work of Soviet specialists at the institute. Following the decision, Soviet instructors fundamentally revised the curricula to focus on technical training, and English became the primary language of instruction, largely in a bid to accelerate the transfer of knowledge without interpreters. A new team of Soviet instructors knowledgeable in vocational subjects who could conduct classes in English was sent to Ethiopia, and the school's library was supplemented with Soviet textbooks translated into English. Those countermeasures were implemented in order to continue the training of specialists who invariably understood English better than Russian.

Upon analyzing the situation at the Polytechnic Institute, Soviet specialists indicated that despite the administration's unfriendly attitudes toward the Soviet Union, study plans and courses at the school continued to follow Soviet models.[57] At the same time, some modifications clearly revealed the school's gradual adoption of the U.S. education system. For example, the grading system was modified to a 100-point scale, the U.S. grading system was introduced, and the system of credits was initiated as well.[58] Notable changes in instruction also occurred. For example, the Soviet tradition of culminating a course of study with a thesis was replaced with a final exam, which Moscow interpreted as the Americanization of the institute. Soviet experts concluded that

---

56   Report on the Work at Bahar Dar Polytechnic Institute, 1971–1974, folder 6461, records group 9606, GARF, p. 10.

57   Ibid, p. 9.

58   Ibid, p. 12.

AFRICA

Ethiopia's Ministry of Education, having been in close contact with U.S. advisors in Addis Ababa, had decided to reform the institute with reference to U.S. norms.[59]

It bears mentioning that, in all of the situations described, the Soviet Union demonstrated considerable patience and even passivity in engaging in talks, if any, with Ethiopia's Ministry of Education. Such tolerance allowed the Soviet specialists and the Embassy of the Soviet Union to maintain contact with students, who would soon contribute significantly to the fall of Ethiopia's monarchy in 1974. Only after that year's revolution did the Polytechnic Institute regain its status as an institution of higher education and reinstitute five-year courses of study. Moreover, throughout the Cold War, the Soviet Union never abandoned the Polytechnic Institute but continued to provide it with financial assistance as well as instructors. In 1983, the institute was given a final grant of $8 million to fund its ongoing projects of modernization and construction.

3.2 *Professors: Sabotage against Russians*

The most persistent problem for Soviet education policy in Ethiopia was the local teaching staff. At the Polytechnic Institute, from 15 to 18 local instructors formed half or slightly more of the total faculty, the rest of which were Soviet or from another country. All local instructors had been selected by Ethiopia's Ministry of Education according to their qualifications and, as Soviet advisors indicated in their reports to Moscow, had been educated in the United States or Germany. Despite approximate equality in monthly salaries and the affordance of comfortable housing for instructors, the institute repeatedly reported about a shortage of teachers. For example, though the Faculty of Agriculture, among others, consistently needed six instructors, only two to four were ever employed at the same time.[60]

According to Soviet reports, most local instructors were careless in their daily work as teachers and undermined the suggestions, efforts, and aspirations of Soviet specialists. The Russian instructors noted that "some teachers consider themselves temporary employees of the institute and do not demonstrate any interest in teaching students; they do not even try to participate in educating prospective specialists."[61] Such behavior irritated the Soviets as much as it jeopardized the institute's principal goal of training a new generation of specialists for Ethiopia's modernization. Ethiopian staff even subverted the

---

59   Ibid, p. 19.
60   Ibid, p. 9, 14.
61   Report by Soviet Advisor, folder 1943, records group 9606, GARF, p. 21.

142   CHAPTER 3

continuity of instruction by knowingly providing Soviets with false information about the number of local instructors available. As one Soviet instructor
noted:

> By the beginning of the academic year, it became known that the Ethi-
> opian side had no instructors for training in the fields of plumbing and
> woodworking. In order to avoid disrupting the classes, it was decided to
> deliver the classes by our [Soviet] specialists. Moreover, a lack of essential
> materials and the simplest instruments and tools caused great difficulties
> in implementing that type of training. The institute's administration and
> instructors on the Ethiopian side did not provide any assistance. They
> showed indifference despite our requests and demands.[62]

As another observed:

> The most difficult part in organizing vocational training was the glass-
> blowing workshop. The Ethiopian instructors asked for demonstration
> classes but later refused participation and did not come. The classes for
> students were conducted by us with the help of translators.[63]

Moreover, when the college's first director, an important link with the Ministry of Education in Addis Ababa and the Soviet team, unexpectedly left the
position on the eve of a new academic year, the college was forced to operate
without a director for several months. The Soviet professors had their hands
full with disorganized classes, oversized classrooms, students' daily problems
with living and dining, and different challenges with the institute's infrastructure. Meanwhile, the team of Soviet specialists assumed control of the administrative functions and all teaching responsibilities, and when a new director
was finally appointed by the Ethiopian government, the Soviets transferred the
administrative functions to him and returned to their teaching duties. Much
to the surprise of the Soviets, the new director, though educated in the United
States, established warm relations with the staff and the Soviet specialists and
"always consulted with us [the Soviets] about questions concerning teaching
before making any decisions."[64]

From the perspective of the Soviet advisors, the subordination of the Polytechnic Institute to the Ethiopian government posed considerable obstacles

---

62   Ibid.
63   Ibid, p. 22–23.
64   Ibid, p. 9–10.

AFRICA   143

for teaching and threatened the quality of instruction. Still responsible for
teaching, the Soviets could not oversee decisions made by Ethiopia's Ministry
of Education concerning the teaching staff and maintenance of the campus.
Without a doubt, the Ministry sought to limit Soviet participation in resolving
the institute's problems, and the instructors' and the Ministry's covert sabotage
of Soviet visions and ideas for vocational education were evaluated by Moscow
as the most urgent problem facing the Sovietization of Ethiopia. To minimize
such sabotage, the Embassy of the Soviet Union appealed to the Ministry of
Education to allow the director of the institute to select instructors or replace
them as necessary. Soon after such permission was granted, the director, at the
suggestion of the Soviet specialists, "dismissed some of the instructors who
did not show a desire to work and did not understand the goals of the college"
and instead employed new instructors who "could contribute to educating and
training national cadres for the country."[65]

Such action relieved some of the tension in the academic life at the Polytechnic Institute between Ethiopian instructors and Soviet experts. By the
mid-1960s, the Soviet specialists seemed to have expanded their authority
at the college, and the director consulted them before issuing any decisions.
Beyond that, the instructors even seemed to officially support the curricula and to enthusiastically deliver lesson. At the same time, however, Soviet
advisors sensed that their Ethiopian counterparts did not seek to establish a
mutual understanding with them and preferred to eschew Soviet ways of completing institutional tasks. Their lack of creativity and unwillingness to impart
high-quality knowledge to students especially irritated the Soviet advisors:

> The instructors from the Ethiopian side worked cooperatively with the
> Soviet specialists during the academic year. To resolve problems, they
> turned to us [Soviet personnel] for help. We were treated with confidence
> and respect. However, it should be noted that most instructors did not
> take part in writing textbooks or in preparing workshops or laboratory
> work for students. That definitely illustrates a lack of experience. But
> after numerous meetings, it became clear that the instructors did not
> have any theoretical knowledge or a high level of education.[66]

Referring to Ethiopian colleagues, another advisor added that "they do not
pay any attention to extracurricular activities and do not take any initiative

---

65   Ibid, p. n/n.
66   Ibid, p. 8.

144   CHAPTER 3

to improve the skills of students."[67] Other advisors later complained to Moscow that Ethiopian staff members began sabotaging nearly all Soviet proposals relative to educating students. In a typical case, for example, the dean of the Department of Agriculture, who, according to a Soviet report, neglected the department, did nothing to assist with instruction and was interested only in activities related to volleyball. Though compelled to leave the institute, to the utter amazement of the Soviets he was later approved to work in the Ministry of Agriculture.[68]

As the sources reveal, the Soviets sought to understand the reasons behind the resistance of their Ethiopian coworkers. Aside from anti-Sovietism, the chief problem concerned the reluctance of the Ethiopian teaching staff to teach classes according to Soviet syllabuses and models, for most of them had been educated at U.S. or European universities and thus exposed to other pedagogical models. The Soviet faculty had to negotiate with and persuade the locals to realign their classes to accommodate Soviet approaches. In perhaps the most illustrative example:

> A team of Soviet specialists worked in difficult conditions, and it was necessary to persistently resolve certain educational problems with the instructors on the Ethiopian side, who had mainly been trained in the West. We [Soviet staff] made massive efforts to convince them to revise their teaching approaches. A lack of textbooks in English prevented us from convincing the Ethiopians to teach subjects in accordance with our programs. Foreign textbooks have fundamental differences with ours, and to date, there are no satisfactory textbooks [at the Polytechnic Institute]. Our failure could persuade the Ethiopians to purchase new textbooks in the United States and England. In that case, the study of all subjects would go awry and not comply with our programs.[69]

As that case demonstrated, Soviet and Ethiopian instructors could not agree upon approaches to teaching students that were supported by divergent models.

Of course, Soviet experts in Ethiopia also confronted fierce anti-Sovietism from Ethiopian instructors. One such instructor, a graduate of the Polytechnic Institute and, later, from the University of Wisconsin, turned out to be "an ardent anti-Soviet inspirer for a protest against foreign instructors proclaiming

---

67   Ibid, p. 9.
68   Report on the Work at Bahar Dar Polytechnic Institute, 1971–1974, folder 6461, records group 9606, GARF, p. 15.
69   Report by Soviet Advisor, folder 1943, records group 9606, GARF, p. 38–39.

AFRICA 145

the purge. He hated the work at the institute and dreamed about getting a new position at HSIU."[70] At the same time, that instructor's case remains unique in Soviet reports about the aspirations of local staff for Ethiopianization. For the most part, the local instructors at the Polytechnic Institute, unlike their counterparts at HSIU, did not advocate a policy of Ethiopianization or of purging foreign staff. They did, however, sabotage the proposals of Soviet specialists concerning teaching and extracurricular activities. In that context, the Soviets pinned great hopes on three Ethiopian students who returned from their studies at Soviet universities and became instructors beginning in the 1973–1974 academic year. Although two of them followed Soviet ideas in higher education and were politically loyal, the third became a great problem for the Soviets when he disseminated anti-Sovietism among students and convinced them that low-quality education was being provided by the Soviet Union. However, the students, who would soon participate in the Ethiopian revolution guided by Marxist thinking, admired the Soviet advisors and even asked the administration to relieve the instructor of his duties, which the administration did shortly thereafter.[71]

Ultimately, as at HSIU, where U.S. specialists were worried that their equipment, laboratories, and other materials from the United States were falling into the hands of unqualified local staff, the Soviets at the Polytechnic Institute faced a similar problem. Neglecting the labs in favor of pursing their chief task of teaching, Soviet instructors urged Ethiopians at the school to maintain the laboratories and to prevent the instruments and machines from being stolen or otherwise compromised. Soviet specialists spent a tremendous amount of energy on convincing Ethiopia's Ministry of Education to introduce positions for technical personnel who would maintain the equipment:

> We have repeatedly voiced concerns about the correct operation of the institute and its equipment. However, the Ministry of Education has not made any technician responsible for the exploitation of the materials. To date, we have had to deal with the maintenance of the institute's equipment. Following our persistent demands, the institute hired an electrician but one with poor qualifications who is currently undergoing training. Unfortunately, that person spends more time, by the order of the director, cleaning up the institute [than maintaining the equipment].[72]

---

70 Report on the Work at Bahar Dar Polytechnic Institute, 1971–1974, folder 6461, records group 9606, GARF, p. 16.

71 Ibid, p. 16–17.

72 Report by Soviet Advisor, folder 1943, records group 9606, GARF, p. 24.

146   CHAPTER 3

As a result of such negligence, the school's equipment was often broken, and "Due to the lack of qualified personnel, at the beginning of the academic year, a large refrigerating chamber (Freon leaked) broke down, and an electric boiler was disabled (its heaters were burned)."[73]

The Soviet specialists eventually realized that Ethiopians did not want to be engaged in maintaining or repairing the equipment whatsoever. As the leader of the Soviet team reported:

> Some instructors from the Ethiopian side claim that our equipment installed in a woodworking workshop doesn't work properly. Unfortunately, they do not accept any explanation that the equipment does work well when it's well cared for. Moreover, it has been repeatedly demonstrated to them in practice that the machine refuses to work due to the lack of maintenance. As a rule, the vague answer has been followed with reference to the director, that he should recruit technicians.[74]

The behavior and sabotage surprised the Soviet specialists, who began believing that the maintenance of labs would not be done after their departure in Moscow. Moreover, they were not able to press the director to guarantee the maintenance that bred misunderstanding between the local and Soviet staff.

To somehow persuade the Ethiopian instructors, the Soviet Union engaged in a few activities involving propaganda. A group for the study of Russian was organized, Soviet films were shown, and Soviet advisors delivered lectures on Soviet foreign policy. However, Ethiopian instructors generally avoided such forays into the use of soft power, and only three local instructors studied Russian.[75] Although the Polytechnic Institute's director, citing spurious reasons, did not allow Soviet staff members to install a photo exhibition, the Soviet films garnered genuine interest from Ethiopian students. All of the films screened in Amharic were shown several times at the request of students and a handful of instructors. The most popular one was *The Fate of a Man*, a film about a Soviet soldier taken to a German concentration camp in the first days of World War II who managed to escape and return to the Soviet army but ended up losing his family when German soldiers burned his village. His older son, a soldier in the Soviet army, was the protagonist's only hope but was killed on the final day of the war. To prevent his grief from prevailing, the hero ventures far from his native village and eventually meets an orphan boy whom he

---

73   Ibid., p. 24–25.
74   Ibid, p. 25.
75   Ibid, p. 27–28.

AFRICA   147

claims is his father, which convinces the protagonist to believe in life again. The film, adapted from a book by the famous Soviet writer and Nobel prize winner Michael Sholokhov offers a compelling representation of the soul and destiny of Russians, and as Soviet experts noted in the reports, unlike many other films, *The Fate of a Man* was always awaited with great anticipation. Other documentaries shown to Ethiopians as propaganda included *The Visit of Haile Selassie I to the Soviet Union* and *Valentina Tereshkova*, a film about the first woman cosmonaut, as well as *America Welcomes Russian Ballet* and *The World Youth Festival in Moscow.* The Soviet Union recognized that films were shown to Ethiopian instructors and students "in order to familiarize them with a Soviet reality and to exert a certain impact" upon them.[76] In other attempts at Sovietization, Ethiopian faculty members were encouraged to participate in classes hosted by the Soviet Embassy's staff on current international events, on Soviet–Ethiopian relations, and in the late 1970s, on Moscow's position in the war between Ethiopia and Somalia.

However, Ethiopian academics, generally dissatisfied with the presence of Soviet colleagues, were not convinced by the Soviet stance until the end of the Cold War. By 1988, the institute employed 31 Ethiopian instructors and 19 Soviet specialists, and many instructors were graduates of the Polytechnic Institute or had been educated in the Soviet Union, which ensured Moscow of their loyalty. Nevertheless, the subversion of Soviet prerogatives, though not so loudly voiced at the Polytechnic Institute as against U.S. advisors in Addis Ababa, limited Moscow's influence. Propaganda projects and classes on Soviet ideology and Marxism were overshadowed by the need to keep the school's infrastructure and equipment in working condition, to instill in students applicable professional skills, and to teach local instructors how to properly use laboratory equipment. At the same time, the Soviet advisors did not encounter any overt aspirations for Ethiopianization among local instructors as had happened with their U.S. counterparts, though the subtle sabotage nevertheless affected the impact of teaching, undermined the quality of education, and ultimately compromised the success of Sovietization.

3.3   *Students: Between Government Repression and Soviet Marxism*
The students at the Polytechnic Institute presented a special problem for attempts at Sovietization in Ethiopia. As was the case for U.S. personnel at HSIU, a low level of pre-existing knowledge and a lack of progress in learning among students became dual dilemmas for Soviet advisors. However, unlike

---

76   Ibid, p. 28.

148   CHAPTER 3

their U.S. counterparts, the Soviet specialists took care to improve the students' knowledge and attempted to revise the position of the directors of Ethiopia's Ministry of Education and the institute regarding the introduction of a more rigid admissions system.

For several years during the 1960s, the Soviet Union could not exert any influence upon student admissions. As mentioned, Ethiopia's institutions of higher education were open to all applicants, and the inclusiveness of students at the school engendered a range of problems for academic life at the institution. In particular, Soviet specialists observed how the student dropout rate—more than 20 percent cited uncomfortable living conditions, the lack of textbooks, and heavy course loads—dried up the pool of skilled graduates needed for Ethiopia's industrialization. However, Soviet specialists were also convinced that the reasons cited for dropping out were not as responsible as disorganized admissions processes that ended up selecting students either unprepared for, or not wholly committed to, higher education. Reportedly, neither Ethiopia's Ministry of Education nor the director of the Polytechnic Institute were engaged in the selection of students, and, moreover, during the academic year, Ethiopian instructors did not extend their classes to assist students who lagged behind. All of those factors worked against the Soviet approaches to vocational education. When Soviet advisors began lobbying the Ministry of Education to alter the admissions procedure, the Ministry of Education refused to concede that weak or unprepared students were being admitted:

> The Ministry of Education and Arts stated that the best students were selected for the institute. However, many students were not able to succeed in their study plans and subjects. The situation attests to problems with teaching pupils at Ethiopia's schools and to the unsatisfactory selection of students for study at institutions of higher education by the Ministry.[77]

The Soviet advisors were especially appalled by the behavior of Ethiopian instructors who would not hold additional classes for students who needed help, which contradicted Soviet pedagogical practices: "Some Ethiopian instructors do not demonstrate an intention to arrange additional classes for weak students. Our proposals for a number of learning activities aimed at improving student performance did not find any support among those instructors. Therefore, only 76 percent of students passed exams."[78] That position of

---

77   Ibid, p. 32.
78   Ibid.

AFRICA 149

the Ethiopian staff did not align with Soviet goals, nor did the quality of the vocational education, which required the strict selection of students with a certain level of proficiency upon matriculating as well as patience from the instructors. To improve the selection of students, Soviet specialists agreed with Moscow to hold an additional exam and interviews with students, and special admissions committees were established to conduct admissions exams for mathematics, physics, chemistry, and foreign languages. As a result, the Soviet advisors only admitted students less than 23 years old who had received full secondary school education and passed the additional exams. Ultimately, those measures contributed to reducing student dropouts.

From 1970 to 1974, many students at the Polytechnic Institute took part in strikes and demonstrations that had significant impacts upon their lives as well as on the life of the institute and Ethiopia as a developing nation. As result of their participation, some students were prohibited from studying, some became visible revolutionaries who aided the dissolution of the monarchy, and some went on to assume important political positions after returning from the Soviet Union after the revolution. Soviet sources scarcely provide information about the protests that unfolded at HSIU in Addis Ababa and the Polytechnic Institute in Bahar Dar. The official history of the Polytechnic Institute mentions some protests against the rising tide of unemployment and the lack of social mobility for graduates. The students involved in the protests were reported to have occupied an administrative building of the university, to have clashed with police, and, more importantly, to have been expelled from the institute by the Ministry of Education. In sum, more than 100 students at the Polytechnic Institute were forever barred from studying at the school.[79]

The student protests became a foundation for the evolution of the Polytechnic Institute into a vocational college. To halt the demonstrations, the Ministry of Education decided to transform the institute into a college with the right to significantly lower the number of students in attendance. The transition to a two-year college education prompted a reduction of students from approximately 1,000 to anywhere from 150 to 200. According to Soviet reports, this weakened development-related policy in Ethiopia.[80] To combat student strikes, Ethiopia's Ministry of Education reduced the number of students and length of their studies as well as telling Soviet specialists that the country needed more specialists in vocational education but not in higher education. The Ministry of Education added that only if all of the students had 12 years

---

79 Fantahun Ayele, "A Brief History of Bahir Dar University," p. 7.
80 Report on the Work at Bahar Dar Polytechnic Institute, 1971–1974, folder 6461, records group 9606, GARF, p. 10.

150   CHAPTER 3

of secondary school education would it be possible to educate them in two years.[81] However, the expulsion of students and an unprecedented reduction in new student admissions only served to radicalize students in Ethiopia, a country where unemployment was rampant, even for graduates with university diplomas. Soviet specialists noted that

> the expulsion of students from the Polytechnic Institute was a special campaign undertaken by the Ethiopian Ministry of Education. It was provoked by the fact that the students of the Polytechnic Institute participated in strikes to demand political freedom, the democratization of the country, the legalization of progressive organizations, and guaranteed work placement after graduation.[82]

Because all of the student strikes were suppressed by the police, increasingly more students were expelled, and, consequently, the institute lost from 80 to 85 percent of the student body. The most dramatic purge occurred after the 1972 strike, when the institute, recently converted from the college, had only 36 students. The hostility of authorities in Addis Ababa to Soviet specialists was fueled by rumors that Soviets had incited students to pursue revolutionary activities. Although the sources furnish no evidence to the truth of that claim one way or the other, some papers indicate the political activity of Soviets at Ethiopia's schools and universities. From another angle, the social and economic situation in the country became so dire that ideas about socialist revolution and Marxism found fruitful soil even without Soviet encouragement.

On the contrary, other documents testify to the passivity of Soviet instructors who had no intention of interfering in revolutionizing the institute or in threatening relations with Addis Ababa despite anti-Soviet actions. Ethiopia's Ministry of Education, which cooperated with U.S. advisors, had indeed advocated the Americanization of the Polytechnic Institute, as the introduction of the 100-point assessment system, the institutionalization of credits, and the elimination of cumulative theses attest. Perhaps a rivalry between the United States and the Soviet Union in the field of education catalyzed the Ministry of Education's intervention into the affairs of the institute. At the same time, the reason for the interference might have been Ethiopian and U.S. attempts to eliminate the center of antigovernment sentiments following suspicions that the Soviet Union would disseminate socialist ideas among students. All of those assumptions can be indirectly justified by the decision of the institute's

---

81   Ibid, p. 11.
82   Ibid.

AFRICA

administration to block all contact between students and the Soviet specialists. For example, when Soviet instructors opted to expand some practical classes and internships that would place students in Soviet company, the director of the institute refused to sign a contract that would end up "increasing Soviet influence in the institute."[83] On top of that, as the Soviet specialists pointed out, "the showing of Soviet films for students became nearly impossible because the authorities of the institute created obstacles and formalities."[84] Eventually, in 1972, a curfew was introduced at the Polytechnic Institute that placed students under the supervision of police, imposed a strict daily schedule for them, prohibited them from visiting bars and similar establishment on weekdays, and barred them from leaving campus after 9 p.m. Moreover, it forbade outsiders from entering the dormitories at all times.[85]

On their part, students at the Polytechnic Institute were excited about the work of the Soviet instructors and interested in learning about the Soviet political system, socialism, and the life of young Soviets. In that light, the denial of student–Soviet advisors contacts imposed by the authorities was belated.[86] Not only did the students study Russian and receive extra classes, but Moscow also expanded its exchange programs with each passing year and even sent Ethiopian students to study in the Soviet Union. After the Ethiopian revolution in 1974 that put a leader loyal to Moscow in power, the Soviet Union was allowed to make a revanche in Ethiopia, and the number of Ethiopian students in the Soviet universities rose rapidly. From 1974 to 1988, about 7,500 Ethiopians—considerably more than the number of students arriving from other developing countries—were trained, and even if not all were loyal to Marxism or the new regime, many graduates occupied high positions of power after the revolution. Some graduates became members of the government, of the Central Committee of the Communist Party of Ethiopia, of the General Prosecutor Bureau, or of departments of mass media and information. About 30 percent of the members of Ethiopia's Ministry of Foreign Affairs were graduates of Soviet universities, and many other graduates worked in embassies and cultural institutions. The staff of Ethiopia's Ministry of Culture employed 16 graduates during the 1970s and the 1980s, and a graduate from Leningrad State University, the author of a Russian national hymn, even headed the Academy of Ethiopian Languages. Beyond that, graduates of Soviet performance institutes headed the National Theater of Ethiopia and the Musical School, and 90

---

83 Ibid, p. 6.
84 Ibid, p. 14.
85 Ibid, p. 12.
86 Report by Soviet Advisor, folder 1943, records group 9606, GARF, p. 3.

percent of teachers at the School of Arts were graduates of Soviet universities. Further still, many graduates of medical institutes held the positions of chief physician or clinical director in Ethiopia.[87]

At the same time, Moscow observed the limited influence of former graduates in economics and politics in the years following the Cold War. Only 1,138 graduates of Soviet universities took jobs in the industrial, agricultural, healthcare, or cultural sectors of Ethiopia's economy. Soviet experts noted that "the number of graduates remains insignificant in the party and state apparatus. In the upper echelons of the government, a significant number of employees originate in the petty bourgeois strata who had been trained in the West and still have a caste isolation, deny new cadres, and make obstacles to the advancement of our graduates."[88]

Another problem involved students who defected from their homeland by not returning to Ethiopia after studying in the Soviet Union. Only 69 percent of Ethiopians returned home during the 1970s, most often due to their reluctance to again live amid poverty and hunger, to participate in the Ethiopian–Somalian war, or to engage in the political games of the pro-Marxist regime. Only 52 of 444 Ethiopian graduates from Soviet schools in 1980 returned home, compared with 15 of 392 in 1981, 82 of 408 in 1982, 208 of 533 in 1983, and 248 of 566 in 1984. In subsequent years, however, the situation evened out as increasingly more Ethiopian students returned to the country after studying abroad in the Soviet Union.[89]

Up through the end of the Cold War, the Polytechnic Institute received assistance from the Soviet Union in the form of Soviet specialists, equipment, and books. After 1988, Ethiopian–Soviet cooperation quickly began to fade, and after the 1991 regime change, Soviet specialists left the institute. In 1999, the Polytechnic Institute became part of the new Bahar Dar University.

4 Conclusion

A unique case in the education policies of the United States and the Soviet Union during the Cold War, Ethiopia required the superpowers to develop education in the country as a means to develop the country itself, as well as forge

---

87 Documents on the Foreign Graduate and Alumni of Soviet Higher Educational Institutions, 1988, folder 337, Documents on the Alumni's Connections, entry 1, records group 9661, State Committee on Education, p. 1–6.

88 Ibid, p. 5.

89 Ibid, p. 9–10.

special relationships between experts from Washington or Moscow and the local academic community.

First, establishing an education system in Ethiopia did not afford either superpower the opportunity to indoctrinate its institutions or students with their rival ideologies, disciplines, and values as had been the case elsewhere during the Cold War, particularly in Europe. Without a doubt, projects of politicization and indoctrination were salient in the U.S. and Soviet education policies pursued in Ethiopia, albeit to a lesser extent than construction projects that responded to the sheer need for infrastructure, the maintenance of equipment and dormitories, and the training of qualified specialists, which absorbed all of the time and energy of U.S. and Soviet advisors. As a consequence, propaganda projects remained underdeveloped, and value-oriented disciplines such as Russian, English, Marxism, political science, literature, and history were sidelined to accommodate, for example, vocational education and engineering courses.

Second, problems riddling interactions between Ethiopian staff and either Soviet or U.S. experts were uncommon in relation to the usual implementation of education policies in other countries during the Cold War. The local teaching staff was formed entirely by foreign advisors who improved the professional level of Ethiopians. Relative to experiences elsewhere during the period, it would have been unsurprising had the Ethiopian instructors treated U.S. and Soviet aid, embodied in the faculty and experts at their respective institutes, with respect. However, the Ethiopians showed signs of alienation to the superpowers and were liable to respond by sabotaging their attempts at Americanization or Sovietization. In interpersonal relations, they did not establish close, trusting communication with U.S. or Soviet newcomers and even actively pursued a policy of Ethiopianization in the academic community as the institutions of higher education were strengthened from the late 1960s to the early 1970s. The behavior of Ethiopian academics differed from that of the local professoriate, for example, in Germany or Afghanistan. In Germany, professors restrained Americanization and Sovietization by struggling for academic freedoms; in Afghanistan, professors sabotaged proposals from Americans and, later on, from Soviets. However, the academic communities of those and other countries never openly called for the Germanization or Afghanization of the teaching staff, whereas the Ethiopian academic community overtly sought to purge foreigners from their ranks and advocated a purely Ethiopian composition of the university staff. Undoubtedly, such outright resistance presented a new challenge for both the United States and the Soviet Union; though having witnessed resistance from conservative professors in various ways and heard their various slogans, neither superpower had been exposed to any policy advocated by local authorities that sought to purge them and their forms of aid from their academic environments. Perhaps most fascinating is that Washington and Moscow conceded to the aspirations of their Ethiopian counterparts and even expanded the ranks of local academic communities despite the fact that such action significantly diminished the quality of education.

Third, the superpowers faced unique sentiments among students in Ethiopia, who were sorely divided in their preferences for U.S. versus Soviet policies. Ethiopian students in Addis Ababa devised slogans against the supremacy of U.S. faculty and Peace Corps volunteers at universities and schools as well as U.S. support for the monarchy. Meanwhile, students in Bahar Dar did not oppose Soviet specialists who endorsed socialistic values and supported the slogans of their fellows in Addis Ababa against the corrupt government and U.S. imperialism. In contrast, students in other countries where the United States and the Soviet Union waged the Cultural Cold War were more open to contact with the superpowers or else opposed both of them. However, attacks on U.S. representatives and the support of Soviet ideas enacted by Ethiopian students were not seen in other countries. Arguably, the reason for the shift was the close cooperation between the United States and Emperor Selassie, if not also social and economic problems that outraged Ethiopian students and endeared them to the Soviet ideology.

Altogether, Ethiopia became a case that illustrates the possibilities and limitations of foreign powers to revise local institutes of higher education and establish new ones. On the one hand, both powers were able to open universities and schools, build academic facilities, and equip laboratories and libraries. On the other, the case shows how the need for development and the behavior of local professors restrained policies bent upon imposing values, culture, and ideology in studies and research at the university level. Thus, the Cultural Cold War attributed to European countries, when U.S. and Soviet experts imposed rival disciplines, values, and ideologies at universities in Europe, became transformed into Developmental Cold War attributed to African countries, in which both Americans and Soviets were limited in how they could impose rival ideas in the institutes of Africa due to the urgent need to build, maintain, and develop the infrastructure of universities. The values and aspirations of local academic communities conflicted with those of U.S. and Soviet policies, and in Ethiopia's case, professors had their own views on effective teaching methods. They not only undermined close communication with foreign advisors and demanded the purge of foreign specialists but also resisted transformations at their institutions toward U.S. or Soviet models, sabotaged reforms, and openly advocated their positions while being both under pressure from and in dialogue with the superpowers. Ultimately, local professors were able to shift the educational policies of both powers, namely by pressing the Soviet Union to alter its reforms at the Polytechnic Institute and by pressing the United States to diminish its reformist appetite at HSIU.

Returning to the theoretical framework discussed in the introduction to the chapter, it must be emphasized that the clash of values was liable to form new constructs in social or academic environments during the Cold War and that various small, marginalized groups and communities, rarely taken into account by researchers in previous studies, were able to act as key drivers in the policies of the superpowers. The clash between U.S. and Soviet advisors and the Ethiopian professors restrained those policies and made them more pliable to the demands of local professors even at the expense of the development of academic institutions and the quality of higher education.

CHAPTER 4

Asia-Pacific

Sabotage of Academics against U.S. and Soviet Strangers in Vietnam

1 Introduction

This chapter examines U.S. and Soviet education policy in Vietnam, where the superpowers sought to gain influence from the 1950s through the 1980s. Vietnam was chosen as a case for analysis due to its unique position in international politics during the Cold War, a position that prompted the intensification of a variety of educational projects proposed for the Vietnamese by both the United States and the Soviet Union. Of all cases investigated in this book, Vietnam alone was subjected to Americanization and Sovietization as civil war ravaged its population, which impacted not only U.S. and Soviet attempts at reform but also Vietnamese responses to those reforms. Moreover, Vietnam is the only case country where both U.S. and Soviet professors and advisors relocated from target universities and institutions of higher education to work in and with local Vietnamese schools. Although both superpowers pursued that strategy in a bid to mitigate a widespread crisis in education in Vietnam, neither U.S. nor Soviet efforts ended in success.

Formal independence from France and civil war led to the international partition of Vietnam into two parts in 1954. The north of Vietnam was controlled by pro-communist leaders inclined to China and the Soviet Union, and the south of Vietnam was controlled pro-democracy government supported by the West, particularly the United States. The division of the country expanded cultural and educational aid programs and contacts between North Vietnam and its capital in Hanoi and the Soviet Union, and between South Vietnam and its capital in Saigon and the United States. Both powers helped their clients to address problems in education, while transferring their rival models of education to Vietnam.[1]

In the early 1960s, the situation became aggravated when North Vietnamese army started helping South Vietnamese guerrillas. The leader of North Vietnam, Ho Chi Minh, received considerable military aid from China and, to a

---

1 George Herring, "The Cold War and Vietnam," *OAH Magazine of History* 18, no. 5 (2004): 18–21; Jeffrey Whyte, "Psychological War in Vietnam: Governmentality at The United States Information Agency," *Geopolitics* 23, no. 3 (2018): 661–89.

© NATALIA TSVETKOVA, 2021 | DOI:10.1163/9789004471788_006

ASIA-PACIFIC

lesser extent, the Soviet Union and aspired to unify the country. The government of South Vietnam asked Washington for increased military and technical assistance. The Eisenhower and Kennedy administrations expanded their assistance but were very cautious against involvement in possible military conflicts.[2]

However, several provocations in the mid-1960s, and more importantly a domino theory about the expansion of communism in Southeast Asia, became premises for the beginning of an initially small and then large-scale military operations against North Vietnam initiated by the Johnson administration after approval of the Gulf of Tonkin resolution by the U.S. Congress in 1964. The United States believed that the expansion of communist Vietnam would create more pro-Soviet countries in the Asia-Pacific region that would weaken the prestige of democracy and American values. The Soviet Union decided to help the loyal regime of Ho Chi Minh within the framework of the international communist movement. Vietnam, a small and nonstrategic country, turned out to be a hot battlefield between two rival ideologies during the Cold War.[3] When active military operations flared up, Moscow displaced all its advisors from North Vietnam. Washington, despite the war, continued sending advisors to South Vietnamese schools and universities, who orchestrated a number of various projects and reforms in the field of education.

In 1969, the Nixon administration began negotiating with representatives of the North to stop the war and leave Vietnam. Finally, in 1973, the American army withdrew from Saigon, and in 1975, Vietnam was united under the leadership of communists, opening an opportunity for the Soviet Union to be engaged in the reformation of schools and universities until 1986.

The case of higher education in Vietnam during the Cold War invites discussion about U.S. and Soviet cultural diplomacy at play in universities around the world, especially as part of discourse about the theory of constructivism developed in international relations studies. While adherents of realism agree that education as a part of public diplomacy or soft power helps to promote foreign policy aims, followers of constructivism argue that education and academic exchanges shape a system of values and norms that, in turn, shape identity, perceptions, and social, political, and economic constructs of the world.[4]

---

2   Lien-Hang Nguyen, *Hanoi's War: An International History of the War for Peace in Vietnam* (Chapel Hill: The University of North Carolina Press, 2016).

3   David Schmitz, *Richard Nixon and the Vietnam War: The End of the American Century* (Lanham, MD: Rowman & Littlefield Publishers, 2014).

4   For additional details, see Giles Scott-Smith, "Mapping the Undefinable: Some Thoughts on the Relevance of Exchange Programmes Within International Relations Theory," *Annals of the Academy of Political and Social Science*, no. 616 (2008): 173–95.

158   CHAPTER 4

Moreover, the webs of traditions, practices, identities, and interests of other entities can limit the intentions of a political power and its foreign policy. Finally, constructivism offers insights in the binary system of perception as constructed in such terms as "we/they," "strangers," or "another" that is widely applied in the study of international relations.[5]

In the context of the Cultural Cold War, Vietnam's education system and universities were viewed by Washington and Moscow as strategic resources for spreading their ideologies in a land that had unexpectedly become the epicenter of ideological containment and the site of violent civil conflict. The United States and the Soviet Union invested massive funding and effort into reforming the educational systems of the two Vietnams according to their rival values and models of university education. However, while instituting their projects via ordinary U.S. or Soviet professors, teachers, and experts, both superpowers encountered a host of obstacles, shortcomings, and setbacks created by the Vietnamese academic community to undermine their proposals and actions. The strategic goals of both powers were often thwarted at Vietnamese universities; visiting advisors from both sides were sometimes unable to realize their objectives, no matter how minor; and the local academic community regularly attempted to undermine Americanization or Sovietization by sabotaging the superpowers' reforms. Consequently, the goals of both the United States and the Soviet Union were often jeopardized by the local academic community's system of values, interests, and traditions, as well as by the inability of their advisors to deal with local academics.

Indeed, documents concerning U.S. and Soviet education policy at work in Vietnam during the Cold War reveal some remarkable interactions between the local academic community and either U.S. or Soviet advisors. Some documents showcase the kind of relations forged between strangers, especially between foreign advisors and Vietnamese university staff, and the latter's responses to U.S. or Soviet reforms at universities that limited the policies of the powers in Vietnamese institutions of higher education. As mentioned, the available documents, mostly reports written by U.S. or Soviet specialists involved in reforming those institutions and other schools in Vietnam, reveal problems in local–foreign relations, including U.S. and Soviet interpretations of Vietnamese responses to reform as sabotage by passively resisting work, study, and implementing projects. Beyond that, in no other case country but Vietnam did the United States and the Soviet Union confront not only plain resistance

---

5   Ted Hopf, "The Promise of Constructivism in International Relations Theory," *International Security*, 23, no. 1 (1998): 171–200.

ASIA-PACIFIC

and sabotage but also the local perception that their projects were unimportant and utterly unessential to academic life and work at Vietnamese universities. Perhaps the conditions of the Vietnam War provoked the ignorance and apathy of the Vietnamese, even if the foreign advisors, much to our surprise, never cited the war as a factor of their failure to reform education in Vietnam. Whereas professors in other countries reacted either positively or negatively to U.S. or Soviet proposals, the Vietnamese seem to have disregarded them. The documents even suggest that Vietnamese academics perceived U.S. and Soviet advisors as the bearers of alien cultures, of projects and reforms not perceived as hostile by the Vietnamese but as plainly inappropriate and unnecessary for the universities of Vietnam. In that way, the grand national interests, as well as security interests, of the two powers clashed with local traditions and culture at Vietnamese universities and schools.

The chapter has two sections. The first section reviews U.S. policy at Vietnamese universities and schools from the 1950s to the early 1970s. The second part considers USSR policy with respect to Vietnam from 1975 to the 1980s. The chapter will conclude with a brief discussion of the limitations that shaped teachers for the superpowers in terms of the approaches of constructivism.

2   Making Teachers of English: U.S. Education Policy in Saigon

Vietnam became the target of U.S. educational policy when the country was divided into two parts following the bloody liberalization from the French colonial regime in 1954. Many universities, schools, and their staff of teachers left the north part of Vietnam, where the government inclined politically and ideologically towards communist China and the USSR, and moved south, where semi-democratic leaders sought the support of Washington. These refugees re-established universities and reopened schools. One such educational institution in exile was the University of Saigon, refashioned by professors from the older Indo Chinese University of Hanoi.[6]

Despite the permanent political crises, the growth in university and school enrollment was rapid; however, the number of educational institutions left by the French colonists remained abysmally inadequate. The situation was

---

6   U.S. Agency for International Development, "Project Agreement between The Department of State, Agency for International Development, The United States of America, and The Directorate of General for Budget and Foreign Aid, Vietnam, 1969–1971," accessed June 10, 2018, www.usaid.gov.

160   CHAPTER 4

so critical that U.S. diplomats decided to help South Vietnam's government in the development and modernization of the education system. Since the mid-1950s, new schools, public universities, and the Ministry of Education were opened at the expense of the U.S. government.[7]

Over the next seventeen years, from 1955 to 1972, the U.S. government, its advisors, and professors from American universities were involved in the reform of the Vietnamese educational system.[8] To transform the educational system, American specialists and politicians pursued a variety of goals, but one goal persisted: educating a new generation of qualified Vietnamese teachers of English at the university level. The University of Saigon turned out to be a primary target of this policy. Moreover, schools also underwent crucial reforms. American advisors were eager to introduce comprehensive education, revise study plans, and make schools more suitable for the needs of the country.

United States policy in South Vietnam can be divided into two periods. The first period lasted from the mid-1950s to the mid-1960s, when the reforms moved very slowly, and American advisors built new educational institutions and studied the specifics of education in Vietnam. The second period corresponds with the Vietnam War, approximately from the mid-1960s up to the early 1970s, when the reforms at schools and the University of Saigon intensified and a number of wide-ranging projects were initiated. American advisors left Vietnam, when it became clear that the county would be united under the power of pro-communist leadership.

2.1   *The University of Saigon and the Faculty of Pedagogy: Making a Teacher*

In the territory of South Vietnam, the United Stated engaged a special diplomatic and semi-military mission—U.S. Operations Mission—that was engaged in technical assistance of Saigon's government. The Mission housed the Education Division, which consisted of only one employee in the mid-1950s but expanded remarkably by the early 1970s. In its most vigorous period of reforms, the Division was manned annually with more than 20 advisors from the government and more than 15 professors and teachers from American universities,

---

7 Completion of Assignment Report. Daryle E. Keefer, Chief Education Advisor, USOM [United States Operation Mission]/Vietnam, 1957–1960, box 27, records group 286, Agency for International Development, entry 578, USAID Mission to Vietnam. Executive Office, National Archives Records Administration (hereafter NARA).

8 U.S. Agency for International Development, "Evaluation and Planning for Secondary Education in South Vietnam by Ralph Purdy, Educational Consultant, part I, August 1971," accessed June 10, 2018, www.usaid.gov.

ASIA-PACIFIC 161

with the Education Division comprising the General Education section and the Teacher Training and Higher Education section.[9]

Until 1961, when the Agency for International Development was established, the International Cooperation Administration encompassed all the American advisors, consultants, and professors sent by the US government to Vietnam and managed the policy of reforms. The head of the Education Division at the U.S. Operations Mission reported directly to Washington, to the Administration for International Cooperation, and from 1961 onwards, to the Agency for International Development.

The face and leader of American educational policy in Vietnam was the head of the Education Division and Southern Illinois University professor Daryle Keefer. He led the first team of American educationalists in South Vietnam who elaborated a plan for training English teachers, developing the university, and remolding the curriculum at schools.[10] The teams from the universities of Michigan, Ohio, Wisconsin, and Southern Illinois were involved in implementation of the projects at different periods of America's engagement in Vietnam.[11] The American advisors established confident everyday relations with both the professoriate of the University of Saigon and the teaching staff at South Vietnamese schools. The head of the Education Division and American professors appealed to Washington for greater financial support for Vietnamese institutions due to the fact that "overwhelming majority of the advisors or technicians are well-received by the Vietnamese."[12] However, Vietnam turned out to be not a very welcoming country. Unexpectedly, the climate of the country caused several advisors to return home. Moreover, Vietnam turned out to be the only country during the Cold War in which American advisors lost their lives. In 1967, fifteen deans and professors of American universities, alongside representatives of the American government, died in a plane crash while inspecting schools located in the distant provinces of South Vietnam.

---

9   Completion of Assignment Report, 1957–1960, box 27, records group 286, NARA; U.S. Agency for International Development, "Evaluation and Planning for Secondary Education in South Vietnam by Ralph Purdy, Educational Consultant, part II, August 1971," accessed June 10, 2018, www.usaid.gov.

10 Letter from Dr. Daryle Keefer, Head, Education Division, to Dr. Arthur Gardiner, Chief, USOM, American Embassy, Saigon, box 27, records group 286, NARA; Quarterly Technical Service Report, Education Division, USOM to Vietnam, April to June 30, 1961, box 27, records group 286, NARA.

11 Completion of Assignment Report, 1957–1960, box 27, records group 286, NARA; Completion of Assignment Report. William Shelton, Teacher Education Advisor, Education Division, USOM/Vietnam, October 30, 1958–April 3, 1961, box 27, records group 286, NARA.

12 Letter from Dr. Daryle Keefer, box 27, records group 286, NARA.

Despite these severe problems and obstacles, American diplomats and the members of the Mission put great emphasis on the work of the Education Division. American advisors set out to accomplish the following in Vietnam: "The modernization and upgrading of higher education in Vietnam involves many substantive areas such as modification of the structure and programs, developing improved teaching techniques, <...> reorganizing curricular offerings, developing the potentials of the available manpower talent pool through study abroad <...>."[13] In the mid-1950s, the American advisors elaborated the following significant projects in the field of education. First, they would teach prospective secondary school teachers at the university level, and English-language teachers were prioritized. For this goal, the American advisors proposed opening a new Faculty of Pedagogy at the University of Saigon. Moreover, they intended to "feed" all the educational establishments with new textbooks, and particular those for study of English and American literature.

Most Vietnamese teachers did not have a professional pedagogical education, and English was certainly not taught at schools. Vietnamese teachers had a primary school education or, at best, they had completed a year of studies at colleges for teachers built by France and named according to the French model of the *école normale*.[14] In 1957–58, the United States initiated the *English Teacher Project* to introduce a system of pedagogical education at universities in Vietnam and to produce qualified teachers with a university diploma. The University of Saigon was said to open the first department of education.[15]

However, the University of Saigon had insufficient capacity to allow the American advisors to implement this idea. The university building was small, lacked adequate equipment and modernized classrooms, and had no space for a new department. After consultations with Washington, the head of the Education Division decided to construct a new building that would house the prospective faculty. Moreover, Soviet education projects in North Vietnam, where they constructed the Polytechnic Institute in Hanoi in 1959, enlarged the American advisors' ideas in terms of building a new campus for the university. In 1959, they articulated proposals about a new education department and

---

13   U.S. Agency for International Development, "Project Agreement."

14   Completion of Assignment Report, 1957–1960, box 27, records group 286, NARA. See in details about the policy of French and American cultural missions in Vietnam during the Cold War: Thuy-Phuong Nguyen, "The Rivalry of the French and American Educational Missions during the Vietnam War," *Paedagogica Historica* 50, no. 1/2 (2014): 27–41.

15   Ibid.; U.S. Agency for International Development, "Report. English Language Programs of the Agency for International Development," accessed June 10, 2018, www.usaid.gov.

ASIA-PACIFIC

a new campus to the Minister of Education in South Vietnam.[16] The Minister of Education of South Vietnam and the Education Division agreed on a site for the campus, including a building for the Faculty of Pedagogy, and a group of American architects and engineers arrived in Vietnam the same year to create a project and construct the campus. They were asked to give special attention to the design and engineering to the classrooms for the Faculty of Pedagogy, and new English-language laboratories, libraries, and special equipment were reserved for a new English Section of the Faculty of Pedagogy.[17]

Unexpectedly, the talks with the Vietnamese authorities began to slow down and were suspended in 1960. The Minister of Education terminated the negotiations, explaining to Daryle E. Keefer that he would revise his mind about the place for the campus.[18] In order not to interrupt the English teacher project, some of old university buildings were rebuilt, and the first students began their studies as prospective English teachers. Daryle Keefer informed Washington that

> the temporary Faculty of Pedagogy building of the University of Saigon has been remolded. <....> Teaching and advisory services have been furnished to the Faculty of Pedagogy, Saigon, especially in the field of English language instruction.[19]

Only in the mid-1960s was a new campus of the University of Saigon, including the Faculty of Pedagogy, finally constructed. The Faculty accommodated the English Section that aimed to foster a new generation of teachers of English. American engineers built new and modernized language labs, tape recorders, classrooms, and a new demonstration secondary school.

The staff of the new English section mainly comprised American professors and advisors from the Agency for International Development. Additionally, instructors from France, England, and Australia worked there. These academics shaped a new curriculum for training English teachers, taught the students, maintained the equipment, wrote manuscripts of new textbooks for both students and teachers, and, most fascinatingly, published books in English for children, something that happened in no other countries where Americans

---

16   Report. Status of proposed New Faculty of Pedagogy and Secondary School, Saigon, [from] Carl Cress, Acting Deputy Chief Education Advisor [to] Mr. Donald Coster, Acting Director, July 1, 1960, box 26, records group 286, NARA.

17   Completion of Assignment Report. William Shelton, October 30, 1958–April 3, 1961, box 27, records group 286, NARA.

18   Ibid.

19   Quarterly Technical Service Report, Education, 1961, box 27, records group 286, NARA.

164   CHAPTER 4

introduced English.[20] The Americans and other foreign specialists outnumbered the local, Vietnamese members of the university staff.[21] Perhaps for this reason, the American professors and advisors somehow neglected the University of Saigon's local teaching staff. In comparison to universities in Europe and the Middle East, where American advisors encountered a community of professors who resisted and restrained some American reforms, the Vietnamese teachers did not demonstrate their disaffection with American projects openly and complied with the American reforms. The reports noted the conservative nature of a few old professors trained by French colonialists who tried to preserve some traditional teaching methods, but the reports also noted many young teachers who were eager to modify the educational system. These young Vietnamese teachers were sent to study at American universities and would replace American advisors in the university's academic positions at the end of that 1960s:

> The faculty of the University of Saigon is older and more mature. Many of the faculty members have taught at the University of Hanoi or in France" <...> The younger faculty has enthusiasm, zeal and experimental mind of youth. This faculty is less interested in tradition and more in building a new and vigorous university.[22]

A study plan included regular coursework in analysis and description of the English language; comparative analysis of Vietnamese and English; general linguistics; techniques for teaching English as a foreign language; and American literature, history, and culture; students also engaged in practice teaching of English at the secondary school level.[23] Students spent four hours in the classroom and one hour in the laboratory each day. However, the American professors often complained in their reports that the students frequently failed to distinguish English sounds and that the study of English was very complicated for most of them.[24] About 100 students were enrolled in the English section of the Faculty of Pedagogy, and only about 30 students graduated from it each

---

20   Report. Educational Administration and Finance, Dec. 17, 1959, [from] USOM/Saigon [to] International Cooperation Administration, box 26, records group 286, NARA; U.S. Agency for International Development, "Report. English Language Programs."

21   U.S. Agency for International Development, "Report. English Language Programs."

22   Completion of Assignment Report, 1957–1960, box 27, records group 286, NARA.

23   U.S. Agency for International Development, "Report. English Language Programs."

24   Memorandum. Monthly Report, November, 1961, from G.S. Hammond, Education Division, to Mr. Arthur Gardiner, Director, box 27, records group 286, NARA.

year and entered directly into ranks of secondary school teachers of English.[25] The percentage of exclusions was high because the university had no entrance examinations and accepted weak students, which irritated the American specialists. Moreover, maintenance of the English-language laboratories was an additional and time-consuming assignment for the American advisors. An engineer supervised the installation and use of the equipment, and the American professors in English made a number of tape recordings named *English for Vietnamese Speakers.*[26]

Nevertheless, by 1965, the English Teacher Program gained national scope. Throughout South Vietnam, language laboratories promoted English for both children and adults. Increased funding within the framework of unfolding development policy, and the necessity to deter the Russians in the Third World through soft instruments of influence such as culture, education, and foreign aid, made the English language program politically determined: "English is the universal, modern language of trade, science, and technology. It is essential that any country wishing to become a full member of the modern western world member amongst its population a large percentage of persons with a good working knowledge of English."[27] The American mission increased the number of students registered in English classes in secondary schools and universities from 70,000 in 1960 to 450,000 in 1967.[28] Moreover, the American advisors were able to increase the number of the graduates from the Faculty of Pedagogy; in 1968 the growth reached 60 graduates, and the program planned to prepare more than 2,000 teachers by 1975.[29]

However, there was a real problem behind these growing numbers of English teachers. The graduates had very low qualifications in both language and pedagogy.[30] The Head of the Education Division acknowledged this problem for the first time in 1969, concluding that the low qualifications permitted by the University of Saigon's archaic examination system were to blame. This system did not select students or include an entrance examination, and in opinion of the American specialists, had to be remolded, revised, and Americanized. The American advisors planned to introduce entrance exams and a credit system for evaluation; they further sought to remold the structure of the university, including the introduction of the departmental system instead of faculties.

---

25   Completion of Assignment Report, 1957–1960, box 27, records group 286, NARA.
26   U.S. Agency for International Development, "Project Agreement."
27   Ibid.
28   Ibid.
29   Ibid.
30   Ibid.

166　　　　　　　　　　　　　　　　　　　　　　　　　　　　　　　　　CHAPTER 4

Moreover, the Ministry of Education, which reluctantly helped the American advisors, also was at risk of a profound transformation due to the establishment of new planning and management divisions. In order to implement these plans, the advisors selected about 40 Vietnamese officials and teachers who had studied in the United States and could therefore contribute to new American reforms in 1969 and 1970.[31]

However, these plans were not realized. In early 1972, American advisors began leaving Vietnam. The future of the University of Saigon turned out to be a dead end. A new communist government dissolved the University of Saigon in 1975, and later, some of its buildings were used for a newly established university named the University of Ho Chi Minh. According to Soviet documents, the Faculty of Education at Saigon University was transformed into the Ho Chi Minh Pedagogical Institute in 1975, which brought about a dramatic increase in the number of students and teaching staff. By the mid-1980s, approximately 5,000 students studied at the Institute under the supervision of 300 faculty members. However, as the United States had previously experienced, the Soviet Union now faced two dilemmas: poorly qualified instructors and a student body with a frustratingly limited knowledge base.[32]

2.2　*U.S. Advisors at Schools: Building Infrastructure*

The English teacher project was not limited to reforms at the universities. Teachers who worked at Vietnamese schools also became targets for American attempts to transform schools and teachers. Vietnamese teachers, as mentioned above, were the graduates of secondary schools or normal schools built by France, and Americans questioned their professionalism.[33] Vietnamese schools were based on cramming, the disciplines were outdated, and the schooling was not compulsory and universal. However, until early 1970s, the American advisors never mentioned the French influence on Vietnamese universities. Before withdrawal, however, documents designated the French traditions as a factor in the failure of American reforms.[34]

31　U.S. Agency for International Development, "Project Agreement between AID and DGBFA, Vietnam. Higher Education, 1971–1973," accessed June 10, 2018, www.usaid.gov.

32　Report on the Visit of the Delegation from the Leningrad State Pedagogical Institute to Ho Chi Minh Pedagogical Institute of Vietnam, 1982, folder 4328, records group 9563, State Archive of Russia Federation (hereafter GARF), p. 2.

33　Completion of Assignment Report, 1957–1960, box 27, records group 286, NARA.

34　See in details: Thuy-Phuong Nguyen, "The Rivalry of the French and American Educational Missions during the Vietnam War," *Paedagogica Historica* 50, no. 1/2 (2014): 27–41. U.S. Agency for International Development, "Evaluation and Planning," part II.

ASIA-PACIFIC

The American educationalists dreamed of the introduction of comprehensive education, widely discussed at that time in many different countries,[35] and of new arts disciplines including civic education, history, English, and other globally accepted subjects that make a school a school. The head of the Education Division intended to liberalize Vietnamese schooling, which implied a profound reform of curricula, the elimination of outdated and irrelevant subjects introduced by French colonialists many years ago, and, the most importantly, the introduction of a comprehensive education system.

However, all these proposals faced one significant problem: the lack of school buildings to accommodate all children who wanted to study. The schools were overcrowded, and before transforming the schooling, the school as a physical and material place needed to be built. By the early 1960s, Americans built three new schools, but this construction did not address the problem of overcrowded schools. In order to hasten their desired educational reforms, the American specialists opened classrooms in appropriate buildings in different Vietnamese provinces. This approach improved school education and contributed to the elimination of illiteracy. Over the next two years, more than 2,000 classrooms for primary and secondary education were opened and staffed with teachers.[36] By the time American specialists left Vietnam in 1972, the number of such classrooms reached 12,225 throughout South Vietnam. These classrooms undoubtedly provided the space and place for English lessons.[37]

However, the American reformers faced another severe problem that enormously hindered their project. The climate of Vietnam and its rains and floods did not allow the Americans to build the schools in time. Not all villages had space to open these American-style classrooms, which led to additional spending on the construction of dormitories for children in other villages. Weather conditions required non-stop building maintenance that, in turn, required additional human resources from the U.S. Construction and maintenance of

---

35   Hilda Amsing, Linda Greveling, and Jeroen Dekker, "The Struggle for Comprehensive Education in the Netherlands: The Representation of Secondary School Innovation in Dutch Newspaper Articles in the 1970s," *History of Education* 42, no. 4 (2013): 460–85; Linda Greveling, Hilda Amsing, and Jeroen Dekker, "Crossing borders in educational innovation: Framing foreign examples in discussing comprehensive education in the Netherlands, 1969–1979," *Paedagogica Historica* 50, no. 1/2 (2014): 76–92; about U.S. policy in schools during the Vietnam War see: Jessica Elkind, *Aid Under Fire: Nation Building and the Vietnam War* (Lexington: University Press of Kentucky, 2016).

36   USOM Quarterly Technical Service Report, July to September 30, 1959 [from] USOM/ Saigon [to] International Cooperation Administration, box 26, records group 286, NARA.

37   Quarterly Technical Service Report, Education, October 1 to December 31, 1961, box 27, records group 286, NARA.

168   CHAPTER 4

school buildings were often slowed due to the slowness and sabotage of Vietnamese partners.[38] However, American specialists rarely mentioned military operations and other factors related to the Vietnam War as an influence that undermined education development or school construction. It was as if there was no war in Vietnam based on the reports of the American professors and advisors.

Additional difficulties stemmed from the project of writing manuscripts for children's textbooks and instructional materials for teachers. The head of the Education Division organized a special team of professors who finalized the first books for schools in 1959.[39] English textbooks were prioritized, and the first materials were sent out to schools. However, the American writing teams unquestionably had limited ability, and the lack of textbooks became an unresolved dilemma for the American reformers who would introduce new disciplines without providing children and teachers with books. Moreover, the Ministry of Education in Vietnam did not have a printing house, and until the mid-1960s all textbooks came from the United States. The Instructional Material Center at the Ministry of Education was finally established in the mid-1960s, and a special writing committee was organized at the U.S. Mission, members of which were primarily engaged in writing and printing school books. The manuscripts of teachers' books on phonetics, grammar, and English practice were printed and disseminated among the schools. Various titles including civic education, Vietnamese culture, chemistry, and geography were also written by American professors.[40] Advisors from Southern Illinois University reportedly made the main contribution in writing schoolbooks.[41] However, the American advisors could not meet the demands of Vietnam's educational system. The numbers of schoolchildren were always much greater than the numbers of copies sent to schools.[42]

---

38   Quarterly Technical Service Report, January 1 to March 31, 1961, Education U-238, [from] USOM/Saigon [to] International Cooperation Administration; Quarterly Technical Service Report, Education, October 1 to December 31, 1960; Memorandum. February Monthly Report, March 9, 1960, from Daryle Keefer, Chief Education Advisor, to Mr. A. Gardiner, Director, box 27, records group 286, NARA.

39   Memorandum. May Monthly Report, June 06, 1960, from Carl Cress, Deputy Chief Education Advisor to Mr. Donald Coster, Deputy Director, box 27; Report. Educational Administration and Finance, Dec. 17, 1959, [from] USOM/Saigon [to] International Cooperation Administration, box 26, records group 286, NARA.

40   Report. Textbook Program, Dec. 24, 1959, from USOM/Saigon to International Cooperation Administration, box 26; Quarterly Technical Service Report, Education, October 1 to December 31, 1961, box 27, records group 286, NARA.

41   Memorandum. Monthly Report, November, 1961, box 27, records group 286, NARA.

42   U.S. Agency for International Development, "Project Agreement."

ASIA-PACIFIC

In this rush for building schools and writing books, the American specialists missed their primary goal: to introduce comprehensive education in Vietnam. Finally, in 1969, the Minister of South Vietnam announced a reform that shattered the American advisors with its limited and revised approach. The reform implied the introduction of compulsory and comprehensive 12-year education with emphasis on polytechnic and labor schooling. The American advisors agreed with the 12 years of education, but they worried about the emphasis on technical and labor education that could undermine those disciplines in the arts introduced by the United States during the previous period.[43] Moreover, this reform neglected the introduction of unified teacher education suitable for comprehensive education. Neither the Vietnamese Ministry of Education nor the American specialists had previously been able to establish a unified system for teacher training. Vietnamese teachers were still recruited from former school graduates. Some had studied at normal schools for teachers or received a certificate from American seminars, and only a few were graduates from the pedagogical departments opened by the United States at universities. Moreover, the prestige of a teaching career was very low in South Vietnamese culture, and the American advisors had no power to improve the image of a teacher or, at least, to make the Ministry of Education increase their salaries.[44]

In order to implement school reform, the unification of teacher education was urgently required, and the American advisors suggested introducing four-year colleges in the American style for all teachers including elementary and secondary teachers. In 1970, American specialists elaborated a plan for the establishment of such pedagogical colleges in 1973, but this plan was never realized.[45] In 1972, the U.S. Agency for International Development terminated the work of the American advisors and professors, and all of them left South Vietnam.

2.3 Successes, Failures, and Consequences of American Reforms
Before leaving Vietnam, the American specialists measured the final results of their activities at universities and schools. They made a survey through interviews with a hundred American and Vietnamese participants in projects, notably advisors, teachers, professors, officials, and students. The results of the

---

43 U.S. Agency for International Development, "Teacher Education. Project Agreement between The Department of State, Agency for International Development, The United States of America, and The Directorate of General for Budget and Foreign Aid, Vietnam, 1970–1973," accessed June 10, 2018, www.usaid.gov.

44 Ibid.

45 Ibid.

170   CHAPTER 4

investigation shocked the Americans. The Vietnamese participants identified problems and failures that the American specialists had never mentioned in their reports and that they had never taken into consideration while making reforms. The reports contained some information about positive and success-ful activities by the American specialists. During the 17-year period of reforms, American advisors had more or less revised the curriculum at universities and schools, convinced the Vietnamese elite that comprehensive education was a main driver for Vietnam's development, taught 64 Vietnamese teachers in the United States, introduced pedagogical education at the university level, and provided schools with textbooks and equipment. Undoubtedly, these achieve-ments were substantial given the fact that the U.S. government had fully sup-ported the reforms starting only in 1965 and they had gained a widespread character, clear objectives, and evaluation criteria. Before American military operations in Vietnam, reforms were enacted by the enthusiasm of the Ameri-can professors and teachers who had worked in Vietnam since 1955.[46]

Nevertheless, the saddest thing was that no reform was fully accomplished. Reform of comprehensive education remained on paper only, schools and universities remained overcrowded, there were insufficient laboratories and textbooks, and the teachers sent to American universities could not adapt their new knowledge to the realities of Vietnam upon their return. The Amer-icanized departments at universities such as the Faculty of Pedagogy pro-duced students who lost touch with Vietnamese traditions and could not find jobs. Despite titanic efforts to train teachers, the quality of teaching was not improved.[47]

The Vietnam War, French colonization, ministerial leapfrog, and hidden sabotage by Vietnamese colleagues were the main factors that limited develop-ment and reforms in education on the American model. The war undoubtedly took away human and material resources, diminished the salaries of teachers, and narrowed the possibilities for building new schools.[48]

The most unexpected result was that the French legacy at Vietnamese uni-versities and schools, including French teachers, textbooks, and approaches to teaching and research, was maintained. French colonization had instilled Vietnamese universities with elitism and the traditions of the French edu-cational system. American advisors did not mention the French influence in their reports to Washington, but in 1969–1970, reports identified the French

---

46   U.S. Agency for International Development, "Evaluation and Planning," part II.

47   Ibid; U.S. Agency for International Development, "Project Agreement."

48   Quarterly Technical Service Report, Education, October 1 to December 31, 1961, box 27, records group 286, NARA.

ASIA-PACIFIC

influence as the primary factor leading to the failure of American reforms. Reportedly, the universities were unable to adopt American patterns of organization and administrative apparatuses. The universities remained patriarchal and retained the features of French education. Some American professors noticed a certain tension in communication with their Vietnamese and French counterparts at universities, who perceived American reforms in their own way. The rectors reportedly had to maintain a balance between requests, aspirations, and reform proposals from French, Vietnamese, and American professors.[49]

The Ministry of Education, in which 15 ministers were replaced, never became a mediator for American reforms nor did it become their supporter. All the efforts to foster qualified staff in project planning and management failed.[50] The American advisors complained to Washington that there was a "failure on the part of the high-level ministry officials to delegate authority to their subordinates"[51] in Vietnam. The United States had difficulties getting its own initiatives to be completed by ministry staff.

Sabotage by Vietnamese citizens engaged in the American reforms turned out to be a significant but overlooked factor. The Vietnamese people's national character and culture made its impact on the Americans' activities. The slowness of the Vietnamese counterparts in the decision-making process, negotiations, and general work greatly slowed down the reforms. Negotiations over publishing textbooks or building new schools, for example, lasted two to three years.[52] The Vietnamese parties postponed appointments, and lower officials did not follow orders from their bosses with whom Americans had formed agreements. The head of the Education Division described the sabotage of Vietnamese counterparts thusly:

> Training and Higher Education project difficulty has been experienced in terms of counterpart arrangements. Often the Project Technician himself could not get to a Vietnamese official who could decide on or recommend a major course of action (or deviation) with reasonable assurance that the decision or recommendation would be acceptable and carried out. Often the technicians had even more difficulty since the Vietnamese officials with whom they worked were of lower rank, than those with

---

49   U.S. Agency for International Development, "Evaluation and Planning," part 11.
50   U.S. Agency for International Development, "Project Agreement."
51   Quarterly Technical Service Report, October 1 to December 31, 1961, Education, box 27, records group 286, NARA.
52   U.S. Agency for International Development, "Project Agreement."

172 CHAPTER 4

whom the Project Technician worked. Because of diverse interests of the Teacher Training and Higher education project, it was difficult to find a Vietnamese counterpart who could professionally serve all of the interests which the project represented.[53]

Vietnamese counterparts did not resist reforms, but, as American advisors noted, something always led to the non-fulfillment of assignments: "no resistance, but always something to prevent accomplishment."[54] The Vietnamese did not trust the Americans and did not understand why reforms were needed. They complained that the Americans were realizing their own plan and values, but did not contribute to development as the Vietnamese wanted.[55]

Finally, the University of Saigon, which became the main foundation for American reforms, neglected certain instructions from the Ministry of Education, and permanent conflicts continued between the two entities. This situation damaged American reforms at the university. The Faculty of Pedagogy, the main offspring of American reforms in Vietnam, turned out to be like an unloved child for the university's administration. Established as an autonomous department, the faculty received privileged and solid funding from the U.S. Operations Mission that created additional tensions among the university staff.[56]

Leaving Vietnam, American advisors made a conclusion about the different ways American and Vietnamese people perceived reforms. What American experts perceived as a success was not perceived in such a way by the Vietnamese: "Success American-style is not applicable to success Vietnamese-style, and the expectations were not appropriate."[57] The United States recognized that their reforms were limited, and the Vietnamese were likely to carry out their own reforms themselves. However, one thing has been accomplished: Saigon understood the importance of comprehensive education: "Even with many limiting conditions, some major accomplishments were achieved, including the official recognition of comprehensive education."[58]

---

53 Completion of Assignment Report. William Shelton, October 30, 1958–April 3, 1961, box 27, records group 286, NARA.

54 U.S. Agency for International Development, "Evaluation and Planning," part II.

55 Ibid.

56 Completion of Assignment Report. William Shelton, October 30, 1958–April 3, 1961, box 27, records group 286, NARA.

57 U.S. Agency for International Development, "Evaluation and Planning," part I.

58 Ibid.

ASIA-PACIFIC 173

3   Making Teachers of Russian: Soviet Education Policy in Hanoi

Once reunited in 1975, Vietnam became a target of Soviet economic, political, and educational reforms. However, the first Soviet specialists had worked in North Vietnam since the mid-1950s and had built the Polytechnic University in Hanoi in 1959. When the Vietnam War broke out, Soviet advisors and professors evacuated North Vietnam and returned only after the country's unification.[59] Like their American counterparts, Soviet specialists sought a corps of Russian-language teachers for Vietnam's schools.

The University of Saigon and other universities in southern Vietnam were dissolved and later rebranded under the socialist model. However, Soviet reformers did not work at universities and schools in southern Vietnam, but mobilized their reforms in the northern part of the country, primarily at universities and schools in Hanoi. This unique situation was a product of the country's division in 1954, when all the USSR's resources were sent to North Vietnam. Moreover, after the country's unification in 1975, the academic life at the universities and schools in the south was almost dead due to purges and repressions, which deterred Soviet politicians from sending Soviet specialists to the bloodless universities and schools of the South.

3.1   *Pedagogical Institute of Foreign Languages at Hanoi: Making a Teacher of Russian Language*

In 1976, the first group of Soviet advisors, professors from various Soviet universities and pedagogical institutes, and teachers of Russian arrived in Hanoi. These academic and nonacademic advisors, together with their families, constituted a group of 200 Soviet citizens. They stayed in a hotel where advisors and teachers from Eastern Europe, Cuba, Japan, France, and Australia also rented rooms. However, the Soviet team's life was not comfortable. They complained to Moscow about permanent economic crisis, shortages of everyday food, and food stamps that affected their living and working conditions. The Pedagogical Institute of Foreign Languages at Hanoi became the main place where Soviet specialists sought to create a new generation of qualified teachers, and particularly teachers of the Russian language, for Vietnam's schools. This institution opened in 1958, and it was often called a university by Vietnamese

---

59   Soviet documents indicate that some projects at universities and schools in North Vietnam were carried out during the Vietnam War. In 1968, for example, the Soviet Ministry of Education asked the Soviet Navy whether it would be possible to transport equipment and specialists to Hanoi's schools by sea, owing to the problem that China often denied Soviet requests to enter Chinese airspace.

174 CHAPTER 4

sources. In Soviet documents, the institution is listed as an institute, a term which refers more precisely to the study plans. Namely, institutes offer a more applied nature of education than universities.[60]

The Institute was located beyond the frontier of the city; some of the buildings were built of bricks, and other ones were made of bamboo.[61] The Pedagogical Institute consisted of four faculties, notably the Faculties of Russian, English, French, and Chinese Languages. Prospective teachers were trained here for five years, but the buildings of the Institute were too small to accommodate all the students. The institute therefore worked in two daily sessions as described in a Soviet report: "English and French Faculties worked from 6:30 to 11:30, Russian and Chinese Faculties—from 12:00 to 17:00 [sic]."[62] The documents do not provide evidence that the Soviet Union planned to build a new building or campus.

The Faculty of Russian Language, where the most of Soviet advisors, professors, and teachers worked, became the largest department in the mid-1970s. In the 1975–76 academic year, 800 students were registered, and 80 teaching staff members worked there. Half of them had graduated from universities, and five of them had received doctorates in the USSR.[63] At the end of the 1970s, 1,000 students had already been trained at the Faculty of Russian Language, 300 new prospective students were enrolled in so-called preparatory courses to pass entrance exams, and 100 teachers worked there.[64] The department produced 200 Russian-language teachers each year.[65] The numbers were higher than those of the Faculty of Pedagogy at the University of Saigon.

The Institute embraced many foreign professors from different countries. A citation from a Soviet professor's report best describes Hanoi's international outlook:

Soviet professors worked at the Faculty of Russian and the Faculty of English; French professors worked at the Faculty of French, and the

---

60 Report on the Work of Instructors and Teachers in Vietnam, 1977–78, by Y. Zatsny, Chief of Soviet Specialists Team at Hanoi, folder 3724, records group 9563, GARF, p. 25.

61 Report on the Trip to Vietnam by Y. Zatsny, Chief of Soviet Specialists Team, October 22, 1976–June 28, 1977, folder 3724, Reports of Soviet Instructors of Russian Language Worked in Vietnam, 1977–1978, entry 1, records group 9563, Soviet Ministry for Education, p. 38.

62 Ibid, p. 37.

63 Report on the Work of Instructors and Teachers in Vietnam, 1977–78, folder 3724, records group 9563, GARF, p. 25.

64 Report on the Work at the Pedagogical Institute for Foreign Languages at Hanoi by Professor K. Naumov, 1978, folder 3724, records group 9563, GARF, p. 50.

65 Report on the Work of Instructors and Teachers in Vietnam, 1977–78, folder 3724, records group 9563, GARF, p. 25.

ASIA-PACIFIC

Chinese professors worked at the Faculty of Chinese. Specialists from England and other English-speaking countries were not invited this year. The reason is that the government can invite members of communist parties while Vietnam is being transformed into socialism. A few members of communist parties from England, France, and Australia work here.[66]

Ten to 20 Soviet professors and associate professors of Russian language and literature were engaged in teaching activities at the Pedagogical Institute. They worked during a period of one or two years, and Moscow assigned them a goal similar to the one the U.S. government had previously designated for its advisors: notably, to train qualified teachers at the university level. However, the disciplines were different. The United States wanted to create English teachers, but the USSR, Russian-language teachers. Like their American counterparts, the Soviet professors had to transform curricula, revise teaching methods, and write textbooks. Like their American rivals, the Soviets mobilized their efforts to write instructional materials for teachers and to develop records of Russian sounds for language laboratories. However, in contrast to the Americans, they spent a lot of time with students engaging them in Russian classes and extra-curricular activities.

The academic load implemented by a Soviet visiting advisor or professor can be summarized as follows: teaching classes for students, supervising Ph.D. candidates among Vietnamese university staff, conducting seminars for Vietnamese teachers, writing and publishing at minimum four textbooks, revising syllabi for disciplines, and modifying the examination system.

In practice, Soviet teachers did not interfere in the work of the departments and did not offer wide-ranging reforms for the administration. Soviet teaching staff worked as visiting professors at the Department of Russian Language and the Department of Russian Literature, and their everyday work aimed to assist "Vietnamese colleagues to improve the methods of teaching."[67] They pointed out that their Vietnamese colleagues had quite satisfactory linguistic and philo-logical knowledge, but the Soviets were not satisfied with their outdated methods of instruction such as the "question-answer method and writing words by dictation."[68] Their Vietnamese colleagues did not develop their students' speaking skills in a way that surprised and irritated the Soviets: "The teaching of the Russian language is dominated by theorizing and studying grammatical

---

66   Report on the Trip to Vietnam, folder 3724, records group 9563, GARF.

67   Report on Work of Instructors and Teachers in Vietnam, folder 3724, records group 9563, GARF, p. 27.

68   Report on the Work at the Pedagogical Institute for Foreign Languages at Hanoi by Associate Professor V. Silina 1977–1978, folder 3724, records group 9563, GARF, p. 65.

categories, which are not appropriate to communication skills of students in the field of common Russian language."[69] To improve the quality of Russian language instruction among their Vietnamese colleagues, Soviet professors wrote dozens of instructional materials for their use.[70] However, in early 1980s, the Soviet professors reported about low qualifications of Vietnamese teachers that created additional difficulties for effective work.[71]

Additionally, the Soviet advisors rewrote, edited, and published new textbooks on Russian literature.[72] The Department of Russian Literature established after the unification of Vietnam had only a few textbooks for students who studied Russian and Soviet literature six hours per week. Soviet teachers had to rewrite and publish new textbooks and instructional materials. One Soviet professor noted in a report:

> Textbooks and books for teachers on Soviet literature were absent. There was a reader on both Russian and Soviet literature. Being convinced that the reader contains a lot of mistakes and misprints and that the texts of Russian classical literature were distorted, I decided to write a new textbook and a reader and did it during the entire academic year.[73]

Or:

> A textbook had a lot of errors in facts referring to Russian literature that made me to rewrite it thoroughly. I have edited 600 pages of the textbook. The first part of it is now in print.[74]

The students were Soviet teachers' main target audience. They paid more attention to the student body than to their Vietnamese colleagues. Reports are full of detailed accounts of how Soviet professors dealt with students in the

---

69   Ibid, p. 70.

70   Ibid, p. 68.

71   Report by Vorobieva O., Instructor of English at Hanoi Pedagogical Institute, 1981–1982 folder 4328, Reports by Soviet Delegations and Specialists about the Visits to Vietnam, 1982, entry 1, records group 9563, Soviet Ministry for Education, GARF, p. 5.

72   Report on the Work at the Pedagogical Institute for Foreign Languages at Hanoi by Professor K. Naumov, 1978, folder 3724, records group 9563, GARF, p. 50.

73   Report on the Work at the Pedagogical Institute for Foreign Languages at Hanoi by S. Bablumyan, Instructor of Russian Literature, 1977–1978, folder 3724, records group 9563, GARF, p. 14.

74   Report on the Work at the Pedagogical Institute for Foreign Languages at Hanoi by M. Altunyan, Instructor of Russian Language 1977–1978, folder 3724, records group 9563, GARF, p. 2.

classroom and beyond.[75] As in Saigon, Hanoi and its educational establishments were overcrowded because there were no entrance examinations. The majority of students were sent to the Institute by military and political party organizations:

> Fresh students are accepted to the Institute according to the requests by factories, military units, and others. A significant portion of students are males 25–35 years old, and most of them are former soldiers. They comprise 25% of the total student body. Many students never studied foreign language.[76]

However, the students were very diligent and responsible:

> Students study with a high sense of duty, they are very conscientious and diligent despite the severe living conditions. Their food is very scare, their scholarship is only 12 rubles [*about $9, Natalia Tsvetkova*], they are compelled to dig canals and build dams after their studies.[77]

The Soviets were eager to teach students speaking skills, and Russian phonetics were therefore prioritized. Students studied Russian phonetics 22 hours a week.[78] However, Soviet teachers, like their American counterparts, noted their Vietnamese students' difficulties in learning foreign languages.[79] Most students struggled to learn Russian, as they had not studied the language before and had entered the Institute by special quotas. One Soviet professor reported: "There is a "C" group at the Institute, which consists of former soldiers. Their age negatively affects their studies of the Russian language."[80]

The Soviet teachers established language laboratories and recorded sounds of the Russian language on tape. However, access to the language labs was

---

75 Ibid, p. 1; Report on Work at the Pedagogical Institute for Foreign Languages at Hanoi by N. Akhmetzyanova, Instructor of Russian Language 1977–1978, folder 3724, records group 9563, GARF, p. 7.

76 Report on Trip to Vietnam, folder 3724, records group 9563, GARF, p. 37.

77 Ibid, p. 40.

78 Report on the Work at the Pedagogical Institute for Foreign Languages at Hanoi by G. Bolshelapova, Instructor of Russian Language 1977–1978, folder 3724, records group 9563, GARF, p. 21.

79 Report on the Work at the Pedagogical Institute for Foreign Languages at Hanoi by N. Oganova, Instructor of Russian Language 1977–1978, folder 3724, records group 9563, GARF, p. 73–74.

80 Report on the Work at the Pedagogical Institute for Foreign Languages at Hanoi by G. Bolshelapova, folder 3724, records group 9563, GARF, p. 22.

178   CHAPTER 4

limited due to their small capacity.[81] In early 1980s, the Soviet instructors noted
the low level of knowledge of Russian due to the lack of manuals, language
labs, and literature.[82]

The Soviet professors' extracurricular activities were another significant
component of their trips to Vietnam and were aimed at promoting the Soviet
way of life among students. They were obliged to arrange student meetings,
conferences, competitions, quizzes, musical and drama groups, and photo
exhibitions and to distribute books as well. Moreover, the Soviet teachers
helped mount theatrical productions conducted by students in the Russian
language.[83]

It is difficult to conclude the extent to which visiting Soviet professors actually carried out these extracurricular activities. Some reports provide a detailed
account of extracurricular life, but some of the reports list events as required
by Moscow. Moreover, some reports repeat each other word for word in this
section. The Soviet professors seemed to copy this section from one other to
compose a suitable but misleading report for Moscow. Here, for example, is
one of the standard descriptions of classes and extracurricular activity in terms
of propaganda work: "During the academic year, 15 evening meetings provided
within discussion clubs, 10 contests held, 150 lectures given to students, 4,500
copies of political books distributed, 22 photo exhibitions installed."[84] Or: "The
classes were structured in such way that the students were instilled with love
for the Russian language, for the Russian people, for Russia."[85]

While students participated in these events with enthusiasm, Soviet advisors
noted the Pedagogical Institute administration's lack of interest in expanding
contacts between students and Soviets. Vietnamese officials tried to prevent
close contact between Soviet teachers and Vietnamese students beyond the
classroom. Unexpectedly, performances, conferences, exhibitions were stymied. One Soviet advisor described such a situation: "Obstacles to broader
propaganda work at the Pedagogical Institute of Foreign Languages at Hanoi
were restrictions imposed on the part of the leadership of the Institute."[86] Or:

---

81 Report on Trip to Vietnam, folder 3724, records group 9563, GARF, p. 38–39.
82 Report by Vorobieva O., Instructor of English at Hanoi Pedagogical Institute, 1981–1982,
     folder 4328, records group 9563, p. 6.
83 Report on the Work of Instructors and Teachers in Vietnam, 1977–78, folder 3724, records
     group 9563, GARF, p. 31.
84 Ibid, p. 31.
85 Report on the Work at the Pedagogical Institute for Foreign Languages at Hanoi by G.
     Bolshelapova, folder 3724, records group 9563, GARF, p. 22.
86 Report on the Work of Instructors and Teachers in Vietnam, 1977–78, folder 3724, records
     group 9563, GARF, p. 31.

"Officials from the Vietnamese side of the Institute interfered with and interrupted extracurricular activities."[87]

The institute's authorities were motivated by their warm attitude toward China, a political and ideological rival of the Soviet Union in that period. The Vietnamese academic community inclined more to China and preferred the Chinese version of communism, eschewing the Soviet version. Beijing blamed Moscow for revising the ideology of Leninism and Marxism and tried to convince the world, and Vietnam in particular, that Beijing, not Moscow, was the center of the world communist movement. The Chinese, therefore, were able to convince a portion of the Vietnamese academic community to discourage Soviet contacts with students. Information emanating from Chinese colleagues was more welcome. However, the situation was cardinally changed after China's attack on the territory of Vietnam in 1979. After the defeat of China, the Vietnamese academic community treated Soviet guests at the institute with greater warmth.

3.2 Soviet Advisors at Schools: Teaching Children

Soviet policy also targeted the Vietnamese school where teachers were trained; the Soviet Union aimed to create a new generation of Russian-language teachers. Like their American counterparts in the south a decade earlier, Soviet specialists arrived at schools to teach the Russian language to children in elementary and secondary schools. Soviet teachers were not involved in any crucial transformations of school life. They did not revise curricula or administer units. Their duty was to educate schoolchildren in the Russian language over a period of two years.

Soviet teachers achieved some success in teaching children in schools. The children very warmly accepted Soviet teachers and participated in various projects. One Russian teacher described such activities in a Vietnamese school:

> I have worked in a school for two years. The pupils are very fluent in Russian, and their knowledge allowed me to give them extra classes. The children are ready to listen and read children's books. They helped a young Vietnamese teacher improve her pronunciation, often translating to her what I wanted to say. They understood my dialogue with her faster than she did.[88]

---

87 Report on the Work at the Pedagogical Institute for Foreign Languages at Hanoi by N. Oganova, Instructor of Russian Language 1977–1978, folder 3724, records group 9563, GARF, p. 76.

88 Report on the Work at the Pedagogical Institute for Foreign Languages at Hanoi by G. Bolshelapova, folder 3724, records group 9563, GARF, p. 17.

180 CHAPTER 4

Schoolchildren learned Russian phonetics more quickly, spoke much better than the students at the Pedagogical Institute, and loved extracurricular projects: "I issued a wall newspaper called *Young Russist*, and each issue was met with joy and interest. My puzzles and quizzes stimulated thought and a search for answers."[89] Additionally: "I have compounded a library of Russian and Soviet children's writers and donated 20 taped records. The Vietnamese children are very fond of singing Russian songs and learning poetry."[90]

However, the Vietnamese schools' administration often overpowered or interfered with these activities by Soviet teachers, as the schools wanted to limit the impact of Soviet ideas on children. Soviet teachers were not allowed to attend some extracurricular activities. The documents describe a case in which a school administration did not let a Soviet teacher attend a performance she had produced. The cause for this cold attitude towards the Soviets is reported to be China's influence on Vietnamese schools. Numerous schools had been evacuated to China, and many teachers knew Chinese, respected China, and wanted to diminish the influence of its main rival, the Soviet Union.[91]

However, the work of the Soviet teachers in schools was interrupted in 1979 when the Vietnamese government announced a school reform, and most Soviet teachers were sent to the southern part of the country in order to contribute to this reform. The introduction of comprehensive education, discussions of which had emerged in many countries in the 1960s and 1970s, was the reform's main goal. The reform's provisions looked very similar to the provisions of the reform announced by the Saigon government in 1969: notably, the introduction of comprehensive and 12-year education, the strengthening of labor and polytechnic education, and the elimination of the French legacy in education. Vietnam planned to unify, at last, two systems of school education developed differently in the southern and northern parts of the country.[92] The reform plan neglected only one thing: professional education of teachers appropriate for this new educational system.

Moreover, the reform demanded huge material resources, and Vietnam asked for aid from the Soviet Union. In early 1980s, the Soviet Union was already an aging empire, with financial resources that were too paltry to transform Vietnam. Soviet specialists, however, warned both governments that it

---

89   Ibid, p. 18.

90   Ibid, p. 19–20.

91   Ibid, p. 18.

92   Report on the Visit of the Team from the Soviet Academy of Pedagogical Science to Vietnam, 10–18 March, 1986 by V. Kozyr, Head of International Cooperation Division, folder 5196, Reports of Soviet Delegations and Specialists on Trips to Vietnam 1986, entry 1, records group 9563, Soviet Ministry for Education, GARF, p. 10–19.

ASIA-PACIFIC 181

was too expensive to revise the education system, to merge divergent schools, and, more importantly, to introduce a unified education for teachers, who were still trained at different levels and most of whom lacked professional education despite all efforts.

Despite the warnings, Moscow and the Vietnamese government began to restructure and merge schools of the north and south. The Soviet specialists and teachers who worked in Hanoi were taken from schools and sent to the south to study the situation in schools there and to make the reform smoother. However, what Soviet teachers saw in the south revealed the profound complexity of the education system's problems and the real powerlessness of the Vietnamese and Soviet efforts to transform schools. Schools were crowded; teachers had low qualifications and extremely low salaries; there were no textbooks; and cramming remained the main method of instruction. These and other problems would necessitate long years of work for development, teaching, and financial investment. All these resources were absent. One Soviet teacher witnessed the following at a school in the city formerly called Saigon:

> The school was built and equipped with the help of the UNICEF funds. It is very overcrowded. There are 2,800 pupils, 50 classes, and 111 teachers. Thirty percent of teachers have worked here since before the liberation, and there are former military personnel and people from the old Saigon administration among the teachers. The teachers have very small salaries. In order to enable the teachers to earn extra money for their families, a sewing factory was built in the city of Ho Chi Minh [*former Saigon, Natalia Tsvetkova*], but the teachers cannot use the factory's equipment. There are also workshops for pupils to make simple furniture for sale.[93]

In addition: "The schools do not have essentials: textbooks, notebooks. It happens that books, paper, and teaching aids are stolen before reaching a teacher."[94] The Russian language was not taught because there were no teachers, textbooks, or language labs. The Soviet teachers tried to ask to Moscow to invest in teaching Russian in the southern part of Vietnam, but there was no money for such large projects in the Soviet Union's budget. Vietnam itself was diving into a harsh economic crisis, but the reform required huge expenditures.[95] A worsening economic situation aggravated the position and image of teachers:

---

93   Ibid, p. 18.
94   Ibid, p. 15.
95   Ibid, p. 19.

182

CHAPTER 4

The life of a teacher remains very difficult. A teacher's salary is 200–400 dongs, with a kilogram of rice [2,2 *lbs, Natalia Tsvetkova*] costing 4 dongs, but the minimum living wage is 13 kg of rice [28,6 *lbs, Natalia Tsvetkova*] per person per month. It's difficult for an ordinary teacher to support a family.[96]

The reform plan was terminated when a huge number of pupils began dropping out of schools. After unification of Vietnam, 15.2 million pupils were enrolled in elementary school classes; only 5 million went to high school, and only 270,000 registered later for the final class of high school. This situation was created by a badly elaborated economic reform that created an unexpected contradiction between the interests of schools and families. The Vietnamese government decided to give the Vietnamese additional pieces of land to allow them to get more rice to feed their families. Each member of a family, including children, was supposed to get an additional 20 hectares [49,4 *acres, Natalia Tsvetkova*]. However, if the children studied at school and stayed separate from their family, the additional land was lost. Hence, many children were compelled to leave schools. Moreover, the economic crisis and the consequences of the Vietnam War led to the emergence of the exploitation of child labor, homelessness, and drug abuse. A number of children, teachers, and families ended up at risk due to ill-considered economic and educational reforms in the mid-1980s.

In 1982, Soviet experts in pedagogy were sent to Vietnam in order to assess the prospects for further reforms. In their reports, the experts, mostly professors from Leningrad State Pedagogical Institute and research institutes in the field of education, concluded that opportunities to continue the reforms were nil, for several reasons. For one, Vietnamese staff could not write textbooks for all levels of education, and teachers were poorly educated. For another, school buildings were in short supply, and, as the experts noted, it would be impractical to conduct reforms in Vietnam's remote mountainous regions, where 54 local tribes and ethnicities lived, all of whom spoke different languages that would demand an entirely different approach to education.[97] The Soviet experts tried to convince both the Vietnamese and Soviet governments that reform demanded the understanding of those local traditions and cultures; however, there was neither time nor political will to pursue such a flexible education policy.

96   Ibid, p. 15.

97   Report on the Visit to Vietnam by the Head of the Laboratory on Ideological and Political Education of the Research Institute of Problems of Education at the Academy of Pedagogical Sciences of the USSR, 1982 folder 4328, records group 9563, GARF, p. 39–40.

ASIA-PACIFIC

In 1986, Vietnam again the Soviet government asked for assistance in reforming its schools, pointing out that "in Moscow, they know the needs of the Vietnamese school well, because this is a Soviet project."[98] The USSR no longer had the ability to resolve such problems. Meanwhile, the economic crisis was unfolding in the Soviet Union, and the empire was approaching the final days of its existence. In the same year, Soviet specialists left Vietnamese universities and schools.

3.3   *Successes, Failures, and Consequences of Soviet Reforms*

In contrast to their American counterparts who elaborated criteria to measure their results, Soviet specialists did not evaluate their results. Visiting professors had their work evaluated by their teaching skills, the numbers of textbooks they produced, and the load of extracurricular work they took on. Thus, it is not easy to evaluate the outcomes of Soviet activities at Vietnamese universities and schools. However, through their reports, Soviet visiting professors have provided for historians their understanding of the main factors that diminished the Soviet influence on local education. They named the three following obstacles: the severe climate of Vietnam, the low professionalism of Soviet teachers themselves, and the shortage of textbooks.

Vietnam's climate turned out to have severely damaged the health of Soviet citizens. Many advisors returned home early or spent months at hospitals. In order to defuse the climate's impact and avoid undermining Soviet foreign aid, professors and teachers were recruited from the USSR's southern republics such as Ukraine, Armenia, Azerbaijan, etc.[99] However, these teachers also noted a deterioration in their health, and many of them left Vietnam ahead of schedule. They complained about the unbearable climate and asked the government to warn prospective visitors in advance. Sharp drops in temperature, hot weather, the lack of air conditioning and central heating, and the negative impact of climate on various devices hampered the ability of Soviet advisors to fulfill their professional duties, as they would miss classes or give up writing textbooks: "our everyday life is severe, because there are no air conditioners. It creates an intolerable life during May and June, and an absolutely heavy one in September and October."[100]

---

98   Report on the Visit of the Team from the Soviet Academy of Pedagogical Science to Vietnam by V. Kozyr, Head of International Cooperation Division, 10–18 March, 1986, folder 5196, records group 9563, GARF, p. 18.

99   Report on the Trip to Vietnam, folder 3724, records group 9563, GARF, p. 43.

100   Report on the Work at the Pedagogical Institute for Foreign Languages at Hanoi by S. Bablumyan, Instructor of Russian Literature, 1977–1978, folder 3724, records group 9563, GARF, p. 15.

184 CHAPTER 4

Moreover, military hostilities and the war, though seldom mentioned in the reports, were nevertheless a key factor constraining the development of universities in Vietnam. Vietnamese ambassadors, who brought news about local situations, appealed to Moscow for help for Vietnamese schools, and Moscow responded positively to their request. Thus, it must be noted that while most Soviet professors left universities in North Vietnam, new teams of advisors began working at local schools, and the teaching of Russian never ceased.[101]

The second problem turned out to be very extraordinary and concerned the qualifications of Soviet professors and teachers in the field of Russian language. As most of the Soviet teachers had been recruited from universities in national republics and the peripheries of the USSR, they spoke Russian with an accent. Vietnamese students and teachers sometimes did not understand the Russian language spoken by Soviet teachers from Armenia, Georgia, Ukraine, etc. The head of a Soviet team in Hanoi reported to Moscow:

> Almost all the teachers had worked at national universities and schools in the USSR before their trips to Hanoi. The Russian language for most of them is not native, their speech is not free from phonetic and grammatical errors, and official Vietnamese representatives have repeatedly noted, for example, their vague pronunciation and hinted that they would prefer to have a native Russian speaker.[102]

Or:

> Teacher Oganova N. A., [sic] who worked in the USSR at a national university, gives classes on phonetics, but her pronunciation makes it very difficult for Vietnamese students to understand the sounds of the Russian language.[103]

Most likely, when making a choice between the professionalism of a Soviet advisor and his/her ability to survive in Hanoi, Moscow made a decision to prioritize the latter. Moreover, the Vietnamese side complained to Soviet officials

---

101 Letter from Minister of Education to Deputy Minister of the Navy, 1968, folder 593, Correspondence about Cultural and Scientific Cooperation in the field of Education with Vietnam, 1968, entry 1, records group 9563, Soviet Ministry for Education, GARF, P. 13; Notes on Conversation with the Ambassador of Vietnam in the Soviet Union, April 8, 1968, folder 593, records group 9563, GARF, p. 7–10.

102 Report on the Work of Instructors and Teachers in Vietnam, 1977–78, folder 3724, records group 9563, GARF, p. 27.

103 Ibid, p. 26.

ASIA-PACIFIC

that the advisors could not teach certain theoretical disciplines related to the Russian language, and they wrote textbooks too slowly: "Soviet specialists could not help the Institute in the field of improving the qualifications of the Vietnamese teaching staff. Soviet specialists wrote no instructional materials or textbooks at the Faculty of the Russian Language, while their teaching load was purposely reduced to 6–8 hours per week to let them to write the textbooks."[104]

Finally, the third problem, which flowed from the second one, was the shortage of literature at the libraries of the Pedagogical Institute. The textbooks were printed at a local publishing house, the capacity of which was limited and the quality of which was low. Published textbooks were "quickly frayed out."[105] All these problems limited the USSR's ability to enact reforms and transmit new knowledge, language, and culture and to shape new, qualified teachers for Vietnamese schools.

To sum up the consequences of Soviet educational reforms in Vietnam, they can be divided into two periods. The first period was 1975–1979, when Soviet specialists did not interfere in reforms initiated by the Vietnamese government in Saigon, working at educational establishments in the northern part of the country. It should be pointed out that this was unusual policy for the Soviet Union, which was accustomed to participating in crucial modifications of education after political regime changes and revolutions in other international contexts. Moreover, the USSR was limited geographically by reforming only the northern part of Vietnam, and the Soviet Union did not offer profound revisions at schools and universities during this period. This approach contrasted with Soviet policy in other countries such as, for example, in Eastern Europe. In Vietnam, Soviet teachers were engaged in teaching students and writing textbooks.

The second period is 1979–1986, when Vietnam's government decided to carry out reforms throughout the country and Soviet advisors were sent to the southern part of the country. However, the USSR's inadequate financial resources at that stage and an economic crisis in Vietnam prevented them from introducing comprehensive education, from training qualified teachers for Vietnamese schools on a professional level, and from taking care of at-risk teachers and pupils.

After the end of the Cold War, Vietnam made crucial reforms at schools and universities enacted by its national experts. Later, the United States and its educationalists returned to the country during the Obama administration

---

104   Ibid, p. 26–27.
105   Ibid, p. 38–39.

186   CHAPTER 4

and assisted Vietnam in transforming and modernizing its universities and schools, significantly improving political relations between the countries in the 2010s.[106]

4   Conclusion

The available documents conclude that both American and Soviet advisors were unable to mold a new, ideal Vietnamese teacher and to transform Vietnamese universities and schools according to their initial goals. Clearly, the main factors for this failure include the permanently unstable political situation in Vietnam, the legacy of French colonization, the war, and mainly, the country's division that made it possible for different values and reforms to flourish. These factors damaged education more than they promoted it. For a long time, the Vietnamese dealt with incoming values of strangers from the United States and the Soviet Union, who tried to revise Vietnam's education according to their own norms, cultures, and values. Hence, in terms of the Vietnamese perception, American and Soviet values and models of education were likely to be alien, not Vietnamese and indigenous.

The concept of constructivism allows for the understanding of why both political powers were not able to instill the Vietnamese with their values. Both superpowers aspired to mold an ideal Vietnamese teacher who would be a bearer of either American or Soviet values, would teach local children and students according to either American or Soviet models of education and textbooks, and would transmit a strange culture to the community of pupils. The constructed communicative field between visiting professors and Vietnamese audiences, and academic and social practices imposed by strangers, did not eliminate the perception of the Vietnamese that American and Soviet guests brought unfamiliar traditions and culture, that they were not *we* but *another*, *not like we*. The web of local traditions and culture restrained the transformations of both political powers in the universities of Vietnam. Hence, the reforms and the molding of a new kind of teacher were destined to fail.

---

106   Natalia Tsvetkova, "Education of Russia in Asia-Pacific Region: Forgotten Lessons from the legacy of the Soviet Union and Recent Experience of American educational Policy, Russian Council for International Affairs," accessed August 04, 2019, http://russiancouncil .ru/inner/index.php?id_4=986.

CHAPTER 5

Latin America and Caribbean

Fear in U.S. and Soviet University Policy in Guatemala and Cuba

1   Introduction

New archival documents have allowed scholars to comparatively analyze the education policies of the United States and the Soviet Union implemented in Latin America and Caribbean during the Cold War—more specifically, U.S. policy in Guatemala and Soviet policy in Cuba. Under the influence of the superpowers, Guatemala and Cuba emerged as unique cases that, over time, demonstrated unprecedented particularities in U.S. and Soviet behavior within the universities and academic communities of foreign countries. It was initially assumed that the universities and other institutions of education in Guatemala, where U.S. political influence swelled after the 1954 coup, and in Cuba, where a constellation of contacts between Moscow and Havana were established after the 1959 revolution, were necessarily and completely co-opted by the Cold War projects of Americanization and Sovietization. The sources, however, largely unconfirm that assumption. Despite its profound influence on political regimes in Guatemala, the United States only marginally impacted Guatemalan traditions of university life. Likewise, any belief that Moscow completely Sovietized life in Cuba collapses in the face of available historical documents showing the Soviet Union's purely nominal influence on traditions of university education in Havana. Indeed, the academic elite in Guatemala and Cuba acted and reacted exceptionally and in stark contrast to their counterparts at universities in other countries within the U.S. or Soviet sphere of influence. In response, the United States and the Soviet Union applied rather unusual policies at Guatemalan and Cuban universities relative to those imposed at institutions of higher education elsewhere in the world during the Cold War. Taken together, the unique behavior of the academic communities and the atypical politics of both superpowers surfaced as significant factors in U.S. policy at Guatemalan institutions of higher education and in Soviet policy at Cuban ones in the second half of the 20th century.[1]

---

[1]   Russell Bartley, "The Piper Played to Us All: Orchestrating the Cultural Cold War in the USA, Europe, and Latin America," *International Journal of Politics, Culture & Society* 14, no. 3

© NATALIA TSVETKOVA, 2021 | DOI:10.1163/9789004471788_007

During the Cold War, the clash between the United States and the Soviet Union shaped a distinct political and cultural context in Western Hemisphere. As a consequence, all universities in the region found themselves captive in a geopolitical game unfolding between Washington and Moscow in the region. As for the superpowers themselves, the United States, on the one hand, was shocked by the growth of Soviet political and cultural sway as part of Moscow's steady advance into what was historically a U.S. zone of influence. In response to the spread of the alarmist slogan "the Russians are coming," the U.S. government acted out of anxiety and, in time, beyond the scope of diplomatic and humanitarian law, namely by participating in coups, political assassinations, and even full-scale military interventions. To U.S. officials, the fear of losing influence in Latin America seemed to justify an unstable, sometimes unpredictable policy that would significantly affect U.S. cultural diplomacy and education policy beyond its borders. At times, the United States had to abandon some of its objectives in cultural diplomacy, including projects at Guatemalan universities, to not irritate Latin American politicians, military officials, and other elites who, according to U.S. politicians, could at any moment notify Moscow about their waning rapport with Washington. Worry and political fear arising from the uncertain behavior of policy-targeting states in the region compelled the United States to appease the elite, including the academic community, in Latin America, and, in our case, Guatemala.[2]

On the other hand, the Soviet Union for the first time saw true potential for large-scale Soviet influence in the region by means of propaganda, cultural diplomacy, and foreign aid, especially after the victory of the Cuban Revolution. Cuba represented an unprecedented challenge in world politics that crucially shifted Soviet foreign policy. In response, Moscow detected an opportunity to destabilize U.S. policy in its traditional zone of influence and to impose a program of Sovietization in local education systems. Against that potential, however, the nationalism of the region's revolutionaries, their independence from both Soviet policy and the Soviet version of Marxism, and their unfavorable position towards Soviet revisionism of revolutionary ideas, terrified the

---

(2001): 571–619; Christopher Darnton, *Rivalry and Alliance Politics in Cold War Latin America* (Baltimore: Johns Hopkins University Press, 2014).

2   Bevan Sewell and Nataliya Petrova, *The US and Latin America: Eisenhower, Kennedy and Economic Diplomacy in the Cold War* (London: I. B. Tauris & Company, Ltd., 2002); Lawrence Freedman, *Kennedy's Wars: Berlin, Cuba, Laos, and Vietnam* (Oxford: Oxford University Press, 2002); Ruth Blakeley, "Still Training to Torture? US Training of Military Forces from Latin America," *Third World Quarterly* 27, no. 8 (2006): 1439–61; Vanni Pettinà, "The Shadows of Cold War over Latin America: The US Reaction to Fidel Castro's Nationalism, 1956–59," *Cold War History* 11, no. 3 (August 2011): 317–39.

Kremlin into believing that the window for such an opportunity could shutter at any moment and that comrades in Latin America or the Caribbean, particularly in Cuba, could halt all cooperation with the Soviet Union. Risking the loss of a new strategic partnership that could help to destabilize the United States, Soviet officials wrestled with anxiety and political fear over the unpredictable behavior of Latin American revolutionaries, and Moscow's shaky influence in the region became a chief driver of policy guiding the development of universities in Cuba as part of Soviet cultural diplomacy in the region. Similar to the United States in Guatemala, the Soviet Union in Cuba was forced to adopt a policy of appeasement toward the Cuban academic elite, even to the point of forgoing projects that Cubans rejected. In sum, both superpowers feared losing sway in such a strategically important region, one doubling as a traditionally vital zone of influence for Washington and as a new opportunity of influence for Moscow. Such political fear affected each superpower's actions at universities in Guatemala and Cuba, actions that diverged significantly from their bolder practices of Americanization and Sovietization at local universities elsewhere in the world.[3]

Before beginning our narrative about how those actions and reactions played out in Latin America during the Cold War, it should briefly address the concept of fear. As a driver of policy in international politics, fear has not been sufficiently recognized in the literature. Of course, studies on international relations and adherents to theories such as realism and constructivism often apply the concept of fear, albeit typically in terms of political or global fear.[4] In that sense, *fear* refers to the concern of actors over geopolitical control, security, and coexistence. Some scholars have also applied the concept in analyzing the behavior of states and nongovernmental entities in the system of international relations, usually by arguing that fear is a cohesive constant in world politics and reminds every state that an ally is capable of betrayal, of interrupting trusted bilateral relations, and of even instigating military conflict. Political realists hold that the unpredictable behavior of various actors in the international arena shapes the concerns, anxiety, and fear of other actors about possible threats and challenges.[5] By contrast, institutionalists more positively maintain that fear can contribute to the establishment of authoritative

---

3 Tanya Harmer, "The 'Cuban Question' and the Cold War in Latin America, 1959–1964," *Journal of Cold War Studies* 21, no. 3 (2019): 114–51.

4 Corey Robin, *Fear: The History of a Political Idea* (New York: Oxford University Press, 2004); Ron Gurantz and Alexander V. Hirsch, "Fear, Appeasement, and the Effectiveness of Deterrence," *Journal of Politics* 79, no. 3 (2017): 1041–56.

5 Shiping Tang, "Fear in International Politics: Two Positions," *International Studies Review* 10, no. 3 (2008): 451–71.

190   CHAPTER 5

international institutions intended to contain the aggressive designs of states in relation to each other. By still further contrast, constructivists emphasize that because political fear can alter the behavior of states, their values, and their presumed identities, it can also facilitate the potential for interstate cooperation.[6]

To be sure, fear has been touched by scholars of the Cold War. Above all, they have provided insights into how the U.S. and Soviet governments exploited the fear of nuclear attack to mobilize their citizens. Added to those insights, numerous studies have demonstrated how U.S. foreign aid programs came into being in response to fear over the spread of communism in the world. Those and other studies have also revealed that fear compelled the United States to establish special development programs in foreign countries as a means to diminish the popularity of leftist ideas. U.S. development programs in Latin America, for example, were propelled by a fear of Soviet-inspired communist expansion in the region. According to such studies, the United States believed that a lack of material assistance would intensify domestic violence and conflicts and, in turn, create conditions ripe for the influence of Soviet ideas.[7]

Despite all of that scholarship, none of the literature shows how fear limits the policy or cultural diplomacy of states in relation to others and causes governments to depart from their initial political objectives and plans in other countries. Our study shows that the Americanization and Sovietization at Guatemalan and Cuban universities, respectively, were cracked by the fear of losing influence in the region, especially in Guatemala and Cuba. Such fear promoted U.S. and Soviet policies of appeasement at Guatemalan and Cuban institutions of education, which ultimately diminished the local appetite for the Americanization or Sovietization of universities throughout the region. Contributing to that trend, the academic elite in Guatemala and Cuba somewhat curtailed the ambitions of U.S. and Soviet policies at their institutions, even by playing on the fears of the two countries and thereby limiting the Americanization and Sovietization of local education. Often, the superpowers were forced to revise, if not abandon, their projects designed to transfer and impose U.S. and Soviet models of education, values, and political and cultural

---

6   Renato Cruz de Castro, "Explaining the Duterte Administration's Appeasement Policy on China: The Power of Fear," *Asian Affairs: An American Review* 45, no. 3/4 (2018): 165–91.

7   Rebecca Clouser, "Facing Fear: The Importance of Engaging with Fear in Development Literature," *Progress in Development Studies* 14, no. 2 (2014): 131–46; Rebecca Clouser, "Security, Development, and Fear in Guatemala: Enduring Ties and Lasting Consequences," *Geographical Review* 109, no. 3 (2019): 382–98.

identities in academia. Such policies were highly unusual compared to those put into action in other regions and countries during the Cold War.

This chapter consists of two sections. The first describes U.S. policy at institutions of higher education in Guatemala, whereas the second describes Soviet policy at similar institutions in Cuba. Each section also accounts for the policies of the superpowers in Guatemala and Cuba, respectively, as well as the reactions and responses of the local academic communities to both Americanization and Sovietization. Together, the sections reveal that such reactions and responses had consequences for the policies of the superpowers, particularly by manipulating U.S. and Soviet fears and thereby forcing Washington and Moscow to tailor their projects to suit the interests of the local communities.

2 The Policy of "Low Gringo Visibility" at Guatemalan Universities

2.1 *Beginnings of U.S. Cultural Diplomacy before the Cold War*

As with all Latin American countries, Guatemala was not under the radar of the United States in terms of cultural diplomacy, exchange, and international education policy. During the 1930s, the United States laid the foundations of its cultural diplomacy agenda, as part of its efforts in public diplomacy, in which exchange programs and projects to transform and modernize Latin American universities played a leading role.

The rise of fascism in Germany and political tensions in Europe before World War II alarmed the United States even to the point of informing U.S. public diplomacy in Latin America. A region of economic and strategic interest to the United States since the proclamation of the Monroe Doctrine, Latin America had become a prime target of German propaganda, especially in radio broadcasts, print media, cinema, theater, German-language schools, and other cultural channels with the power to attract Latin American audiences. By 1941, Germany had built approximately 900 schools in the region, the German language had become fashionable, and vast amounts of German books had been translated into Spanish and Portuguese. Germany's cultural diplomacy in the region at the time was so vigorous that U.S. businessmen and elites encouraged President Franklin Roosevelt to advocate that U.S. cultural diplomacy respond to the intensification of German cultural policy to the south by redirecting the attention of Latin American populations to American values instead.[8]

---

8 U.S. White House, "Address by Franklin D. Roosevelt, 1933," accessed October 11, 2018, http://www.fdrlibrary.marist.edu/aboutfdr/inaugurations.html.

To begin a new cultural offensive in Latin America, the United States needed the consent of Latin American states to participate, a problem that Roosevelt and U.S. Secretary of State Cordell Hull successfully resolved at the Inter-American Conference for the Maintenance of Peace in Buenos Aires in 1936. At the conference, Roosevelt designated exchanges in the fields of education and culture as the effective way for protecting democracy in the Western Hemisphere and for confronting fascism. In agreements and a convention signed at the Conference, 20 Latin American states agreed to participate in U.S. cultural programs that would enroll Latin American students, journalists, and politicians in training at U.S. universities. For the first time, an intergovernmental, international, multilateral agreement was concluded between the United States and a group of foreign countries concerning academic exchange programs: the Convention for the Promotion of Inter-American Cultural Relations. Calling for the "greater mutual knowledge and understanding of the people and institutions of the countries represented and a more consistent educational solidarity," the convention established "an exchange by professors, teachers and students among the American countries, as well as <...> a closer relationship between unofficial organizations which exert an influence on the formation of public opinion."[9]

In 1938, the Roosevelt administration took another historic step by establishing within the Department of State the Division of Cultural Cooperation designed to halt the spread of fascist ideas in North, South, and Latin America.[10] With a staff of eight, the Division of Cultural Cooperation was allocated $27,000 by Congress for cultural and educational programs for all Latin American countries. Although the initial funding was limited, the Division's budget would later be increased to roughly $1 million during the two years that followed.[11] A new position—cultural attaché—was also introduced to the U.S. Foreign Service to manage and elaborate public diplomacy projects against Nazi propaganda in the region. The Division's establishment within the Department of State marked a watershed in the history of U.S. public diplomacy. For the first time, the governmental apparatus was assigned to conduct cultural programs in other countries. Whereas most cultural and educational exchanges had previously been in the hands of private Americans, charitable

---

9   U.S. Congress, *U.S. Statutes at Large 51, 1937* (Wash., D.C.: GPO, 1938), 178–84.

10 Meeting Minute. Interdepartmental Committee on Cooperation with the American Republics, 1939, box 1, records group 353, Records of Interdepartmental and Intradepartmental Committees (State Department), National Archive Records Administration (hereafter NARA).

11 Ibid.

foundations, universities, and nongovernmental organizations, beginning in 1938 the White House took control over the soft power of the United States used for the political interests of the government. Reasons of national security contributed to the dynamic between private independent cultural exchange and the U.S. government, and in time, any challenges to U.S. interests or values would only intensify the government's participation in regulating programs of cultural or public diplomacy.

To counter German propaganda in Latin America, the first projects of the Division of Cultural Cooperation included modernizing the region's universities according to the U.S. model, sending U.S. professors there to deliver lectures on current policy issues, building new centers for English education, and, of course, teaching students in the field of political science and English. The U.S. government not only opened 230 so-called new American schools and colleges but also introduced English as the language of instruction in Latin American universities, all in response to German policy within the education system. Nevertheless, German schools continued to outnumber American schools by three to one. By 1939, the list of public diplomacy events had been expanded to include projects for distributing special films to schools and universities, disseminating information about U.S. foreign policy, and analyzing German propaganda distributed across Latin America. As a consequence, a new trend in U.S. public diplomacy began taking shape: Programs began targeting leading Latin American specialists in all fields, along with university administrators, who could influence other groups of society in the region.[12] In that way, U.S. cultural diplomacy did not embrace all clusters of the population but only the most influential ones, whose members who could impact public opinion.

The faster that Hitler moved across Europe, the more frequently memoranda addressing U.S. public diplomacy mentioned developing democratic political institutions in Latin America. In parallel, the influential local citizens selected to articulate pro-democratic and pro-U.S. sentiments began dominating public diplomacy. The U.S. government suggested that politicians, members of the government and local legislative assemblies, and heads of cultural and educational institutions, libraries, schools, universities, as well as journalists, editors, and publishers, were all actors in society who should be involved in exchanges to promote democracy in the region's countries. To make an impact on individuals in those professional groups, the U.S. government arranged for them to tour the United States and allocated $70,000 per year to that purpose, which, for cultural diplomacy, was a tremendous amount of government funding.[13]

---

12   Ibid.
13   Ibid.

194   CHAPTER 5

In 1940, the first group of Latin American politicians, students, professors, and journalists was invited by the U.S. Department of State to participate in an exchange program known today as the International Visitor Leadership Program. Created to establish and improve relations with representatives of governments and parliaments in the region and, in time, around the world, the program was initially exclusive to foreign citizens in positions of influence who could spread American ideas and political values within their societies. As the program and ones similar to it began to take the lead among U.S. projects of cultural diplomacy, their budgets grew rapidly. Thus, it was in that prewar context that the fundamental principle of U.S. public diplomacy was introduced: to have participants in such programs, upon returning home, sway public opinion in their societies and promote positive attitudes toward the United States, especially with the publication of pamphlets, travelogues, articles, and books. In fact, initial reports from various departmental committees indicate that U.S. diplomats tracked publications issued by Latin American participants in the programs and even contributed to their promotion.[14]

According to reports from the Division of Cultural Cooperation, representatives of all available political, cultural, and educational institutions in Latin America participated in tours and exchanges sponsored by the U.S. government from 1939 to 1940. For that brief period, famous politicians such as Manuel Morales, head of the National Bank of Guatemala, and hundreds of representatives of governmental agencies, writers, and rectors of universities, among others, were involved in the exchanges. The culmination of U.S. public diplomacy came in 1941, when budgets for projects in the fields of information, education, and culture totaled approximately $2 million, and the composition of the participants was articulated as "leaders and specialists," along with "students and professors."[15] Such public diplomacy contributed not only to the rollback of German influence in Latin America but also significantly strengthened the political and economic orientation of the region's countries toward the United States.[16]

During World War II, the U.S. government significantly expanded educational programs throughout Latin America, largely as part of a plan to improve the region's education systems, which also involved raising standards of education in Latin American countries in 1943. To that purpose, the U.S. government

---

14   Meeting Minute, 1939, box 1, records group 353, NARA.

15   U.S. Department of State, *Report of the Division on Cultural Cooperation, 1940–1942* (Wash., D.C.: GPO, 1942).

16   Manuel Espinosa, *Inter-American Beginnings of U.S. Cultural Diplomacy, 1936–1948* (Wash., D.C.: Department of State, 1976).

LATIN AMERICA AND CARIBBEAN 195

invited ministers and administrators of education from those countries to the United States to visit major schools and colleges, sent U.S. consultants to some universities in Latin America to revise their teaching materials, funded the translation of textbooks into Spanish and Portuguese, coached Latin American universities in developing curricula and programs, and helped to expand teachers' colleges and English education in the region. As a whole, the project became the largest in the history of international education policy in the United States. Not only did each country accommodate a special standing committee composed of U.S. advisors, but from 1943 to 1944 several universities received new textbooks and teaching materials as well. Ultimately, more than 500,000 books and other teaching aids became available in the region's schools. On top of that, U.S. professors were sent to universities in Latin America to develop programs in vocational education, health education, rural education, teacher training, and English-language instruction.[17] The United States was especially able to establish close, cooperative relations with rectors of the universities, who, after visiting U.S. universities, published articles on the U.S. education system and planned to adopt some of its models in institutional management, curricular development, student housing, and other aspects of academic life observed during their tours.[18]

Although Roosevelt's wartime policies indeed fueled the engines of U.S. cultural diplomacy at Latin American universities, whose development continued to receive financial support from the U.S. government, the unexpected postwar influence of the Soviet Union in Latin American countries was soon viewed as a threat to the contacts, relationships, and successes achieved by U.S. cultural diplomacy in the region. According to the sources, after World War II, "the urgent and critical problem in Latin America was to counteract the potent attraction which Communism had for the underprivileged, particularly the [sic] semiliterate labor groups."[19]

2.2 Imposing Social Service at San Carlos University: Extending the Functions of a Traditional University

From the standpoint of politics, Guatemala became a priority country for U.S. policy in Latin America early during the Cold War. The popularity of leftist ideas and the policies of Guatemalan President Jacobo Árbenz, some aimed

---

17 U.S. Department of States, *History of the Office of the Coordinator of Inter-American Affairs* (Wash., D.C.: GPO, 1947), 100–102.
18 Espinosa, *Inter-American Beginnings*, 294.
19 U.S. Department of State, *U.S. Advisory Commission on Information. Semiannual Report to the Congress, March 1949* (Wash., D.C.: GPO, 1949).

at nationalizing U.S. companies in Guatemala and cooperating with communist elements, raised concerns in Washington. In response, a coup executed by the United States in 1954 ultimately effected Árbenz's replacement with a U.S. henchman, at which point Guatemala became listed among countries eligible for U.S. assistance programs and cultural diplomacy. One of Washington's typical policy strategies in foreign states such as Guatemala was to eradicate Marxist ideas from their education systems by re-educating teachers and university professors, particularly under the guidance of those named in the National Security Council's Policy Paper #5509 issued in 1959. Shortly after, the revolution helmed by Fidel Castro in Cuba only increased the amount of U.S. funds directed toward developing and transforming Guatemala's education system. To stop the further spread of leftist ideas, Washington was compelled to support unpopular conservative, even authoritarian, leaders in Guatemala throughout the Cold War, despite permanent demonstrations against the Guatemalan and U.S. governments as well as a civil war. In the context of the Cold War and experiencing massive psychological shock caused by the unexpected victory of revolutionaries in Cuba, Washington had no choice but to attempt to halt the spread of revolutionary ideas, which, at the time, seemed to originate in Moscow. Universities and education in Latin America were at the epicenter of that containment policy.

Of the four universities in Guatemala, most were privately funded. In fact, the sole government-sponsored university, albeit with partial private funding nonetheless, was also the oldest: the University of San Carlos. Of the roughly 16,000 students enrolled in Guatemala's four institutions of higher education, nearly 13,000 attended the University of San Carlos, which made the academic institution, along with the national military, the most influential entity in the country.[20] Indeed, higher education in Guatemala was dominated by the University of San Carlos, which any high school graduate in Guatemala could attend and more than 75% of high school graduates ultimately did. At the same time, only 3% of its students graduated each year, thereby making the average length of time from matriculation to graduation a stunning 11 years. Although the institution's connection to the political elite made it dependent upon the government, the permanent, steady growth of the student body also created conditions for the intensification of antigovernment sentiment on its campus. That reality surprised visiting U.S. experts into seeking an agenda of reform for life at the university.

---

20   Education Development (Higher). Airgram from AID/Washington to Guatemala AID, August 14, 1970, box 3, records group 286, Records of the Agency for International Development, entry 420, USAID Mission to Guatemala. Education Office, NARA.

LATIN AMERICA AND CARIBBEAN   197

U.S. assistance programs began supporting the University of San Carlos—Guatemala's largest, oldest, and most famous—immediately after the 1954 coup. A year later, U.S. aid to the institution totaled a whopping $200 million.[21] By the end of the decade, the scope of projects was expanded when the National Security Council issued the above-mentioned policy paper concerning the re-education of teachers, leaders, and youth. Nevertheless, stable financial support for construction projects at the University of San Carlos and the establishment of new departments (i.e., faculties) and, in time, new universities reached Guatemala only after 1961, when the Foreign Aid Act and the U.S. Agency for International Development (USAID) became a part President John F. Kennedy's international policy.

That same year, USAID opened its office in Guatemala City, the nation's capital, and began observing life at Guatemalan universities. In the years that followed, USAID staff in Guatemala regularly reported to Washington about the favorable environment at the University of San Carlos—that is, favorable to the cooperation with the USAID—and the possibility of expanding U.S. funding there. While developing projects for the University of San Carlos, experts of the Education Division at USAID noted some national peculiarities of Guatemala's university system, including the lack of connection between the university, research, the real world, and the needs of the Guatemalan economy. The university was described as being isolated from Guatemalan society, even as an ivory tower, which would later become a problem for U.S. reformers:

> The national university may be characterized as traditional in structure and outlook, with all of the inherent problems of inflexibility, inefficient use of resources, inadequate teaching methods and lack of contact with reality. The national university had no courses whatsoever dealing with present-day Guatemala—that is, no connection between the University and the reality of Guatemala.[22]

Universities in Guatemala, at least according to the opinion of U.S. experts, were supposed to contribute to the country's development and produce qualified specialists for even its most remote provinces. However, the University of San Carlos, the most influential academic institution in the country, had trained only 100 agronomists and 50 veterinarians in the previous 10 years.

---

21   U.S. Agency for International Development, "U.S. Overseas Loans and Grants: Obligations and Loan Authorizations, July 1, 1945–September 30, 2017," accessed, June 05, 2020, https://explorer.usaid.gov

22   Ibid.

198   CHAPTER 5

Such figures shocked U.S. experts, as did the fact that none of the country's sociologists, anthropologists, or secondary school teachers had postsecondary diplomas. Questioning the true influence of Guatemala's entire university system, USAID advisors thus sought to overhaul the University of San Carlos, with the primary goal of eliminating the traditionalism of the university education offered there. As a consequence, transforming the university to serve Guatemala's economy became the principal line of work for USAID and its consultants.

U.S. experts believed that introducing so-called "social services" at the University of San Carlos would create conditions for students and professors to actively assist communities in Guatemala's remote provinces and, as a result, better familiarize themselves with their country. By involving universities in national development, the project was hailed as a key factor of its overarching program, dubbed the "University Extension," which was aimed at mobilizing university resources for the development of those provinces in Guatemala. The advisors announced that new courses in the field of social services would connect the university with real problems in the country and that students would even implement projects in the provinces geared toward helping local populations to meet medical and educational needs. Likewise, professors had to revise their courses so that they could teach students to participate in the development programs.[23] All of those provisions were included in the development plan for the University of San Carlos.[24]

A special social services advisor from USAID was sent to the University of San Carlos in order to identify key individuals who could be involved in further developing social services at the institution. The advisor sought to engage local professors in the project and encourage them to introduce new disciplines that could professionalize the education on offer. Experts working for USAID additionally suggested that attracting so-called "progressive professors" and providing them good salaries for their work would promote the development of disciplines such as geography, sociology, cultural anthropology, and political science.[25] However, it soon became clear that organizing such professors onto a team would be difficult, for 90 percent of the faculty at the University of San Carlos were paid by the hour, taught courses irrelevant to Guatemala at the time, and did not have tenure. As a result of those conditions, the professors neither knew each other well nor had any aspirations to reform the university. Further still, they were not involved in research, which sorely limited their

---

23   Ibid.

24   Ibid.

25   USAID Social Science Program, FY 1968, 1969, box 2, records group 286, NARA.

LATIN AMERICA AND CARIBBEAN 199

ambitions to delve into new fields of study and, at the same time, undermined the goals of U.S. experts to introduce new disciplines.

In response, the United States banked on the loyalty and disposition of the new university rector, Dr. Rafael Cuevas del Cid, who promised to realize the program for the development of social sciences at the University of San Carlos. It was Cuevas del Cid who had informed university professors about details of the reform, including the need to study Guatemala's potential for development, transform curricula, develop social sciences projects, and, ultimately, extend the work of the university into development, an altogether unfamiliar, vague provision for the professors. He had also indicated in a speech that the reform should seek to affect the life of each student and teacher.[26] The United States thus greatly hoped for his support: "Despite the formidable academic culture lag, there is strong evidence that the promise for change will go beyond verbal commitment."[27]

Such reforms were additionally supported by the Ministry of Education in Guatemala, which assured Americans of the project's success and led U.S. specialists toward the idea of establishing centers for social services in Guatemala.[28] Among the professoriate, some also promoted that idea and collaborated with U.S. visitors as well as USAID in Guatemala. As a result, U.S. experts were confident that their "Guatemalan friends" would be able to persuade the rest of the professors about the need for reform:

> There has been also one consultant to the program, an established social scientist with previous experience and contacts in Guatemala. This man is older and can make contact more easily with the upper strata of university administration.[29]

The University of San Carlos soon established the Center of Extension and Social Service, which was designed to provide assistance with training personnel for the provinces of Guatemala and to serve as a hub for specialists, students, and anyone else interested in introducing new sciences and development project into the country. The University of California, Los Angeles, and Texas A&M University were the U.S. government's primary partners in accomplishing such projects in Guatemala. The Center also sought to attract

---

26   Ibid.
27   Higher education—USAID Project, no date, box 3, records group 286, NARA.
28   Education Development (Higher). Airgram from AID/Washington to Guatemala AID, August 14, 1970, box 3, records group 286, NARA.
29   USAID Social Science Program, FY 1968, 1969, box 2, records group 286, NARA.

200 CHAPTER 5

and re-educate professors in each department about curricular development as a means to introduce courses needed to train specialists for Guatemala's remote towns.[30]

To engage the student body in projects for the development of both social sciences and the country overall, summer schools were arranged.[31] Some faculties even began making rural service mandatory for graduating students, most of whom, however, participated rather reluctantly. In the first two years, only 108 of 13,000 students were enrolled in the project.[32] To support the development of new disciplines, the students were offered grants for writing dissertations; as noted in one source, it was "in a sense bribe money to get students into field, but it is worth it."[33] U.S. consultants truly believed that the students would venture into the provinces of their country after graduation and provide assistance. However, they were mistaken, for most students continued to seek work in the nation's capital.[34] Sources nevertheless show that some students in the Department of Medicine did provide temporary assistance by practicing dentistry in Guatemala's remotest areas. Other faculties and students, by contrast, simply abandoned the U.S.-led project.

2.3   Fear and a Policy of Low Gringo Visibility

Although it seemed that the project to extend the functions of the University of San Carlos would succeed, the project generated criticism and anxiety among the professoriate, some of whom claimed that the U.S. advisors were undermining the institution's primary function—that is, to produce fundamental, pure knowledge. In response, U.S. specialists sought to convince them that modernizing the University of San Carlos was not only necessary but also entirely possible, as long as the professors recognized that traditional education in Guatemala did not meet the needs for the country's development and that the university needed to implement reforms. The U.S. specialists added that doing so would require taking some radical departures from the traditional, urban-centered, career-oriented education currently on offer by revising the curriculum, training new cadres, and introducing new teaching

---

30   Education Development (Higher). Airgram from AID/Washington to Guatemala AID, August 14, 1970, box 3, records group 286, NARA; Higher Education, 1971–76, box 2, records group 286, NARA.

31   Ibidem.

32   USAID Social Science Program, FY 1968, 1969, box 2, records group 286, NARA.

33   Greater Involvement with Students at the University Level. Letter from Melvin S. Droubay, Social Science Advisor, to Dr. Peter Wright, Head, no date, box 2, records group 286, NARA.

34   USAID Social Science Program, FY 1968, 1969, box 2, records group 286, NARA.

LATIN AMERICA AND CARIBBEAN 201

methods.[35] However, the academic community refused to participate at the Center of Extension and Social Service; they said that the University's responsibility was to impart fundamental knowledge, not overly professional or narrow expertise.[36] The students, for their part, were also not excited about the prospect of living, even temporarily, in remote towns in Guatemala and refused to travel there.

The attempts of U.S. advisors to continue instituting mandatory social service at the University of San Carlos failed. The experts noted that

> the self-serving elite that has suffered an average of 10 years of university attendance was little interested in the problems of their country. The concept of university extension outside the capital and addressed to national educational needs still contends with the traditional orientation of the faculty and student body toward urban orientation toward urban careers opportunities in medicine, law, engineering, architecture [sic] and the narrow scholarly pursuits of Iberian humanities.[37]

When the U.S. government invited the University of California, Los Angeles, to accelerate the development programs and social services at the University of San Carlos, the professors and administration of the Guatemalan university did not attend the meeting scheduled with the experts from Los Angeles, and the projects were terminated. Describing that opprobrium, USAID staff in Guatemala wrote in a telegram sent to the U.S. Department of State that "they do not want a heavy 'gringo' influence at the University, especially in the field of social service."[38]

The U.S. advisors, sensing sabotage among the local academic community, were concerned that at any moment the professors could completely derail U.S.-led activities and projects at the University of San Carlos . The behavior of the professors also fomented alarmist attitudes and fear among visiting consultants about the possible cancellation of the entire package of projects. The top reason for the rebellion against the project for mandatory social service in particular, at least according to the reports of U.S. experts, was leftist influence:

---

35   Higher education—USAID Project, no date, box 3, records group 286, NARA.
36   Ibid.
37   Greater Involvement with Students at the University Level. Letter from Melvin S. Droubay, Social Science Advisor, to Dr. Peter Wright, Head, no date, box 2, records group 286, NARA.
38   Memorandum from Mekvin S. Droubay, Higher Education Advisor, to Mr. Robert E. Culbertson, Director. April 7, 1970, box 1, records group 286, NARA.

202   CHAPTER 5

The administration, faculty, and student associations at San Carlos have long been dominated by a variety of extreme leftists. Embassy contact with this influential group has been severely restricted in recent years. While some political problems might be encountered in securing participation of university faculty and students, careful selection of programs and participants should minimize it [*sic*].[39]

Such anti-Americanism, expanding so fast and so widely, cautioned experts of the university's possible departure from U.S. oversight. According to the friendly community of professors loyal to U.S. efforts, the ubiquity of U.S. sources of support—equipment, textbooks, and construction projects, to name a few—posed a highly visible threat to faculty and students interested in help from the United States.

In talks with Washington, the U.S. advisors thus recommended obscuring U.S. responsibility for the projects: "There is little likelihood in the politically sensitive university community that such programs because of USAID support will be labeled U.S. programs."[40] A fear that the projects could incite protests among the academic community encouraged the United States to roll back the project that required students to perform social service. The advisors also reduced contact with the University of San Carlos and continuing working on the projects there via local organizations instead. Among the advisors, the approach was called the policy of "low gringo visibility," one that would become popular among U.S. experts and implied minimizing direct contact with the university and its faculty. Thus, programs affiliated with students and faculty were disguised to conceal any apparent connection with USAID.[41] Additionally, U.S. Secretary of State William P. Rogers supported the idea of obscuring the fact of direct funding for universities in Guatemala and indicated in a cable that "the approach to the project appropriately de-emphasizes the visibility of the U.S. role in university education as the USAID undertakes joint project implementation with the Guatemalan institutions."[42]

However, the approach did not work well, and in 1971, the United States admitted that the extension program had failed at the University of San Carlos, chiefly due to both the reluctance of professors there to revise their

---

39   Intensive Review Activities—Higher Education. Airgram from Guatemala to AID/Washington, August 31, 1971, box 2, records group 286, NARA.

40   Higher education—USAID Project, no date, box 3, records group 286, NARA.

41   Greater Involvement with Students at the University Level, no date, box 2, records group 286, NARA.

42   PROP—Educational Development (Higher Education). Airgram from AID/Washington to Guatemala AID. October 12, 1970, box 3, records group 286, NARA.

LATIN AMERICA AND CARIBBEAN 203

courses and introduce new ones and the reluctance of students to leave the capital: "The concept of university extension outside the capital [addresses] to national educational needs, still contends but weakly with the traditional orientation of the faculty and student body."[43] The faculty did not want to change the traditional role of Guatemalan universities—namely, produce fundamental scientific knowledge—and, in the opinion of U.S. experts, became the principal obstacle to the overall project's successful development.

Those problems were accompanied by an economic crisis in the United States that contributed to significant reductions in funding for foreign aid programs. Although diplomats indicated in cables to Washington that funding cuts would lose the United States "points" in the political game being played at San Carlos, fear of the loss of contacts and cooperation with some professors at the university had already forced U.S. specialists at USAID to curtail their projects in 1972.[44]

Before leaving the University of San Carlos, U.S. experts described the situation in Guatemala in exceptionally bitter terms:

> Four centuries of university tradition created a proud defense of the status quo. Efforts by multi-national and bi-lateral groups to bring the national university into the 20th Century have met most often with indifference if not hostility: visiting professors from the U.S. have found themselves isolated; AID supported contracts have left the system unchanged; audio visual laboratories have lapsed into disuse when U.S. technicians left the country; the most effective criticism of a general studies program at the University of San Carlos was that the idea originated in the United States [sic].[45]

The visiting experts did not have reliable professors who could effect reform at the university:

> The difficulty of effecting any significant change in direction at the University of San Carlos is underlined by the fact that less than 10% of university teachers are employed full-time. The traditional curriculum is supported by a traditional structure: classes largely based upon the

---

43 Higher education—USAID Project, no date, box 3, records group 286, NARA.

44 Letter. Mr. Robert E. Culbertson, January 21, 1971, box 2, records group 286, NARA; Intensive Review Activities—Higher Education. Airgram from Guatemala to AID/Washington, August 31, 1971, box 2, records group 286, NARA.

45 Higher education—USAID Project, no date, box 3, records group 286, NARA.

204   CHAPTER 5

old lecture notes of part-time teachers, administration that performs a
house-keeping function [*sic*].[46]

Against the milieu of the elite, traditional, and inflexible University of San Carlos, other private, independent universities were relatively young and vibrant.
Their commitment to depart from the norms of the traditional Guatemalan
university were thus a breath of fresh air, and U.S. experts thus shifted their
project of Americanization to their campuses.

2.4   *Leaving the Traditional University: The Shift to Alternative Academies*

Difficulties experienced at Guatemala's University of San Carlos urged the
U.S. government to focus its attention on other universities in the country. In
the early 1970s, as anti-Americanism spread throughout the student body and
professoriate at the national university, private universities that were independent as well as dynamic seemed relatively eager to collaborate with the United
States. Such institutions were therefore cast as appropriate sites for implementing U.S. projects designed to create a pool of specialists for the development of the country.[47]

One such institution was the Universidad del Valle, a private university
whose dynamic nature and clear opportunities for transformation were noted
by U.S. experts. In fact, many professors employed at the University of San Carlos who supported U.S. innovations and projects eventually transferred to the
Universidad del Valle, which had grown out of an American school that had
operated in Guatemala from 1938 to 1945.[48] In USAID documents, the Universidad del Valle receives the most positive assessment, largely because its professoriate was open to new curricula, new courses, and alternative means of
instruction.[49]

U.S. consultants also believed that the success of the transformation at
the Universidad del Valle would later prompt the implementation of similar
reforms at the University of San Carlos:

Several high-level administrators, deans, and professors from the National
University are also on the Del Valle staff, where they are more free to

---

46   Ibid.
47   Education Development (Higher). Airgram from AID/Washington to Guatemala AID,
        August 14, 1970, box 3, records group 286, NARA.
48   Ibid.
49   Ibid.

experiment [*sic*]. Thus, programs which have organized at del Valle have found their way into San Carlos [*sic*].[50]

And:

> It [the University] has been very successful in attracting research and training support from the U.S. and other foreign sources. From its inception, the institution has been committed to offering strong undergraduate and graduate programs in the sciences, humanities, education, and the social sciences. It is located on a fifty-two-acre campus which is also the site of the American High School, of which the Del Valle is an affiliated institution [*sic*].[51]

Thus, the Universidad del Valle became the platform for educating a corps of teachers for schools in Guatemala, which solved a few pressing problems in the country. For one, the training of primary school teachers in mathematics had become a major deficit in Guatemala; for another, several students and prospective teachers had been forced to drop out of universities and other institutions due to their weak knowledge in mathematics. In response, several U.S. professors were sent to the Universidad del Valle to teach the teachers at the university.

The Universidad del Valle also profoundly contributed to the U.S. university extension project that trained and mobilized teachers for work in Guatemala's provinces, as well as developed courses for training teachers in the social sciences.[52] Beyond that, U.S. professors visited the institution to work with students in preparation for developing courses in various areas of the social sciences. U.S. specialists managed to teach mathematics to more than 500 university students majoring in the discipline and to re-educate more than 1,500 local school teachers. In those ways, the U.S. program at the Universidad del Valle contributed substantially to the development of Guatemala as a country.[53]

Even so, the most successful development-oriented projects were implemented by universities opened and built by the U.S. government in Guatemala.

---

50 Ibid.

51 U.S. Agency for International Development, "Guatemala. Education Sector Assessment, 1985. USAID Report," accessed June 05, 2020, https://pdf.usaid.gov/pdf_docs/PNAAY130 .pdf, p. 368.

52 Higher Education. Letter from Mr. R.E. Culbertson, Director to Peter C. Wright, Chief, Education Division, USAID, September 28, 1970, box 3, records group 286, NARA.

53 Educational Development (University). USAID Project, 1970–1972, box 3, records group 286, NARA.

The Universidad Francisco Marroquin, for instance, an institution built by the United States in 1971, provided U.S.-style higher education with an emphasis on disciplines such as economics, business administration, management, law, the social sciences, computer science, architecture, dentistry, and medicine. Funded by USAID, the Universidad Francisco Marroquin served as a center for the study and demonstration of U.S. ideas and practices.[54]

In the early 1980s, another private university, the Universidad Rafael Landivar, also demonstrated its effectiveness in executing U.S. projects. With several affiliations across Guatemala, the Universidad Rafael Landivar became a major contributor to the education of the country's indigenous Mayan population. During the Cold War, the United States paid scant attention to the living conditions of indigenous people in Guatemala, and only after leaving the University of San Carlos and shifting to the private universities in the mid-1970s did U.S. experts propose to expand access to university education to indigenous individuals. The Universidad Rafael Landivar thus became an active participant in the U.S. project aimed at extending education to more Guatemalans. The institution developed and implemented a higher education program for Mayan-speaking students that also provided them with financial support for the completion of associate's and/or bachelor's degrees. As part of that program, USAID planned to sponsor approximately 266 indigenous professionals in earning bachelor's degrees and 400 indigenous technicians in earning associate's degrees.[55]

In those ways, young, dynamic universities, particularly in Guatemala, became major partners of the United States. By contrast, traditional universities such as the University of San Carlos opposed the projects, for their faculty stifled the activity of U.S. experts in order to save the traditional features of education in Guatemala. To maintain contact with the University of San Carlos, the U.S. government pursued a policy of appeasement, which sometimes even involved obscuring the very presence of its projects. Such unusual behavior, compared to the implementation of U.S. education policy in other countries, was determined by a fear that Guatemala could disrupt its relations with the United States in favor of policies sympathetic to the Soviet Union or

---

54   U.S. Agency for International Development, "University Francisco Marroquin, Guatemala. Contract. USAID, 1984–1985," accessed June 05, 2020, www.usaid.gov.

55   U.S. Agency for International Development, "Project Agreement between the Department of State, Agency for International Development of the United States of America and the Ministries of Education and Economy, Guatemala, 1954. Educational Project, 1973;" U.S. Agency for International Development, "Educational Development, Guatemala. Contract. USAID, 1974," accessed June 05, 2020, www.usaid.gov.

LATIN AMERICA AND CARIBBEAN 207

leftist movements, as had occurred in Cuba. The fear of losing a partner in the fight against communism forced the United States not to enter into conflict with professors or pursue the radical transformation of Guatemala's largest university.

3 The Policy of Appeasement by "Russo Soviético" in Cuba

3.1 *Approaching the Universities of Latin America*

While USAID and global assistance programs were being developed, the Soviet Union elaborated its own cultural diplomacy and development programs for the countries of Latin America. For the first time in Russian history, full-scale exchange and construction programs for universities in the countries of the Western Hemisphere were introduced. The chief reason for the new development policy was a communist revolution in Cuba, the new government of which sought help from Moscow. As time would tell, the request catalyzed the expansion of assistance programs for Havana and other countries throughout Latin America. Beginning in 1961, Soviet policy prescribed increased flows of financial support to the region, and the Soviet Union constructed 380 factories, university buildings, and other facilities around the world, including in Latin American countries. The Soviet Union also provided assistance to 17 developing countries, including Ghana, Mali, Pakistan, Brazil, Ceylon, and Nepal. In India and Indonesia, Soviet aid in the form of equipment doubled, while it tripled in South Africa and Iraq. The total supply of equipment and materials amounted to 118 million rubles ($129.8 million) in 1961 and 223 million rubles ($245.3 million) the following year. Between the same years, revenues from Soviet exports to Cuba skyrocketed from 1.8 million rubles ($1.98 million) to 10.8 million rubles ($11.8 million), and the number of Soviet specialists sent abroad—to 25 countries, to be exact—grew from 4,900 in 1960 to 6,510 in 1961 and exceeded 10,000 by 1962.[56] At the same time, equipment and materials were supplied to new targets of Soviet assistance such as India's Bombay Institute of Technology, Burma's Institute of Technology in Rangoon, and (North)

---

56 Letter by A. Mikoyan, the Council of Ministers of the USSR. August 26, 1961, folder 162, Materials on the Establishment and Technical Assistance, the Hanoi Polytechnic Institute: Minutes of the Meetings of the Commission for Foreign Economic Affairs at the Presidium of the Council of Ministers of the USSR, 1961–1965, entry 2, records group 9606, Soviet Ministry for Higher Education, State Archive of Russian Federation (hereafter GARF), p. 2–3.

Vietnam's Polytechnic Institute in Hanoi, as well as to institutes in Ambon, Indonesia and in Guinea, Ethiopia, and others.[57]

In that context of new technical assistance projects and cultural diplomacy programs, the Soviet State Committee of the Council of Ministers for Cultural Relations with Foreign Countries decided in 1961 to expand relations with Latin American nations by increasing exchanges in vocational education.[58] For some of the countries of Latin America, expanding contact with the Soviet Union had certain appeal as well. In 1961, a Soviet delegation visited Brazil at the invitation of the government, with which diplomatic relations had not yet been restored. In conversations with members of the Soviet delegation, the rectors of Brazilian universities assured the delegates that popular interest in the Soviet Union and in the Russian language was growing in Brazil, even to the point that Brazilian intellectuals and students had aspirations to study and visit the USSR. Beyond that, representatives of leftist movements whom members of the Soviet delegation also met asked the Soviets to assist with constructing schools in the *favelas* of Brazilian cities.[59] That same year, a delegation of communists from Chile arrived in Moscow with a rather interesting story about how the rector at the University of Santiago, though having signed an agreement to cooperate with Moscow State University, had failed to have the agreement ratified by the Chilean university's "reactionary" academic council. Nevertheless, the delegation asked Moscow not to annul the agreement, because the rector was ready to implement its provisions concerning the establishment of a Department of Russian, the publication of textbooks on Soviet history, and the exchange of students, all with or without the academic council's consent.[60]

---

57 Informational Letter on the Soviet Assistance to Foreign Countries, 1960, folder 249, Memoranda, Notes, Letters of the Council of Ministers of the USSR, entry 1, records group 9606, GARF, p. 2.

58 The State Committee of the Council of Ministers of the USSR for Cultural Relations with Foreign Countries. Secret Report. June 2, 1961, folder 48, Correspondence with Embassies, Missions, Consulates of the USSR, Ministries, Departments, Universities and Other Organizations about Cultural, Scientific and Technical Relations with the Countries of America, and about the Training of Citizens of these Countries in the USSR, entry 2, records group 9606, GARF, p. 46.

59 Report on the Visit to Brazil and the Work Accomplished in the field of Cultural Relations between the USSR and Brazil by of the Student Delegation. July 3, 1961, folder 48, records group 9606, GARF, p. 55.

60 Notes on a Conversation with the Secretary of the Central Committee of the Communist Party of Chile, Comrade Orlando Mills. Secret Report, April 7, 1961, folder 48, records group 9606, GARF, p. 32.

LATIN AMERICA AND CARIBBEAN 209

Those and numerous other examples illustrate that Soviet ideas had gained traction in Latin America. Going forward, the modernization and industrialization of countries in the region would allow Moscow to help with developing their education systems, constructing new universities, and revising disciplines, courses, and textbooks across Latin America. Such transformations were typically occurring in countries with highly unstable political situations and, moreover, in direct competition with the United States, which had long been active at universities in Latin America and regarded them as being within their sphere of influence. In that context, Cuba, no longer under that influence, was to become a model of the Sovietization of education systems, curricula, and textbooks during the Cold War.

In requesting help from the Soviet Union, Cuba's young revolutionaries articulated a desire to train specialists needed to develop the Cuban economy currently under sanctions. Havana did not ask Moscow to reform Cuban universities but instead wanted its national specialists to be trained at Soviet institutions of education. The Soviet Union, realizing the importance of the island in the context of the Cold War, readily validated the requests and aspirations of the Cuban government. In the field of education, Cuba even became the top Soviet priority for the training of specialists. In 1961, when the Cuban–Soviet exchange program was introduced, the USSR invited 300 Cubans to be taught engineering, 100 to become teachers, and 400 to be trained as skilled professional workers and technicians.[61] The Soviet Ministry of the Navy even allocated a ship, the *Cooperation*, to transport the first wave of Cuban students at the astounding cost of 180,000 rubles ($198,000).[62]

On its own initiative, the Soviet Union proposed to foster of a corps of Russian-language teachers at Cuban universities. Moscow encouraged the Cuban government to identify 80 Cubans to receive training in the USSR. However, in 1961, the Soviet Minister of Education stated that "it will be difficult for the Cuban government to do it. Cuba will not be able to recruit 80 people who have at least a secondary education. If we find such Cubans, we will expose the very important positions in the state apparatus and areas of work."[63] Instead, Cuba proposed that Moscow send Soviet teachers of Russian to Cuba, which explains how visiting Soviet professors began appearing on the island.

---

61 Secret Letter from the Deputy Minister of Finance of the USSR to the Deputy Minister of Higher and Vocational Education of the USSR. January 2, 1960, folder 48, records group 9606, GARF, p. 3.

62 Ibid, p. 4.

63 The Visit of the Inspector Y. Paporov to the Republic of Cuba. Secret Report. July 13, 1961, folder 48, records group 9606, GARF, p. 65.

3.2 Soviets at the University of Havana: Fear of Loss

The University of Havana was the first university to which visiting Soviet professors and consultants were sent. Among the oldest in the region, the University of Havana had been established by the Spanish in 1728 and remained under the control of the Catholic Church until the mid-19th century, when it dissolved its relationship with the Church. After the Spanish–American War of 1898, won by the United States, the University of Havana endured the influence of the U.S. model of education. Professors from Harvard University had introduced the social sciences into the University of Havana, established three departments—the Department of Liberal Arts, Medicine, and Law—and organized distinct bachelor's and master's levels of education. Student revolts seeking the university's democratization won autonomy for the University of Havana in 1933, after which the participation of students in high-standing official committees and in academic affairs was expanded. Autonomy was lost, however, after General Batista rose to power in 1952. Although two other universities were opened—one in Oriento (Santiago de Cuba), the other in Las Villas—Batista closed all universities in Cuba in 1956. The reason for such a severe policy was the political, often antigovernment activity of university students and graduates, including Fidel Castro, who led the revolutionary coup in 1959 and immediately reopened the University of Havana after the uprising's success.

Following the Cuban Revolution and during the Cold War, four universities operated in Cuba: the three mentioned above and another, the University of Camaguey, opened in 1975 in the province of Camaguey. The majority of Cuban students—more than 70 percent—studied at the University of Havana. Clearly, the young government led by Fidel Castro and Ernesto "Che" Guevara understood the importance of universities in Cuba's national development, for the country lacked specialists and teachers who, according to the Cuban Minister of Education, "shamefully leave Cuba." Seeking help from the USSR, the minister complained to Soviet diplomats about the situation: "One day <...> the rector of the University of Las Villas and his deputy left secretly the territory of the Republic by motorboat. There are many recent examples of the escapes of engineers and teachers."[64]

As all entities and elements in Cuban society, Cuban universities had to undergo a series of reforms proposed by the young government. To set the

---

64 Notes on a Conversation with the Deputy Minister of Education of Cuba, José Aguilera Maceiras. Secret Report. From the Diary of Y. Gavrikov, the Third Secretary of the Embassy of the USSR in the Republic of Cuba, December 15, 1960, folder 48, records group 9606, GARF, p. 6.

LATIN AMERICA AND CARIBBEAN

direction of reforms at the universities, a representative delegation of the Republic of Cuba, led by Minister of Education Armando Harto, arrived in the USSR in 1961. At the same time, Castro and Guevara visited the University of Havana, where they explained to students and professors the need to reform the institution. However, changes at the university were ultimately rather slight; trade unions and student organizations were re-established, the academic collegial councils and all departments were reinstated, semesters as the divisions of the academic year were introduced, students' attendance at lectures was made mandatory, the practice of attending college indefinitely was eliminated, and research programs related to Cuba's development were initiated. Other changes included that young people from low social strata, along with children of workers and peasants, received the right to apply to and attend the University.

To Moscow's surprise, Castro's government did not abolish the U.S. system of education or the levels of education awarding bachelor's and master's degrees, which had never existed at Soviet universities. Moreover, U.S. textbooks, a U.S. testing system, and the departments created by U.S. professors were all being preserved and maintained. In fact, after visiting Soviet institutions of education, the Cuban government had decided not to apply the Soviet model of higher education, which stipulated five years of study, the awarding of specialist degrees, the absence of institutional autonomy, and, of course, Marxist–Leninist disciplines. Members of Cuba's government repeatedly told Soviet experts that "maintaining autonomy is more appropriate than abolishing it, because eliminating the autonomy of the University would raise voices of a counter-revolutionary nature."[65]

Although many universities in various countries visited by Soviet experts had sought to protect traditions of local education and teaching,. Cuba had succeeded to the most extent. Moscow was anxious that Cuba, as China once had, would shift its foreign policy against the Russians. After all, the Cuban government had developed an independent perspective on international events, articulated its own version of Marxism, and pursued foreign policy without including Moscow. The Soviet government quickly recognized that it would be better to use soft power, even a policy of appeasement, toward Cubans, for if Cuba balked at instituting Soviet reforms at the University of Havana, then acquiescing to Cuban prerogatives could be worthwhile. Political stakes were extremely high, and Moscow did not want to relinquish relations with an island located so near its rival, the United States, over mere disagreements about reforming universities.

---

65   Ibid, p. 7.

212   CHAPTER 5

Such anxiety and even fear over losing influence in Cuba also decelerated some rather radical Soviet-proposed transformations at the University of Havana. Ultimately, the Soviets were able to negotiate only two changes: the establishment of the Department of Workers and Peasants for Cubans who aspired to enter the university and the introduction of a Chair of Russian. In 1963, Soviet specialists also managed to open that office, whose chief purpose, according to sources, was not preparing Cubans to enter the university but readying citizens and students to be sent to study abroad in the USSR. Cubans allowed the Soviet Union to establish the Chair of Russian not as a distinct academic division, however, but within the Department of Non-Spanish Languages, wherein only one or two Soviet professors were assigned to teach courses on the history of literature and Russian.

Within those circumscriptions, visiting Soviet professors faced some problems that cast doubt on the idea of a strong Cuban–Soviet alliance. For one, studying Russian was not as popular among students, as usually described by scholars, but mostly undertaken by students and other Cubans sent to study in the USSR. For another, the attitude of students toward Soviet professors was one of slight suspicion. In one instance, after listening to a lecture on socialist realism as the dominant frame of artistic representation, students told their Soviet professor that expressionism, abstractionism, and surrealism were more innovative frameworks in contemporary art. Puzzled, the professor, upon reporting to Moscow about the comment, noted that her "work had to be carried out in extremely difficult conditions, because most Cuban students and professors thought in that way."[66] To revise the views of students, Soviet visitors sought to arrange seminars for studying the works of Lenin or to disseminate propaganda; however, the administration immediately reduced all of those classes along with the ones taught by Soviet professors, which thoroughly shocked the Soviets.[67] The Soviets were nevertheless compelled to stay silent so as not to damage otherwise friendly political relations with Cuba.

The denial of Soviet ideology at the universities of socialist Cuba has been attributed to the well-known position of many Cuban Marxists that Soviets

---

66   Report by I. Ivanova, the Instructor of Russian Language and Literature, Department of
      Modern Non-Spanish Languages at the University of Havana. August 5, 1965, folder 2317,
      Reports on Trips of the Soviet Professors and Researchers to Cuba in 1965, entry 2, records
      group 9606, GARF, p. 49/227.

67   The Summary of the Report by V. Grigoriev, the Chief of the Soviet Professors Group in
      Cuba and the Representative of the Ministry of Higher and Vocational Education of the
      USSR. Report by I. Ivanova, the Instructor of Russian Language and Literature, Department of Modern Non-Spanish Languages at the University of Havana. August 5, 1965,
      folder 2317, records group 9606, GARF, p. 51/229.

LATIN AMERICA AND CARIBBEAN   213

were revisionists who had abandoned the principles of the world revolution in favor of following the policy of peaceful coexistence with the West or, as would become visible in the 1970s, a policy of détente. Thus, Soviet professors and their classes were not models for Cuban students, and the University of Havana, which had forsaken neither its autonomy nor traditions of freedom, was not going to tolerate Soviet ideas disseminated as exclusively correct and undeniably true. Because Soviet propaganda had dissatisfied local professors and students alike, visiting Soviet consultants, though allowed to work in the Department of Workers and Peasants and at the Chairs of Russian, were prohibited from establishing traditional departments and from offering courses on Soviet history and Soviet communism. Moscow was compelled to agree with those restrictions out of fear of losing a political partner in the strategic region.

To subordinate the University of Havana, Moscow therefore decided to open a separate university to train ideologically loyal teachers and translators of Russian. It was assumed that the university's graduates would "conquer" the University of Havana and that Sovietization would follow. In 1962, a separate pedagogical institute named after Maxim Gorky, a famous Soviet writer, was established—the Maxim Gorky Russian Language Institute—where an elite, highly qualified group of translators and teachers of Russian were to be trained. The Institute became a hub for elaborating common approaches to teaching Russian and to writing textbooks for all institutions of education in Cuba, including schools, vocational colleges, and universities. Approximately 140 students were enrolled in the Institute's first year, and classes were taught by both Cuban and Soviet specialists. The Department of Workers and Peasants was also established at the Institute in the case that the same department at the University of Havana became a casualty of upended Cuban–Soviet cooperation.

The Maxim Gorky Russian Language Institute was designed to disseminate Soviet ideology, culture, and history in Russian-language classes and, in the process, undermine the significance of the University of Havana as the primary source of specialists for Cuba.[68] However, to the Soviet specialists' surprise, the Institute encountered unprecedented difficulties in elaborating a unified model for teaching Russian. It proved impossible to launch a system for writing textbooks in Russian, and the first graduates could not secure jobs, for Russian as a discipline had been introduced too slowly at Cuban schools and universities. Describing Cuba throughout the mid-1960s, Soviet experts noted that

---

68   Report on the Teaching of the Russian in the Republic of Cuba by Head of the Educational Center in Havana Ievleva [sic]. June 5, 1966, folder 2317, records group 9606, GARF, p. 249–50.

214 CHAPTER 5

the Russian language was introduced as a compulsory discipline only at technical institutes. In schools, Russian was learned as elective, and there was low attendance. The institutions of education where attending Russian lessons was compulsory had the groups with the highest numbers of students (30–35 people).[69]

Moscow had attempted to provide each Cuban province with teaching aids and textbooks, but despite sending books, syllabi, and other materials by mail to every Cuban town, they were rarely, if ever, used in practice: "The materials sent from the Institute including a syllabus and a textbook with teaching instructions for lessons remained unopened and idle at the homes of teachers."[70]

In the early 1980s, rising interest in learning English in Cuba became a new threat to Sovietization, one that Soviet specialists even made official. However, according to documents from both the 1960s and the 1980s, the problematic rivalry between English and Russian had existed throughout the Cold War. Nevertheless, in the early and mid-1980s, the problem seemed dire as described in the reports of Soviet professors, who characterized the rising popularity of English at the University of Havana as a betrayal of the Cubans:

> We are dissatisfied with the reduction of Russian studies at universities and schools and the introduction of English, with the sporadic dissemination of information about the Soviet Union on TVs, on the radio, in cinema, and in theaters, and hence with the lack of interest in our cultural programs.[71]

In many institutions of education, including schools and institutes established and governed by the Soviets, Russian was even eliminated as a discipline.[72]

Having positioned Russian as a political driver for expanding Sovietization at the University of Havana, the Soviets agonized over the popularity of

---

69 Report on the Teaching of the Russian in the Republic of Cuba, 1966, folder 2317, records group 9606, GARF, p. 241.

70 Ibid, p. 243.

71 Report on the Visit the Soviet Delegation of Ministry of Higher Education, including Associate Professor and Head of the Department of Russian as a Foreign language at Tula State Pedagogical Institute V. Kolodeznev, to Cuba, November–December 1987, folder 355, Reports on the Work of Soviet Specialists at Educational Institutions of the Republic of Cuba, 1987, entry 11, records group 9606, GARF, p. 14.

72 Report on the Visit of a Group of Educationalists to the Republic of Cuba. February 1986, folder 5203, records group 9563, GARF, p. 30.

English in Cuba and sought to rectify the situation. In 1987 and 1988, Moscow sent Soviet experts to the Cuban Ministry of Education to clarify the need to teach and learn Russian. In turn, the Soviet specialists visited the University of Havana, where Russian was the primary discipline in the Department of Workers and Peasants and, of course, in the Chair of Russian. There, the experts received the shocking information that the Cubans planned to dissolve those pro-Soviet units at the University, even after the Soviets had invested heavily in teaching 600 Cubans in the department each year. In reality, the situation with enrollment had become so dismal that the department had not attracted any new students in 1987, and 60 other students and 68 teachers were set to lose their jobs.[73] The Cubans claimed to the Soviet visitors that "there is a reduction in the number of students in all units dealing with Russian, and the reduction of those structures is inevitable."[74] The most serious blow, however, came from the Cuban Ministry of Education: "The measures to eliminate the Russian language from institutions of education in the Republic while spreading English are consistent with the guidelines of the Central Committee of the Communist Party of Cuba."[75]

The Soviet specialists insisted on maintaining the Chair of Russian and the Department of Workers and Peasants at the University of Havana despite a sharp drop in students and Cubans who wanted to learn Russian. It was thus proposed to retain the current teaching staff and publish a new textbook as a Soviet–Cuban project. The Soviet experts hoped that such collaboration would inspire Cubans to resume pursuing Russification.[76] However, the fate of Russian in Cuba was sealed by the policy of the University of Havana. Shortly after, in 1987 and 1988, all structures dealing with Russian, notably the Department of Workers and Peasants and the Chair of Russian, were dismantled, and the Department turned into an evening education division for students who worked during the day.

---

73 Report on the Visit the Soviet Delegation of Ministry of Higher Education, including Associate Professor and Head of the Department of Russian as a Foreign language at Tula State Pedagogical Institute V. Kolodeznev, to Cuba, November–December 1987, folder 355, Reports on the Work of Soviet Specialists at Educational Institutions of the Republic of Cuba, 1987, entry 11, records group 9606, GARF, p. 51–52.

74 Ibid, p. 51.

75 Ibid.

76 Report on the Visit of the Delegation of the Soviet Ministry of Higher Education to the Preparatory Departments (The Departments for Workers and Peasants) of the Republic of Cuba. November 23 – December 03, 1987 (Universidad de la Habana), no date, folder 355, Reports on the Work of Soviet Specialists at Educational Institutions of the Republic of Cuba, 1987, entry 11, records group 9606, GARF, p. 71.

3.3 *Soviets at Alternative Academies: Facing Opposition and Denial*

The Soviet government recognized that its projects at the University of Havana neither constituted the Sovietization of the institution nor contributed to the training of new cadres. Moreover, it was too expensive and time-consuming to train Cubans in the USSR. A permanent fear and concern that Moscow would lose influence in Cuba drove the Soviets to identify new institutions of education to renew their influence. To avoid additional failures at the stubborn University of Havana and to develop an education system based on the Soviet model, Moscow targeted institutes in the field of pedagogy newly established by the Soviet Union or else transformed from older pedagogical schools opened prior to the Cuban Revolution.

For their part, Fidel Castro and the Cuban government did not perceive anything threatening in the work of Soviet consultants at Cuba's pedagogical institutes and schools. The head of Cuba even invited Soviet teachers to Cuban schools and Soviet professors to the pedagogical institutes to improve the literacy and academic performance of students. The first consultants were Spanish-speaking nationals who had long lived in the USSR, if not born there. Speaking two languages, such specialists effected some transformations at Cuban schools and in higher pedagogical education according to the Soviet model. They issued the first syllabi and introduced disciplines such as mathematics, drawing, physics, and chemistry.

Later, the first and largest team of Soviet specialists arrived in Cuba to train school teachers, prospective university staff, and interpreters at the pedagogical institutes. In three years, "190 Soviet specialists, including 64 translators, 16 laboratory assistants, and 104 teachers of the Russian language" were sent to Cuba.[77] Indeed, it was a large number of Soviet vising professors.

Twelve pedagogical institutes in Cuba operated within the Soviet sphere of influence, although each had different names and statuses at different times during the Cold War. Soviet specialists tried to impose the model of Soviet education, especially the five years of study, and eliminated the bachelor's and master's degrees previously established at the schools. Instead, most pedagogical institutes introduced five- or six-year courses of study and awarded Soviet-patterned specialist degrees that had never before existed in Cuba.[78]

A particular concern for the Soviets was the pedagogical institutes for foreign languages that trained teachers in both Russian and English. The most

---

77 Pino Estevez, *Distant Education of Secondary School Teachers at Higher Pedagogical Institutes of Cuba*. PhD Thesis (Minsk, 1984), 41.

78 Report on the Visit of a Group of Educationalists to the Republic of Cuba, February 1986, folder 5203, records group 9563, GARF, p. 27.

famous was the Paul Lafargue Pedagogical Institute of Foreign Languages, named after Paul Lafargue, a renowned Marxist thinker who had been born in Cuba, where his father owned plantations, and had married Karl Marx's daughter. Established in 1977, the Lafargue Institute trained both teachers and translators and rapidly gained a reputation as the core source for translators and highly qualified teachers. The Institute had two faculties: the Faculty of Germanic Languages, which was engaged in teaching English, and the Faculty of Slavic Languages, which taught Russian. Both faculties in turn staged a miniature cultural confrontation between English and Russian and between Cuban professors who clashed over whether to prioritize English or Russian in academic life.

The number of students enrolled in the two faculties became the primary indicator of the popularity and significance of Soviets in Cuba. Immediately after the Institute's opening and until the end of the Cold War, the number of students aspiring to study English exceeded the number of students in the opposite faculty where Russian was taught. In 1983, for example, the Faculty of Germanic Languages accepted 421 students instead of the 320 planned, whereas the Faculty of Slavic Languages accepted 70 instead the expected 130. In sum, 1,049 students studied English while 730 studied Russian.[79] The imbalance annoyed the Soviet specialists, but no measures were taken to reduce admissions to the English faculty or to intensify admissions to the Russian one. The Soviet consultants attempted only once to expand the quota of students for the Russian faculty, but when seats remained vacant, the Institute's administration relocated those vacancies to the English faculty. Such independent, defiant behavior, if committed in another country under Soviet influence, would have been perceived by Soviet specialists as clear opposition to Sovietization and would have justified certain consequences in terms of pressure and hard policy toward the professoriate. In Cuba, however, Moscow behaved with restraint, even by allowing Cubans to perpetrate such disobedient behavior, which ultimately worked to critically wound Soviet influence at the Institute.

At the same time, the Institute's administrative staff, including the rector and deans of the faculties, who had studied and received doctoral degrees in Moscow, were friendly and loyal to the Soviet visitors. The young staff, including a 29-year-old rector and teachers no older than 33, as pointed out by the Soviet specialists, were open to Soviet reforms and to Soviet inquiry. Although

---

79   Report on the Work as an Advisor in the Field of English Philology at the Havana Higher Pedagogical Institute of Foreign Languages by L. Berdnikova, the Head of the English Language Department at the Pyatigorsk State Pedagogical Institute of Foreign Languages, 1983–1986, July 11, 1986, folder 5203, records group 9563, GARF, p. 59–60.

218   CHAPTER 5

pliable and friendly in personal communications, the Cubans were stubborn
about academic reforms proposed by the Soviets: "The team is young and
interested in everything, listens to advice, and creatively implements it in practice."[80] Another source adds that one staff member "is lively, quickly reacts,
and listens to advice."[81] At the same time, the Cubans did not comply with
Soviet demands to expand the instruction of Russian at the expense of English
or to diminish the number of students at the Faculty of Germanic Languages.
Preference for the English language thus became a sensitive dilemma between
the Institute's young staff and the Soviet experts.

The most emotionally trying attitude among Cubans for the Soviet consultants turned out to be the denial of Soviet experience in teaching English. The
Cuban teaching staff questioned and even rejected the practice and theory of
teaching English proclaimed in Soviet universities. For the first time in the history of their policy, Soviet specialists encountered highly professional staff flu-
ent in English who had published textbooks and teaching instructions but did
not instruct in British English, so highly appreciated by the scientific school of
Soviet philologists, but its American counterpart. The approach clearly humiliated the Soviets, who promoted their own approach but realized that students
wanted American English, despite its utter absence in Soviet pedagogy and
philology. One source describes the situation as follows:

> The team of professors in the English faculty is young and energetic.
> They speak fluent English. [However] the professors have professionally
> endorsed the theoretical positions of American language schools, with-
> out giving information to students about the viewpoints of other linguis-
> tic schools, without showing the development of the theory of language,
> and without demonstrating the contributions of Soviet and European
> linguistic schools to its development. I had to fight to improve the con-
> tent of theoretical courses.[82]

Another added:

> When I was introduced to leading Cuban experts and heads of depart-
> ments at the Institute, who demonstrated dozens of textbooks written

---

80   Report on the Work Accomplished by a Consultant on the Teaching of Mathematics at
      the Higher Pedagogical Institute in Guantanamo by N. Chikantseva, 1985–1986, folder
      5203, records group 9563, GARF, p. 95.

81   Ibid, p. 98.

82   Report on the Work as an Advisor in the Field of English Philology at the Havana Higher
      Pedagogical Institute of Foreign Languages by L. Berdnikova, 1983–1986, July 11, 1986,
      folder 5203, records group 9563, GARF, p. 63.

LATIN AMERICA AND CARIBBEAN 219

by them and spoke excellent English, it became clear that I had to help and teach not staff who were weak in English and its theory, not those who believe that they needed my help, but professors who assumed to know everything about the theory and practice of English, in its American version in particular. So, I had to teach the strongest, most respected professors not only at the institute but also from across Cuba.[83]

Most Cuban professors and lower-level teaching staff, having been taught with U.S. textbooks, used similar textbooks to teach students despite the flow of Russian manuals translated into Spanish. The Soviet advisors could not tolerate that practice, and using scholarly arguments, they tried to persuade the Cubans to stop teaching American English. For instance, the Soviets emphasized the "weaknesses" of textbooks from the United States: "American textbooks available in Cuba used for teaching and written by Americans to prepare students for any profession are inappropriate for the Institute."[84] The Soviet advisors considered the textbooks especially unsuitable for prospective translators and teachers of English. In addition, the Soviet visitors tried to convince the Cubans that American English, in terms of theory of linguistics, was poorly studied by scholars and could never become the version of English to dominate instruction. The students, in their opinion, as prospective translators or teachers, needed to know theoretical phonetics and grammar; however, theoretical courses were not taught by the Cubans, even if they were extremely popular in Soviet linguistic institutes that pushed Russians to introduce them in Cuba. On top of that, the Soviet professors were embarrassed by the approaches used to study the grammar of American English, which were "based on the transformational and generative grammar of the American linguist N. Chomsky."[85] Therefore, the Soviet advisors asked the Cubans to forget their previous studies and teaching, switch to British English, and introduce more courses in theoretical phonetics, theoretical grammar, and passive reading at the expense of the communication practice. The Cuban professors who had grown up learning from textbooks in American English could not understand why their students needed pure theoretical linguistic courses if the purpose of language was communication.

To promote their approach, the Soviet professors introduced their textbooks on lexicology and phonetics that only served to confuse students and classes at the Institute. There, first-year students studied British English, whereas older ones studied American English. In time, the efforts of the Soviet instructors

---

83   Ibid.
84   Ibid, p. 65.
85   Ibid.

220 CHAPTER 5

proved to be senseless, and the Cubans did not switch to British English: "They [students] work with tape recordings in British English, but the instructor persistently articulated his Americanized options of the sounds to the audience."[86]

The problem of instructing in American English at the Institute was never resolved, and the Cubans never agreed to revise their approaches to the teaching and learning of English. Consequently, the academic community became increasingly less interested in the Russian language, and visits by the Soviet advisors, rendered largely useless, were reduced. U.S. textbooks and disciplines remained in the pedagogical institutes, and Soviet syllabuses translated into Spanish proved unable to uproot the tradition of teaching according to the U.S. model. One Soviet professor evaluated the situation in a report as follows: "Throughout the first half of the 20th century, the educational system of Cuba was under the impact of American pedagogy. American textbooks and syllabuses used in Cuban schools and institutions of higher education remained almost unchanged. Most scholars and pedagogical staff had been educated in American or pro-American institutions of education that drive the development of socialist pedagogy in the education system of the country."[87]

Moscow was never able to arrange the publication of textbooks for students based on the Soviet model, and Cuba's universities continued to be dominated by books arriving from the United States and other countries:

> Pedagogical literature comes from abroad in Spanish and English. The editions of the United States, Spain, France, and Japan prevail. There is no Soviet pedagogical literature translated into Spanish. Pedagogical journals from capitalistic countries are in great demand, since they are published in English and Spanish; Soviet magazines are hardly read, because the problem with translating them into Spanish has still not been resolved. The situation contributes to the domination of bourgeois pedagogy in Cuba.[88]

More broadly, the problem was never resolved during the entire Cold War. In a report from 1986, the problem was discussed in bitter terms: that the

---

86 Ibid.

87 Report on the Work of Soviet Experts at the Cuban Ministry of Education, 1972, folder 1786, Reports on the Work at the Cuban Ministry of Education and on the Summer Courses at the Havana National Institute for Advanced Teacher Training by Soviet Experts, April–December 1972, entry 1, records group 9563, GARF, p. 15.

88 Ibid, p. 9.

"pedagogical institutes, not to mention the universities, have many textbooks brought from different countries but only a single Soviet textbook on pedagogy."[89]

Moreover, the Soviet Union failed to disseminate its own textbooks on history and Marxism–Leninism in Cuba as had been accomplished in other countries. Many universities, pedagogical institutes, and schools on the island continued to reproduce knowledge according to U.S., British, and Spanish textbooks, among others, which embraced "the ideological, political, scientific and methodological principles that are alien to the socialist school and contain obvious falsifications of historical facts."[90] The Soviet advisors were not able to revise even the textbook for the study of history:

> The course of history is taught without the basic principles of historical materialism, without the classic works of Marxism–Leninism. There is no Marxist periodization of the history of Cuba, and the role of the proletariat and the international workers' movement is poorly covered. Textbooks contain mistakes. Thus, the creation of the old Russian state is explained by the invasion of the Normans into the territory of Kievan Rus.[91]

The Soviet Union additionally failed to eliminate the U.S.-inspired testing system, considered to be so destructive, as the primary approach to evaluating students' knowledge: "The vicious practice of tests borrowed from the United States, Spain, and Mexico remains acceptable."[92]

To revise the situation, a separate hub for producing unified syllabuses, textbooks, and disciplines was created in Havana. Having to prepare lecture courses and textbooks on various subjects for current and newly established pedagogical schools and institutes, the hub tried to train a new corps of teachers in Russian and Marxism–Leninism and to introduce the subjects into

---

89 Report on the Visit to the Republic of Cuba by Associate Professor and Vice-Rector at Tula State Pedagogical Institute N. Shaidenko in April, 1986. April 15, 1986, folder 5203, records group 9563, GARF, p. 41.

90 Ibid.

91 The question has still recently remained sensitive in scholarly discussions. One group of historians claimed that the Russian state was founded by ancient Russian called the Slavic people themselves. Other group claimed that Vikings or Normans visited the north part of current Russia and contributed to the establishment of the statecraft. The second approach was criticized during the Soviet times for its diminishing the ability of ancient Russians to create their own state. So, the first position was promoted in all the textbooks and books.

92 Report on the Work of Soviet Experts at the Cuban Ministry of Education, 1972, folder 1786, records group 9563, GARF, p. 8.

schools and pedagogical institutes.[93] Although instructors from a number of Soviet universities worked to re-educate Cuban teachers and university professors in Marxism–Leninism, the Soviet specialists constantly complained to Moscow that the students, teachers, and professors did not understand Marxism–Leninism as a scientific methodology and, in any case, did not want to study it.[94]

When an education reform was initiated in 1971 in Cuba, Soviet experts conducted an examination of all institutions of education, textbooks, and teaching materials in Cuba. As a result, they came to the discouraging conclusion that the statements in the curricula, syllabi, and textbooks differed from the tenets of Marxist–Leninist ideology.[95] The Cuban government formally conceded to conduct a rigorous reform of education on the basis of the Marxist–Leninist ideology, and the strategy was drafted by Soviet specialists.[96] However, the reform remained on paper and did not alter any real content in the education of students. The Soviet reports repeat time and again that the "knowledge of many works of classical Marxism–Leninism [of both students and university professors] leaves much to be desired."[97] For example, a Soviet professor of history, who worked at the Pedagogical Institute in Santa Clara, noted that he had to deliver classes to professors but not to students on topics such as "the history of the labor movement," the "development of the world socialist system," "the capitalist world in the third stage of the general crisis of capitalism," and "the ecological crisis of 1970–1980s," all because the professors did not understand the discipline.[98] The lack of research on Marxism–Leninism discouraged the Soviet specialists. Although they proposed research topics, organized conferences, and sent young instructors to the Soviet universities, the Cuban academic staff mostly denied Marxism–Leninism as the sole scholarly foundation for research. Nearly all Cubans who discussed the matter with the Soviet consultants "did not pay any mind to the Marxist–Leninist worldview and did

---

93   Report on the Work as Instructor in Cuba by I. Semenov, 1965, folder 2317, records group 9606, GARF, p. 48/226.

94   Report on the Work of Soviet Specialists at Summer Courses at the Havana National Institute for Advanced Teacher Training, Cuba. August–October 1972, folder 1786, records group 9563, GARF, p. 35.

95   Report on the Work of Soviet Experts at the Cuban Ministry of Education, 1972, folder 1786, records group 9563, GARF, p. 18–19.

96   Ibid, p. 15.

97   Report on the Work as an Advisor at the Higher Pedagogical Institute in Santa Clara in Cuba by Associate Professor at the Kiev State Pedagogical Institute T. Ladychenko. November 1985, folder 5203, records group 9563, GARF, p. 8–9.

98   Ibid.

LATIN AMERICA AND CARIBBEAN

not elaborate propaganda or ideological work."[99] Such statements riddle documents from the 1960s to the 1980s.

Attempts to introduce courses in the field of Marxism–Leninism to pedagogical institutes in Cuba continued throughout the Cold War but ultimately failed. In other countries, including East Germany, by contrast, such courses had been introduced rather quickly and painlessly. In Cuba, however, the Soviet experts were afraid of exerting pressure on the local academic elite, and the fear of a possible breach in contact and cooperation at the hands of the Cubans made Moscow act extremely cautiously, despite such an appeasement policy largely undermining the process of Sovietization. Even in 1985, Soviet advisors reported to Moscow that a course on Marxism–Leninism distinct from other disciplines had been introduced in a study plan at a pedagogical institute. Without a doubt, the introduction of Marxism–Leninism in the mid-1980s versus the 1960s showcases the failure of traditional Soviet goals of education policy. In Cuba, indoctrination proceeded at a crawl, which was attributed to the position taken by the Cuban government, which, as indicated, was highly suspicious of the Soviet version of Marxism and Soviet propaganda. All of those factors distinguished Sovietization in Cuba from the process in other countries. Moscow did not seek to pursue a policy of pressure in Cuba, for any careless move was liable to precipitate the denial of cultural diplomacy and, in turn, damage the political goals of Moscow in Latin America.

The success of the policy of sabotage pursued by Cuban professors was determined by their full recognition of the place and role of Cuba in Soviet politics. The Soviet fear of losing Cuba allowed the academic community to ignore Soviet demands as well as proposals. Another motive for their noncompliance, however, was their professionalism as scholars and educators, which allowed them to rival the Soviet model of education. The Cubans were highly qualified instructors, and assured in their knowledge and local traditions, they had no incentive to modify the education that they considered to be better than the Soviet counterpart. Therefore, unlike the case in other countries, visiting Soviet professors could not offer anything more attractive than socialist realism, Marxism–Leninism, and British English, none of which widely appealed to the Cubans.

Compared to people in other countries, Cubans enjoyed communicating with the Soviets but transformed and revised nothing in their practices of higher education. The Cuban professors were open to dialogue, highly

---

99   Report on the Work as an Advisor in the Field of English Philology at the Havana Higher
     Pedagogical Institute of Foreign Languages by L. Berdnikova, 1983–1986, July 11, 1986,
     folder 5203, records group 9563, GARF, p. 87.

224 CHAPTER 5

adaptive, and professional but also quite choosy. They understood Moscow's fear of losing ground on the island, and that fear, along with ideas of nationalism, independence, and Cuban Marxism, created conditions for the minimal influence of the Soviet Union on the Cuban academic community. Undoubtedly, there were professors who completely refused to cooperate and even communicated the underlying sentiment to the Soviet consultants:

> The partner [a Cuban] shows extreme passivity and is brought to consultations almost on a lasso. And such partners are not so rare in the practice of our consultants.[100]

Unlike in other cases of Soviet policy observed at the universities of East Germany, Vietnam, and Afghanistan, no measures were taken against such Cuban professors. There were no instructive conversations with them, and the Soviet Union approached such situations rather gingerly. Political stakes were high, and Moscow did not want to lose the favor of the Cuban government.

Soviet instructors also faced a range of difficulties due to special nature of Soviet–Cuban relations. Deconstructing the identity of the Cuban professors and their national character, the Soviet consultants noted that the Cubans, unlike professors in other countries, demanded not only the informal settlement of any issue before the exchange of papers or official negotiations but also their involvement in drafting those materials:

> The effectiveness of the recommendations depends on the level of involvement of Cuban specialists as coauthors, even their formal participation. Therefore, the participation of Cuban experts in the development of teaching materials was expanded as much as possible. Any documents to be transmitted to the Cuban side first needed to be agreed upon with the Cuban experts through oral talks in order to avoid misunderstanding.[101]

Moscow itself also created similar obstacles. Quite often, in the 1960s in particular, when aid to Cuba had only begun to be distributed, the Soviet government delayed the delivery of the necessary consultants, literature, and equipment,

---

100   Report on the Work as a Consultant of the Department of Biology at the Higher Pedagogical Institute in Camaguey by A. Elenevsky, 1984–1986. June 5, 1986, folder 5203, records group 9563, GARF, p. 51.

101   Report on the Work as an Advisor in the Field of English Philology at the Havana Higher Pedagogical Institute of Foreign Languages by L. Berdnikova, 1983–1986, July 11, 1986, folder 5203, records group 9563, GARF, p. 80.

LATIN AMERICA AND CARIBBEAN

thereby breaking its promise to the Cubans. That misstep hurt the image of the Soviet Union: "The Soviet agencies did not fulfill their obligations according to the plan of cultural cooperation with Cuba, which affects the reforms of the education system and higher education, as well as damages the prestige of the USSR."[102] For a long time, the Soviets could not arrange the translation of the necessary textbooks and literature for students into Spanish. Finally, the Soviet government wanted Spanish to be studied by the visiting Soviet professors in order to accelerate informal communication between the Soviet and Cuban professors. However, learning the language required time, and even though some Soviet professors managed to learn Spanish and even deliver lectures in the language, most of the Soviets worked with an interpreter, which only further complicated the work. It often happened that translators did not possess the necessary knowledge: "Translators often don't have a special vocabulary. Giving classes with translators is not very effective, and not knowing the language prevents efficient contact between partners."[103]

In 1986, the Soviet specialists noted that Cuba disdained Moscow and did not officially thank the Soviet Union for its assistance in the field of education:

> In none of the speeches were any words about the aid of the USSR in the field of public education of Cuba. That came out of a desire not to publicize the facts of cooperation in front of the countries of Latin America and the United States.[104]

That statement finally assured the Soviet advisors that perhaps their fear and alarmist attitudes were justified, even if the policy of appeasement toward the Cubans had been unnecessary and failed.

4 Conclusion

As a whole, Latin American countries represent a unique case in the education policies of both superpowers during the Cold War. The policy of the

---

102 Secret Resolution on the Cultural and Scientific Relations with the Republic of Cuba by the State Committee on Cultural Relations with Foreign Countries at the Council of Ministers of the USSR. November 20, 1961, folder 48, records group 9606, GARF, p. 31/99.

103 Report on the Work as a Consultant of the Department of Biology at the Higher Pedagogical Institute in Camaguey by A. Elenevsky, 1984–1986, June 5, 1986, folder 5203, records group 9563, GARF, p. 45.

104 Report on the Work of Soviet Experts at the Cuban Ministry of Education, 1972, folder 1786, records group 9563, GARF, p. 14.

United States and the Soviet Union in the region was based on the fear of losing influence in the targeted countries—in this chapter, Cuba for the Soviets and Guatemala for the Americans. In both cases, such fear stemmed from the political and military context of the Cold War. For its part, the United States was shocked by the approach of the Soviet ideology into the zone of their vital interests. The popularity of the Soviet Union and of Marxist ideas in Latin American perspectives and attitudes was liable to destabilize any country in the Western Hemisphere and invite the USSR and its nuclear arsenal to the borders of the United States. Indeed, the Cuban Revolution accelerated that potential reality. For the first time, the Soviet Union's policy in terms of large-scale cultural diplomacy gained a foothold in the countries of Latin America and sought, at all costs, to also gain political advantages in the region. Therefore, any loss of influence or any denial of cooperation was viewed by the Kremlin as a defeat.

Facing the political context of the Cold War, both superpowers pursued a policy of appeasement in their cultural diplomacy, which involved abandoning many of the principles upheld in transforming universities in other countries at the time. A void of traditional sources of pressure on the faculty at the universities of Guatemala and Cuba in the field of teaching politically oriented courses such as political science, American studies, Marxism–Leninism, and Soviet studies ironically, and for the first time, allowed the superpowers to be pressured by local universities, which, without any obvious struggle, could deny the services and reforms offered by their U.S. or Soviet partners. The University of San Carlos, for instance, refused to create university extension projects and to revise various courses, while the University of Havana denied Marxist–Leninist interpretations of ideology, denied the Russian language, and, perhaps most fascinating, denied the Soviet approach to teaching English. The superpowers, however, felt that they had little choice but to tolerate such conduct and did not implement any hard policy toward the universities, all in order not to shatter their fragile but strategically necessary partnerships.

The academic communities of Guatemala and Cuba were aware of their peculiar position in the strategic calculations of the two superpowers. They witnessed the anxieties and fears in the policies that Washington and Moscow had implemented and exploited those concerns to their advantage. As a result, academia in Latin America received real financial and technical support in the construction and development of university infrastructure, the development of national cadres, and the improvement of the work of teachers. Such structural changes became the chief visible results of the unique political situation and the rival forms of cultural diplomacy. To maintain influence in the foreign countries and in their education systems, both superpowers made massive investments and readily validated any requests from their partners in Latin America.

As a result, fear and a policy of appeasement rendered neither the United States nor the Soviet Union capable of achieving full Americanization or Sovietization at the respective universities in Guatemala and Cuba. Faced with the reluctance of the universities to implement their projects, they were compelled to step back.

Conclusion

The United States and Soviet Union were able to make some structural revisions in the target universities, contributing to the development and modernization of education systems. However, the transformations could not alter the modes of thinking and the values of academic communities, namely professors, who, in most cases, continued to maintain local traditions in education. The transformations offered by both the United States and the Soviet Union were often met with resistance from this part of the academic community, which did not want to see changes in their universities based on American or Soviet models. Thus, the book shows that the transfer of patterns of education from one nation-state to another can influence some constructional and institutional changes but cannot profoundly change minds and hearts in the university community.

Corps of professors in the countries located in five regions turned out to be able to accommodate and even tame the ambitions of the two superpowers, referring to their intentions to revise universities and, consequently, the life of the local academic community. The professors, quiet and unyielding, thus came to be recognized as the main impediment to the plans of the U.S. and the Soviet Union. It was they who initiated sabotage against Americanization and Sovietization, refusing to adopt new statutes, deliver courses, and conduct research on newly proposed themes. The reformers exerted a great amount of effort to introduce political science, American studies, English, Marxist-Leninist philosophy, Soviet history, or the Russian language to target universities. Moreover, the successful introduction of new disciplines or the establishment of new and independent departments on the American or Soviet models did not guarantee that new disciplines, new teaching methods, or new research topics would be implemented properly by local educators. Consequently, the professors supported development projects, the construction of new buildings or dormitories, and took part in exchange and training programs, receiving degrees from prestigious U.S. and Soviet universities. However, they refused to take any steps suggested by the reformers to diminish the power of the local academic community in university senates or governing bodies, including revisions to charters, curricula, admission rules, and other factors that could destabilize local traditions and their powerful positions. Hence, U.S. and Soviet reforms unexpectedly came up against professors on the grassroots level who were unwilling to lose influence, and as a result, these reforms were not successful.

© NATALIA TSVETKOVA, LEIDEN, 2021 | DOI:10.1163/9789004471788_008

CONCLUSION 229

Hence, small groups and communities, rarely taken into consideration by researchers in previous Cold War studies, were able to act as key drivers in the grand international policies of the superpowers. The professors at the target universities made impacts on the policies of both the United States and Soviet Union, pushing them to accommodate their goals to align with the needs of local communities. Returning to the theoretical discussion started in the introduction, it must be stated that conceptual frameworks relative to realism, Americanization, and Sovietization explain only part of the picture—namely the political and cultural plans, intentions, strategies, and actions of the U.S. and the Soviet Union at foreign universities—while neglecting the reactions of and feedback from recipients, that is, professors, students, and administrative staff.

The realist explanations the reasons and motives of U.S. and Soviet policies in terms of national security limit the scholarly understanding of what happened at universities under the influence of the two nations and how target communities responded and limited their interventions. The concepts of Americanization and Sovietization were broadly contrasted as the soft and hard notions in the historiography. However, the new archival records and analysis show that both superpowers had similar aims in the cultural Cold War and exploited the same methods in order to deal with universities worldwide. In order to understand the limitations of Americanization and Sovietization, it is necessary to take into consideration both the successes and failures of the policies accomplished by American and Soviet advisors. The advisors of both countries were able to change university structures, introduce new management, and develop a new infrastructure for students and teaching staff. The assistance provided by both governments in these developments was welcomed by local publics, but the reaction to the introduction of new disciplines was restrained. American and Soviet advisors were not able to transform traditional ways of teaching, convince professors and departments to develop and offer new courses, make students study new subjects, etc. Both silent and open resistance on the part of university communities undermined American and, later, Soviet cultural influences. Both superpowers recognized the fact that universities had only formally acquiesced to the imposed revisions, while a part of the university community did not believe in the ideas put forth by either the American or Soviet powers.

Therefore, the exploration of reactions coming from the receiving ends can overcome one-sided approaches in studies on the cultural Cold War. The concepts of constructivism, fear, and response discuss the theses about the impacts of values, local entities, and groups with their own identities on international politics and can tell more about the behavior of such recipients—in this case, professors. Differences in values; everyday clashes between experts from either the U.S. or Soviet Union with local professors, who perceived the visiting advisors from Washington and Moscow as strangers; and divergent identities and traditions in education had crucial impacts on the final results of the transformations proposed by both superpowers.

In Germany, the professoriate, while demonstrating its loyalty to both American and Soviet reforms, nonetheless protested both the Americanization and Marxification of universities in both parts of Germany and limited the implementation of the proposed transformations. American advisors were unable to overcome this strong opposition and were forced to admit that American influence was undermined in German universities. In East Germany, Soviet reforms were blocked by the stubborn disobedience of a segment of the professoriate, making Moscow admit the failure of its efforts to produce a generation of pliable professors. Both the West German and East German professoriate believed that American democracy and Soviet Marxism undermined the concept of academic freedom and other traditions of German university life, and academic communities in both parts of that country were able to retain certain traditional features of the German university system throughout the entire period of the Cold War.

In Afghanistan, the development of Kabul University went along with the imposing American or Soviet values, English or Russian language, American or Soviet disciplines, etc., with local traditions being ignored by the superpowers. The policies of both Washington and Moscow were resisted by the university community, and neither superpower could subdue the localism and conservatism peculiar to Afghan universities. Professors and students resisted silently and openly, with their resistance taking different forms—notably sabotage, student strikes, and an Islamic movement that rolled back the impacts of both the Americanization and Sovietization of Afghanistan and its educational system.

In Ethiopia, the United States and the Soviet Union were compelled to develop education as part of modernization. Construction projects, the maintenance of equipment and dormitories, and the training of qualified specialists absorbed all of U.S. and Soviet advisors' time and energy. As a consequence, value-oriented disciplines such as Russian, English, Marxism, political science, literature, and history were sidelined to accommodate vocational education and engineering courses. Moreover, Ethiopians showed signs of alienation in regard to the superpowers and pursued a policy of Ethiopianization in the academic community. Washington and Moscow conceded to the aspirations of their Ethiopian counterparts in order to maintain connections to local universities they had built. Both superpowers were able to open universities and

CONCLUSION 231

schools, build academic facilities, and equip laboratories and libraries. However, the case of Ethiopia can be used to demonstrate how the need for development restrained policies bent upon imposing values, culture, and ideology in studies and research at the university level. The local academic community resisted transformations at their institutions toward U.S. or Soviet models, sabotaged reforms, and openly advocated their positions while being under the pressure of and in dialogue with the superpowers.

In Vietnam, both American and Soviet advisors were unable to mold a new, ideal Vietnamese teacher and to transform Vietnamese universities and schools according to their respective initial goals. Both superpowers aspired to mold an ideal Vietnamese teacher who would be a bearer of either American or Soviet values, would teach local children and students according to either American or Soviet models of education and textbooks, and would transmit a new culture to the student community. Clearly, the main factors for this failure included the permanently unstable political situation in Vietnam, the war, and mainly, the country's division. Everyday communication between visiting professors and Vietnamese audiences, as well as academic and social practices imposed by U.S. and Soviet advisors, did not eliminate the perception of the Vietnamese that American and Soviet guests proposed unfamiliar and alien traditions and cultures. In terms of the Vietnamese perception, American and Soviet values and models of education were likely to be alien, not Vietnamese and indigenous. The web of local traditions and culture restrained the transformations of both political powers in Vietnam's universities.

In Guatemala and Cuba, both superpowers had strong concerns about losing influence in these target countries, based on the concept of political fear. It is evident that this fear stemmed from the political and military context of the Cold War. For its part, the United States was shocked by the encroachment of Soviet ideology into zones marking their own vital interests. The popularity of the Soviet Union and of Marxist ideas in Latin American perspectives and attitudes was liable to destabilize any country in the Western Hemisphere and invite the USSR and its nuclear arsenal to the borders of the United States. Indeed, the Cuban Revolution accelerated that potential reality. For the first time, the Soviet Union's policy in terms of large-scale cultural diplomacy gained a foothold in the countries of Latin America and sought, at all costs, to also gain political advantages in the region. Therefore, any loss of influence or denial of cooperation was viewed by the Kremlin as a defeat.

Facing the political context of the Cold War, both superpowers pursued a policy of appeasement in their cultural diplomacy, which involved abandoning many of the principles upheld in transforming universities in other countries at the time. The universities in Guatemala and Cuba could adopt or even deny the services and reforms offered by their U.S. or Soviet counterparts, and their academic communities were aware of their peculiar position in the strategic calculations of the two superpowers. They witnessed the anxieties and fears in the policies of Washington and Moscow and exploited these to their advantage. The superpowers, fearful of shattering their fragile but strategically necessary partnerships, tolerated such conduct. As a result, academia received real financial and technical support in the construction and development of university infrastructure while, at the same time, preserving their local traditions. Thus, in the grand international game and high politics known as the Cultural Cold War, professors and students were able to tame the United States and Soviet Union and reduce their attitude of arrogance in pursuing their political and national interests in universities worldwide.

Bibliography

Archival Sources

National Archives Records Administration (NARA), College Park, MA, United States

Records group 59, General Records of the Department of State

Central files, 1950–54
  box 2451
Central Files, 1967–1969
  box 345
Confidential Central Files. Germany. Internal and Foreign Affairs 1945–1969, microfilms
  reels 7, 30
Culture and Information, 1970–1973
  boxes 392, 403
Decimal Files
  boxes 5, 2447, 2449
International Information Administration. Field Program for Germany 1945–1953
  boxes 1, 2437
Office of Educational, Cultural Affairs, Lot 98D 252
  box 206
Records of the Plans and Development Staff, Evaluation Branch, 1955–1960
  box 44
Records of the U.S. Board of Foreign Scholarships, 1971–1980
  box 27

Records group 260, Records of US Occupation Headquarters. World War II. Office of Military Government of the United States

Berlin. Education and Cultural Relations Branch, 1945–49
  boxes 128, 134
Hessen. Education and Cultural Relations Division, 1947–48
  box 702
Bavaria. Office of Education and Cultural Relations Division
  box 57
Württemberg–Baden. Records of Education and Cultural Relations Division, 1945–1949
  boxes 913, 915, 916, 917A

234   BIBLIOGRAPHY

Records group 286, Agency for International Development

USAID Mission to Afghanistan, Education Division (entry 66)

boxes 2,4

USAID Mission to Ethiopia. Education Division (entry 254)

box 2, 3, 4, 5

USAID Mission to Guatemala, Education Office (entry 420)

boxes 1, 2, 3

USAID, American University in Cairo and American University of Beirut (entry 549)

box 11

USAID Mission to Vietnam, Executive Office (entry 578)

boxes 26, 27

Records group 353, Records of Interdepartmental and
Intradepartmental Committees (State Department)

box 1

University of Arkansas Library, Fayetteville, AR, United States
Special Collections, Bureau of Educational and Cultural Affairs
Historical Collection

box 317, folder 17 (Germany)

State Archive of Russian Federation (GARF), Moscow, Russia
Records group P–7317, Files of the Soviet Military Administration
in Germany

folders 2, 3, 6, 11, 12, 14, 27, 37, 107

Records group P–7133, The Main Office of the Soviet Military
Administration in Germany, Sachsen–Anhalt

folder 273

Records group 9518, The Committee on Cultural Ties with Foreign
Countries at the Council of Ministers, 1957–1987

folder 883

Records group 9563, The Ministry of Education of the USSR,
1966–1988

folders 593, 1786, 2032, 3724, 4150, 4328, 4974, 5186, 5196, 5203

Records group 9606, The Ministry of Higher and Vocational
Education of the USSR

folders 48, 65, 128, 147, 162, 249, 301, 353, 354, 355, 1942, 1943, 2317, 6461

BIBLIOGRAPHY   235

Records group 9661, State Committee on People's Education,
1988–1991
folders 337, 589

*Russian State Archive of Social–Political History (RGASPI), Moscow,
Russia*
Records group 17, Central Committee of the Communist Party
folder 90

Russian State Archive of Modern History (RGANI), Moscow, Russia
Records group 5, Central Committee of Communist Party. Records
of the Education and Science Commission, 1949–1991
folders 55, 102, 180, 208.

Interviews

Shiriaev, Boris. *Soviet Advisor at Kabul University, 1983–1987.* Interviewed by Natalia Tsvetkova, September 25, 2013.

Published Documents

Department of State. 1988, 1989. *International Exchange and Training Programs of the
U.S. Government. Annual Reports.* Wash., D.C.: Bureau of Educational and Cultural
Affairs, United States Information Agency.
Espinosa, Manuel. 1976. *Inter-American Beginnings of U.S. Cultural Diplomacy, 1936–
1948.* Wash., D.C.: Department of State.
Kellermann, Henry. 1978. *Cultural Relations as an Instrument of US Foreign Policy: The
Educational Exchange Program between the United States and Germany, 1945–1954.*
Wash., D.C.: GPO.
National Council of Educational Statistics. "Digest of Educational Statistics 1997."
Accessed April 14, 2001. http://nces.ed.gov/pubs/digest97/d97t410.html.
National Security Council. "National Security Decision Directive 32. U.S. National
Security Strategy, May 20, 1982." Accessed July 08, 2020. www.fas.org.
National Security Council. "National Security Decision Directive 54. U.S. Policy Toward
Eastern Europe, September 2, 1982." Accessed July 08, 2020. https://fas.org/irp/
offdocs/nsdd/nsdd-54.pdf.
National Security Council. "National Security Decision Directive 223. Implementing
the Geneva Exchanges Initiative, April 02, 1986." Accessed July 08, 2020, https://fas
.org/irp/offdocs/nsdd/nsdd-223.htm.

National Security Council. "National Security Directive 194. Meeting with Soviet Leader in Geneva: Themes and Perceptions. October 25, 1985." Accessed July 08, 2020. https://fas.org/irp/offdocs/nsdd/index.html.

National Security Council. "National Security Directive 23. US Relations with Soviet Union. September 22, 1989." Accessed July 08, 2020, https://fas.org/irp/offdocs/nsd/nsd23.pdf.

Public Papers of President Ronald W. Reagan. "Statement by Principal Deputy Press Secretary Speaks on Soviet–United States Cultural and Educational Exchanges. August 05, 1986." Accessed July 08, 2020, http://www.reagan.utex.edu/archives.

Turner, Jim. 1988. *United States Foreign Assistance to Afghanistan. A History by Sector, 1952–1979.* Wash., D.C.: GPO.

U.S. Agency for International Development. "Altiplano Higher Education Development. A.I.D. Evaluation Summary. Part I, 1989." Accessed June, 05, 2020. www.usaid.gov.

U.S. Agency for International Development. "Contacts with Government of Afghanistan. Report. USAID/Kabul, April–May 1974." Accessed July 08, 2020. www.usaid.gov.

U.S. Agency for International Development. "Education Sector Support Project, AID Evaluation, 1986–1990." Accessed July 08, 2020. www.usaid.gov.

U.S. Agency for International Development. "Educational Development, Guatemala. Contract. USAID, 1974." Accessed June 05, 2020. www.usaid.gov.

U.S. Agency for International Development. "Evaluation and Planning for Secondary Education in South Vietnam by Ralph Purdy, Educational Consultant, part I, II August 1971." Accessed June 10, 2018. www.usaid.gov.

U.S. Agency for International Development. "Examination of USAID Assistance to the Afghanistan Education Sector. Audit Report, September 30, 1972." Accessed July 08, 2020. www.usaid.gov.

U.S. Agency for International Development. "Guatemala. Education Sector Assessment, 1985. USAID Report." Accessed June 05, 2020. www.usaid.gov.

U.S. Agency for International Development. "Higher Education – Kabul University. Revised PROP. Airgram from USAID/Kabul to AID/W, March 1, 1973." Accessed July 08, 2020. www.usaid.gov.

U.S. Agency for International Development. "Higher Education/Kabul University. Project Appraisal Report. University of Nebraska at Omaha, 1973–1976." Accessed July 08, 2020. www.usaid.gov.

U.S. Agency for International Development. "Kabul University Administration Improvement. Airgram, from AID/W to Kabul, November 11, 1969." Accessed July 08, 2020. www.usaid.gov.

U.S. Agency for International Development. "Letter by Olaf Bergelin to Education Office. USAID/Washington, November 05, 1970." Accessed July 08, 2020. www.usaid.gov.

BIBLIOGRAPHY

U.S. Agency for International Development. "Project Agreement between AID and DGBFA, Vietnam. Higher Education, 1971–1973." Accessed June 10, 2018. www.usaid .gov.

U.S. Agency for International Development. "Project Agreement between The Department of State, Agency for International Development, The United States of America, and The Directorate of General for Budget and Foreign Aid, Vietnam, 1969–1971." Accessed June 10, 2018. www.usaid.gov.

U.S. Agency for International Development. "Project Agreement between the Department of State, Agency for International Development of the United States of America and the Ministries of Education and Economy, Guatemala, 1954. Educational Project, 1973." Accessed June 05, 2020. www.usaid.gov.

U.S. Agency for International Development. "Report of Visit to the United States Engineering Team (USET) Kabul, Afghanistan by R.G. Carson, Chairman, Kabul Afghan-American Program Steering Committee, March 12–28,1970." Accessed July 08, 2020. www.usaid.gov.

U.S. Agency for International Development. "Report. English Language Programs of the Agency for International Development." Accessed June 10, 2018. www.usaid.gov.

U.S. Agency for International Development. "Retrospective Review of US Assistance to Afghanistan: 1950–1979. Report by USAID, 1988." Accessed July 08, 2020. www .usaid.gov.

U.S. Agency for International Development. "Teacher Education. Project Agreement between The Department of State, Agency for International Development, The United States of America, and The Directorate of General for Budget and Foreign Aid, Vietnam, 1970–1973." Accessed June 10, 2018. www.usaid.gov.

U.S. Agency for International Development. "Technical Education. Faculty of Engineering. Kabul University. Project Appraisal Report, 1970–72." Accessed July 08, 2020. www.usaid.gov.

U.S. Agency for International Development. "Technical Manpower Development for Afghanistan at Kabul University, Report, USAID, October 20, 1977." Accessed July 08, 2020. www.usaid.gov.

U.S. Agency for International Development. "Terminal Project Assessment Report. Education Planning, Administration and Research, 1971–1974." Accessed June 10, 2018. www.usaid.gov.

U.S. Agency for International Development. "The Technical Education Project. Airgram from USAID/Kabul, 1969." Accessed July 08, 2020. www.usaid.gov.

U.S. Agency for International Development. "U.S. Overseas Loans and Grants: Obligations and Loan Authorizations, July 1, 1945–September 30, 2017." Accessed, June 05, 2020. https://explorer.usaid.gov.

U.S. Agency for International Development. "University Francisco Marroquin, Guatemala. Contract. USAID, 1984–1985." Accessed June 05, 2020. www.usaid.gov.

238 BIBLIOGRAPHY

U.S. Congress. "Support Eastern Europe Democracies. Public Law 179, 101 Congress. November 28, 1989." Accessed July 08, 2020. https://www.congress.gov/101/statute/STATUTE-103/STATUTE-103-Pg1298.pdf.

U.S. Congress. 1938. *U.S. Statutes at Large.* Vol. 51. 1937. Wash., D.C.: GPO.

U.S. Department of State. 1942. *Report of the Division on Cultural Cooperation, 1940–1942.* Wash., D.C.: GPO.

U.S. Department of State. 1949. *U.S. Advisory Commission on Information. Semiannual Report to the Congress, March 1949.* Wash., D.C.: GPO.

U.S. Department of States. 1947. *History of the Office of the Coordinator of Inter-American Affairs.* Wash., D.C.: GPO.

U.S. White House, "Address by Franklin D. Roosevelt, 1933." Accessed October 11, 2018. http://www.fdrlibrary.marist.edu/aboutfdr/inaugurations.html.

Literature

Abuza, Zachary. "The Politics of Educational Diplomacy in Vietnam." *Asian Survey* 36, no. 6 (1996): 618–31.

Aguilar, Manuela. *Cultural Diplomacy and Foreign Policy: German-American Relations, 1955–1968.* New York: Peter Lang Inc., 1996.

Aldrich, Richard. "The Struggle for the Mind of European Youth: The CIA and European Movement Propaganda, 1948–1960." In *Cold-War Propaganda in the 1950s,* edited by Gary Rawnsley, 183–203. London: Palgrave Macmillan, 1999.

Alexandre, Laurien. *The Voice of America: From Détente to the Reagan Doctrine.* Norwood, NJ: Ablex Publishing Corp., 1988.

Amin, Tahir. "Afghan Resistance: Past, Present, and Future." *Asian Survey* 24, no. 4 (April 1984): 373–99.

Amsing, Hilda, Linda Greveling, and Jeroen Dekker. "The Struggle for Comprehensive Education in the Netherlands: The Representation of Secondary School Innovation in Dutch Newspaper Articles in the 1970s." *History of Education* 42, no. 4 (2013): 460–85.

Anderson, Betty. *American University of Beirut: Arab Nationalism and Liberal Education.* Austin: University of Texas Press, 2012.

Arndt, Richard. *The First Resort of Kings: American Cultural Diplomacy in the Twentieth Century.* Dulles, VA: Potomac Books, 2005.

Arnove, Robert. *Philanthropy and Cultural Imperialism: The Foundations at Home and Abroad.* Bloomington: Indiana University Press, 1982.

Atkinson, Carol. "Does Soft Power Matter? A Comparative Analysis of Student Exchange Programs 1980–2006." *Foreign Policy Analysis* 6, no. 1 (2010): 1–22.

BIBLIOGRAPHY

Autio-Sarasmo, Sari, and Katalin Miklóssy. *Reassessing Cold War Europe*. New York: Routledge, 2011.

Ayele, Fantahun. "A Brief History of Bahir Dar University." Accessed March 10, 2020. https://bdu.edu.et/sites/default/folders/A%20Brief%20History%20of%20BDU.pdf.

Babiracki, Patryk, and Kenyon Zimmer. *Cold War Crossings: International Travel and Exchange across the Soviet Bloc, 1940s–1960s*. College Station: Texas A&M Univ. Press, 2014.

Barfield, Thomas. *Afghanistan: A Cultural and Political History*. Princeton: Princeton University Press, 2010.

Barghoorn, Frederick. *The Soviet Cultural Offensive: The Role of Cultural Diplomacy in Soviet Foreign Policy*. Princeton: Princeton University Press, 1960.

Bartley, Russell. "The Piper Played to Us All: Orchestrating the Cultural Cold War in the USA, Europe, and Latin America." *International Journal of Politics, Culture & Society* 14, no. 3 (2001): 571–619.

Berghahn, Volker. *The Americanization of West German Industry, 1945–1973*. Leamington Spa: Berg, 1986.

Berman, Edward. *The Influence of the Carnegie, Ford and Rockefeller Foundations on American Foreign Policy: The Ideology of Philanthropy*. Albany: State University of New York Press, 1983.

Blakeley, Ruth. "Still Training to Torture? US Training of Military Forces from Latin America." *Third World Quarterly* 27, no. 8 (2006.): 1439–61.

Bocock, Jean, Lewis Baston, Peter Scott, and David Smith. "American Influence on British Higher Education: Science, Technology, and the Problem of University Expansion, 1945–1963." *Minerva: A Review of Science, Learning & Policy* 41, no. 4 (2003): 327–46.

Bogatyrev, Nikita. *Democratization of German Schools after the Liberation of Germany: Materials of the Ministry of Education in Thüringen, 1945–1949*. PhD Dissertation. Moscow: Academy of Education Sciences, 1951.

Bourdieu, Pierre. "Cultural Reproduction and Social Reproduction." In *Power and Ideology in Education*, edited by Jerome Karabel and A. H. Halsey, 487–510. New York: Oxford University Press, 1977.

Braithwaite, Rodric. "The Russians in Afghanistan." *Asian Affairs* 42, no. 2 (2011): 213–29.

Brind, Harry. "Soviet Policy in the Horn of Africa." *International Affairs* 60, no. 1 (1983): 75–95.

Broich, Tobias. "U.S. And Soviet Foreign Aid During the Cold War: A Case Study of Ethiopia." *Working Papers* no. 10 (2017). Accessed March 10, 2020. https://www.merit.unu.edu/publications/working-papers/abstract/?id=6367.

Brooks, Chay. "The Ignorance of the Uneducated": Ford Foundation Philanthropy, the IIE, and the Geographies of Educational Exchange." *Journal of Historical Geography*, no. 48 (2015): 36–46.

240 BIBLIOGRAPHY

Bucznska-Garewicz, Hanna. "The Flying University in Poland, 1978–1980." *Harvard Educational Review* 55, no. 1 (1985): 20–33.

Carnoy, Martin. *Education as Cultural Imperialism*. New York: McKay, 1974.

Carr, Graham. "Diplomatic Notes: American Musicians and Cold War Politics in the Near and Middle East, 1954–60." *Popular Music History* 1, no. 1 (2004): 37–63.

Castagneto, Pierangelo. "Ambassador Dizzy: Jazz Diplomacy in the Cold War Era." *Americana: E-Journal of American Studies in Hungary* 10, no. 1 (2014). Accessed March 15, 2020. http://americanaejournal.hu/vol10jazz/castagneto.

Caute, David. *The Dancer Defects: The Struggle for Cultural. Supremacy During the Cold War*. Oxford: Oxford University Press, 2003.

Clay, Lucius. *Decision in Germany*. London: Doubleday & Co., 1950.

Clouser, Rebecca. "Facing Fear: The Importance of Engaging with Fear in Development Literature." *Progress in Development Studies* 14, no. 2 (2014): 131–46.

Clouser, Rebecca. "Security, Development, and Fear in Guatemala: Enduring Ties and Lasting Consequences." *Geographical Review* 109, no. 3 (2019): 382–98.

Coldren, Lee. "Afghanistan in 1984: The Fifth Year of the Russo-Afghan War." *Asian Survey* 25, no. 2. A Survey of Asia in 1984: Part II (February 1985): 169–79.

Connelly, John. *Captive University: the Sovietization of East German, Czech, and Polish Higher Education, 1945–1956*. Chapel Hill: University of North Carolina Press, 2000.

Cull, Nicholas. "'The Man Who Invented Truth': The Tenure of Edward R. Murrow as Director of the United States Information Agency During the Kennedy Years." *Cold War History* 4, no. 1 (2003): 23–48.

Cull, Nicholas. *The Cold War and the United States Information Agency: American Propaganda and Public Diplomacy 1945–1989*. Cambridge: UK: Cambridge University Press, 2008.

Cull, Nicholas. *The Decline and Fall of the United States Information Agency: American Public Diplomacy, 1989–2001*. New York: Palgrave Macmillan, 2012.

Cull, Nick. "The Cold War on the Silver Screen." *Diplomatic History* 33, no. 2 (2009): 357–59.

Cullather, Nick. "Damming Afghanistan: Modernization in a Buffer State." *The Journal of American History* 89, no. 2 (September 2002): 512–37.

Curti, Merle. *American Philanthropy Abroad*. New Brunswick, NJ: Transaction Books, 1963.

Daniel, Robert. *American Philanthropy in the Near East, 1820–1960*. Athens, Ohio: Ohio University Press, 1970.

Darnton, Christopher. *Rivalry and Alliance Politics in Cold War Latin America*. Baltimore: Johns Hopkins University Press, 2014.

David-Fox, Michael. *Showcasing the Great Experiment: Cultural Diplomacy and Western Visitors to the Soviet Union, 1921–1941*. New York: Oxford University Press, 2014.

BIBLIOGRAPHY

241

David-Fox, Michael. "The 'Heroic Life' of a Friend of Stalinism: Romain Rolland and Soviet Culture." *Slavonica* 11, no. 1 (2005): 3–29.

David-Fox, Michael. "The Fellow Travelers Revisited: The Cultured West Through Soviet Eyes." *The Journal of Modern History* 75, no. 2 (2003): 300–335.

de Castro, Renato Cruz. "Explaining the Duterte Administration's Appeasement Policy on China: The Power of Fear." *Asian Affairs: An American Review* 45, no. 3/4 (2018): 165–91.

Dizard, Wilson, Jr. *Inventing Public Diplomacy: The Story of the U.S. Information Agency.* Boulder, CO: Lynne Rienner Publishers, 2004.

Drozdova, Katya, and Joseph H. Felte. "Leaving Afghanistan: Enduring Lessons from the Soviet Politburo." *Journal of Cold War Studies* 21, no. 4 (2019): 31–70.

Edwards, David. *Before Taliban: Genealogies of the Afghan Jihad.* Berkeley: University of California Press, 2002.

Elkind, Jessica. *Aid Under Fire: Nation Building and the Vietnam War.* Lexington: University Press of Kentucky, 2016.

Emadi, Hafizullah. "Radical Political Movements in Afghanistan and Their Politics of Peoples' Empowerment and Liberation," *Central Asian Survey* 20, no. 4 (December 2001): 427–50.

Endy, Christopher. *Cold War Holidays: American Tourism in France.* Chapel Hill: University of North Carolina Press, 2004.

Engerman, David. *Staging Growth: Modernization, Development, and the Global Cold War.* Amherst: University of Massachusetts Press, 2003.

Estevez, Pino. *Distant Education of Secondary School Teachers at Higher Pedagogical Institutes of Cuba.* PhD Thesis. Minsk: Minsk State University, 1984.

Fayet, Jean. "VOKS: The Third Dimension of Soviet Foreign Policy." In *Searching for a Cultural Diplomacy*, edited Jessica Gienow-Hecht and Mark Donfried, 33–49. New York: Berghahn Books, 2013.

Feis, Herbert. *Foreign Aid and Foreign Policy.* New York: Dell Pub. Co., 1966.

Foglesong, David. *The American Mission and the "Evil Empire:" The Crusade for a "Free Russia" since 1881.* New York: Cambridge University Press, 2007.

Foglesong, David. "When the Russians Really Were Coming: Citizen Diplomacy and the End of Cold War Enmity in America." *Cold War History* 20, no. 4 (November 2020): 419–40.

Fosler-Lussier, Daniella. "Music Pushed, Music Pulled: Cultural Diplomacy, Globalization, and Imperialism." *Diplomatic History* 36, no. 1 (2012): 53–64.

Freedman, Lawrence. 2002. *Kennedy's Wars: Berlin, Cuba, Laos, and Vietnam.* New York: Oxford University Press, 2002.

Gaddis, John Lewis. *Strategies of Containment: A Critical Appraisal of American National Security Policy During the Cold War.* New York: Oxford University Press, 2005.

Gaddis, John Lewis. *The Cold War: A New History.* New York: Penguin Press, 2005.

Gaddis, John Lewis. 1997. *We Now Know: Rethinking Cold War History*. New York: Oxford University Press, 1997.

Garcia, Oscar. "A Complicated Mission: The United States and Spanish Students during the Johnson Administration." *Cold War History* 13, no. 3 (2013): 311–29.

Geck, Wilhelm. "Student Power in West Germany: The Authority of the Student Body and Student Participation in Decision–Making in the Universities of the Federal Republic of Germany." *The American Journal of Comparative Law* 17, no. 3 (1969): 337–58.

Geoghegan, Kate. "A Policy in Tension: The National Endowment for Democracy and the U.S. Response to the Collapse of the Soviet Union." *Diplomatic History* 42, no. 5 (2018): 772–801.

Gienow-Hecht, Jessica. "Academics, Cultural Transfer, and the Cold War – A Critical Review." *Diplomatic History* 24, no. 3 (Summer 2000): 465–95.

Gienow-Hecht, Jessica. *Transmission Impossible: American Journalism as Cultural Diplomacy in Post-War Germany, 1945–55*. Baton Rouge: Louisiana State University Press, 1990.

Giles, Geoffrey. "Reeducation at Heidelberg University." *Paedagogika Historica* 33. no. 1 (1996): 201–19.

Gilman, Nils. *Mandarins of the Future: Modernization Theory in Cold War America*. Baltimore: Johns Hopkins University Press, 2007.

Glade, William. "Issues in the Genesis and Organization of Cultural Diplomacy: A Brief Critical History." *Journal of Arts Management, Law & Society* 39, no. 4 (Winter 2009): 240–59.

Gleijeses, Piero. "Moscow's Proxy? Cuba and Africa 1975–1988." *Journal of Cold War Studies* 8, no. 2 (2006): 3–51.

Gordon, Johnston. "Revisiting the Cultural Cold War." *Social History* 35, no. 3 (August 2010): 290–307.

Gramsci, Antonio. *Selections from the Prisons Notebooks*. New York: International Publishers, 1971.

Gregory, Tomlin. *Murrow's Cold War: Public Diplomacy for the Kennedy Administration*. Lincoln: Potomac Books, 2016.

Greveling, Linda, Hilda Amsing, and Jeroen Dekker. "Crossing borders in educational innovation: Framing foreign examples in discussing comprehensive education in the Netherlands, 1969–1979." *Paedagogica Historica* 50, no. 1/2 (2014): 76–92.

Griffiths, Tom G., and Euridice Charon Cardona. "Education for Social Transformation: Soviet University Education Aid in the Cold War Capitalist World-System." *European Education* 47, no. 3 (2015): 226–41.

Gurantz, Ron, and Alexander V. Hirsch. "Fear, Appeasement, and the Effectiveness of Deterrence." *Journal of Politics* 79, no. 3 (2017): 1041–56.

Hafsteinsson, Sigurjóón Baldur, and Tinna Gréétarsdóóttir. "Screening Propaganda: The Reception of Soviet and American Film Screenings in Rural Iceland, 1950–1975." *Film History* 23, no. 4 (2011): 361–75.

BIBLIOGRAPHY

243

Harmer, Tanya. "The 'Cuban Question' and the Cold War in Latin America, 1959–1964." *Journal of Cold War Studies* 21, no. 3 (2019): 114–51.

Hatschek, Keith. "The Impact of American Jazz Diplomacy in Poland During the Cold War Era." *Jazz Perspectives* 4, no. 3 (2010): 253–300.

Heinemann, Manfred. "Interview mit Pjotr I. Nikitin." In *Hochschuloffiziere und Wiederaufbau des Hochschulwesens in Deutschland 1945–1949. Die sowjetische Besatzungszone*, edited by Manfred Heinemann, 75–146. Berlin: Akad.–Verlag, 2009.

Heinemann, Manfred. *Hochschuloffiziere und Wiederaufbau des Hochschulwesens in Deutschland 1945–1949. Die sowjetische Besatzungszone*. Berlin: Akad.–Verlag, 2000.

Herring, George. "The Cold War and Vietnam." *OAH Magazine of History* 18, no. 5 (2004): 18–21.

Hesse, Jan-Otmar. "The 'Americanisation' of West German Economics after the Second World War: Success, Failure, or Something Completely Different?" *European Journal of the History of Economic Thought* 19, no. 1 (2012): 67–98.

Hixson, Walter. *Parting the Curtain: Propaganda, Culture, and the Cold War, 1945–1961*. New York: St. Martin's, 1997.

Hopf, Ted. "The Promise of Constructivism in International Relations Theory." *International Security*, 23, no. 1 (1998): 171–200.

Hopkins, Michael F. "Continuing Debate and New Approaches in Cold War History." *Historical Journal* 50, no. 4 (December 2007): 913–34.

Hornsby, Robert. "The Post-Stalin Komsomol and the Soviet Fight for Third World Youth." *Cold War History* 16, no. 1 (February 2016): 83–100.

Hughes, Geraint. "The Cold War and Counter-Insurgency." *Diplomacy & Statecraft* 22, no. 1 (March 2011): 142–63.

Hyman, Anthony. "The Struggle for Afghanistan." *The World Today* 40, no. 7 (July 1984): 276–84.

Ickstadt, Heinz. "Uniting a Divided Nation: Americanism and Anti-Americanism in Post-War Germany." *European Journal of American Culture* 23, no. 2 (June 2004): 157–70.

Kaiser, Tim, Tobias Kriele, Ingrid Miethe, and Alexandra Piepiorka. "Educational Transfers in Postcolonial Contexts: Preliminary Results from Comparative Research on Workers' Faculties in Vietnam, Cuba, and Mozambique." *European Education* 47, no. 3 (2015): 242–59.

Kalinovsky, Artemy. *Laboratory of Socialist Development: Cold War Politics and Decolonization in Soviet Tajikistan*. Ithaca: Cornell University Press, 2018.

Kanet, Roger E. "Soviet and American Behaviour Toward the Developing Countries—A Comparison," *Canadian Slavonic Papers/Revue Canadienne Des Slavistes* 15, no. 4 (1973): 439–61.

Kelley, John. "U.S. Public Diplomacy: A Cold War Success Story?" *The Hague Journal of Diplomacy* 2 (2007): 53–79.

Kissi, Edward. "Paradoxes of American Development Diplomacy in the Early Cold War Period." *Past & Present* 215, no. 1 (2012): 269–95.

Klimke, Martin. *The Other Alliance. Student Protest in West Germany and the United States in the Global Sixties*. Princeton: Princeton University Press, 2010.

Knauer, Georg. "Professor Knauer's Resignation from the Free University of Berlin." *Minerva* 12, no. 4 (1974): 510–14.

Kuisel, Richard. *Seducing the French: The Dilemma of Americanization*. Berkeley University of California Press, 1993.

Lasch, Christopher. "The Cultural Cold War." *The Nation,* (11 September, 1967).

Lasch, Christopher. *The Agony of American Left*. New York: Alfred A. Knopf, 1969.

Latham, Michael. *Modernization as ideology: American Social Science and "Nation Building" in the Kennedy Era*. Chapel Hill: University of North Carolina Press, 2006.

Latham, Michael. *The Right Kind of Revolution Modernization, Development, and US Foreign Policy from the Cold War to the Present*. Ithaca: Cornell University Press, 2011.

Lebovic, Sam. "From War Junk to Educational Exchange: The World War II Origins of the Fulbright Program and the Foundations of American Cultural Globalism, 1945–1950." *Diplomatic History* 37, no. 2 (2013): 280–312.

Leffler, Melvyn P., and Odd A. Westad. *The Cambridge History of the Cold War*. Vols. 1–3. Cambridge: Cambridge University Press, 2011.

Legesse, Lemma. "The Ethiopian Student Movement 1960–1974: A Challenge to the Monarchy and Imperialism in Ethiopia." *Northeast African Studies* 1, no. 2 (1979): 31–46.

Liddell, Helen. "Education in Occupied Germany: A Field Study." *International Affairs (Royal Institute of International Affairs 1944–)* 24, no. 1 (1948): 30–62.

Loth, Wilfried. "The German Question from Stalin to Khrushchev: The Meaning of New Documents." *Cold War History* 10, no. 2 (May 2010): 229–45.

Lunden, Rolf. *Networks of Americanization: Aspects of American Influence in Sweden*. Uppsala, Stockholm: Almqvist & Wiksell International, 1992.

Martinez, Edda, and Edward Suchman. "Letters from America and the 1948 Elections in Italy." *The Public Opinion Quarterly* 14, No. 1 (1950): 111–25.

McKenzie, Brian. *Remaking France: Americanization, Public Diplomacy, and the Marshall Plan*. New York: Berghahn Books, 2008.

McNair, John. "Winning Friends, Influencing People: Soviet Cultural Diplomacy in Australia, 1928–1968." *Australian Journal of Politics and History* 61, no. 4 (2015) 515–29.

McVety, Amanda Kay. "Pursuing Progress: Point Four in Ethiopia." *Diplomatic History* 32, no. 3 (June 2008): 371–403.

Meisler, Stanley. *When the World Calls: The Inside Story of the Peace Corps and Its First Fifty Years*. Boston: Beacon Press, 2011.

Metaferia, Getachew. *Ethiopia and the United States: History, Diplomacy, and Analysis*. New Your Algora Publishing, 2008.

Mickiewicz, Ellen. "Efficacy and Evidence: Evaluating U.S. Goals at the American National Exhibition in Moscow, 1959." *Journal of Cold War Studies* 13, no. 4 (2011): 138–71.

BIBLIOGRAPHY 245

Mikkonen, Simo, and Pia Koivunen. *Beyond the Divide: Entangled Histories of Cold War Europe*. New York: Berghahn Books, 2015.

Mikkonen, Simo. "Interference or Friendly Gestures? Soviet Cultural Diplomacy and Finnish Elections, 1945–56." *Cold War History* 20, no. 3 (2020): 349–65.

Mikkonen, Simo. "The Finnish-Soviet Society: From Political to Cultural Connections." In *Nordic Cold War Cultures: Ideological Promotion, Public Reception, and East-West Interactions*, edited by Valur Ingimundarson and Rosa Magnusdottir, 109_31. Helsinki, Aleksanteri Institute, 2015.

Mikonnen, Simo. "Mass Communications as a Vehicle to Lure Russian Émigrés Homeward." *Journal of International and Global Studies* 2, no. 2 (2011): 45–61.

Mistry, Kaeten. "The Case for Political Warfare: Strategy, Organization and US Involvement in the 1948 Italian Election." *Cold War History* 6, no. 3 (2006): 301–29.

Mueller, Tim. "The Rockefeller Foundation, the Social Sciences, and the Humanities in the Cold War." *Journal of Cold War Studies* 15, no. 3 (2013): 108–35.

Naimark, Norman. *The Russians in Germany: a History of Soviet Zone of Occupation, 1945–1949*. Cambridge, MA, London: The Belknap Press of Harvard University Press, 1995.

Nguyen, Lien-Hang. *Hanoi's War: An International History of the War for Peace in Vietnam*. Chapel Hill: The University of North Carolina Press, 2016.

Nguyen, Thuy-Phuong. "The Rivalry of the French and American Educational Missions during the Vietnam War." *Paedagogica Historica* 50, no. 1/2 (2014): 27–41.

Nikitin, Andrey. *The Activity of the Soviet Military Administration in the Democratization of German Higher Education, 1945–1949*. PhD Dissertation. Moscow: Moscow State Historical Archival Institute, 1986.

Ninkovich, Frank. *The Diplomacy of Ideas: U.S. Foreign Policy and Cultural Relations, 1938–1950*. New York: Cambridge University Press, 1981.

Oldenziel, Ruth, and Karin Zachmann. *Cold War Kitchen: Americanization, Technology, and European Users*. Cambridge, MA: MIT Press, 2011.

Osgood, Kenneth A., and Brian Etheridge. *The United States and Public Diplomacy: New Directions in Cultural and International History*. Leiden: Martinus Nijhoff Publishers, 2010.

Osgood, Kenneth. "Form before Substance: Eisenhower's Commitment to Psychological Warfare and Negotiations with the Enemy." *Diplomatic History* 24, no. 3 (2000): 405–33.

Pakin, Esra. "American Studies in Turkey during the Cultural Cold War." *Turkish Studies* 9, no. 3 (2008): 507–24.

Paperny, Vladimir. "Hot and Cold War in Architecture of Soviet Pavilions." In *Architecture of Great Expositions 1937–1959: Messages of Peace, Images of War*, edited by Rika Devos, Alexander Ortenberg, and Vladimir Paperny, 81–98. New York: Routledge, 2016.

Paulet, Anne. "To Change the World: The Use of American Indian Education in the Philippines." *History of Education Quarterly* 47, no. 2 (2007):173–202.

Paulus, Stefan. "The Americanisation of Europe after 1945? The Case of the German Universities." *European Review of History* 9, no. 2 (2002): 241–53.

Peacock, Margaret. "Samantha Smith in the Land of the Bolsheviks: Peace and the Politics of Childhood in the Late Cold War." *Diplomatic History* 43, no. 3 (2019): 418–44.

Peacock, Margaret. "The Perils of Building Cold War Consensus at the 1957 Moscow World Festival of Youth and Students." *Cold War History* 12, no. 3 (2012): 515–35.

Pells, Richard. *Not Like US: How Europeans Have Loved, Hated, and Transformed American Culture since World War II*. New York: Basic Books, 1997.

Pettinà, Vanni. "The Shadows of Cold War over Latin America: The US Reaction to Fidel Castro's Nationalism, 1956–59." *Cold War History* 11, no. 3 (August 2011): 317–39.

Phillips, Sarah, and Hamilton Shane. *The Kitchen Debate and Cold War Consumer Politics: A Brief History with Documents*. New York: Macmillan Higher Education, 2014.

Pittway, Mark. "The Education of Dissent: The Reception of Voice of Free Hungary, 1951–1956." In *Across the Blocs: Cold War Cultural and Social History*, edited by Rana Mitter and Patrick Major, 97–116. London: Frank Cass, 2004.

Puddington, Arch. *Broadcasting Freedom: The Cold War Triumph of Radio Free Europe and Radio Liberty*. Lexington: The University Press of Kentucky, 2015.

Reeves-Ellington, Barbara. "Vision of Mount Holyoke in the Ottoman Balkans: American Cultural Transfer, Bulgarian Nation-Building and Women's Educational Reform, 1858–1870." *Gender & History* 16, no. 1 (2004): 146–71.

Reid, Susan. "Who Will Beat Whom? Soviet Popular Reception of the American National Exhibition in Moscow, 1959." *Kritika: Explorations in Russian and Eurasian History* 9, no. 4 (2008); 855–904.

Richmond, Yale. "Cultural Exchange and the Cold War: How the West Won." *American Communist History* 9, no. 1 (2010): 61–75.

Richmond, Yale. *Cultural Exchange and the Cold War: Raising the Iron Curtain*. State College, Pennsylvania: Penn State University Press, 2003.

Richmond, Yale. *Practicing Public Diplomacy: A Cold War Odyssey*. New York: Berghahn Books, 2008.

Rider, Tobe. "A Campaign of Truth: The State Department, Propaganda, and the Olympic Games, 1950–1952." *Journal of Cold War Studies* 18, no. 2 (2016): 4–27.

Robin, Corey. *Fear: The History of a Political Idea*. New York: Oxford University Press, 2004.

Rodden, John. "The Galileo of the GDR: Robert Havemann." *Debatte* 14, no. 1 (2006): 37–48.

Rosenberg, Victor. *Soviet-American Relations, 1953–1960: Diplomacy and Cultural Exchange during the Eisenhower Presidency*. Jefferson: NC: McFarland & Company, 2005.

Rubin, Barnett. "Post-Cold War State Disintegration: The Failure of International Conflict Resolution in Afghanistan." *Journal of International Affairs* 46, no. 2 (January 1993): 469–92.

BIBLIOGRAPHY

Sanjian, Gregory. "Promoting Stability or Instability? Arms Transfers and Regional Rivalries, 1950–1991." *International Studies Quarterly* 43, no. 4 (1999): 641–70.

Saunders, Frances. *Who Paid the Piper? The CIA and the Cultural Cold War*. London: Granta, 2005.

Schmitz, David. *Richard Nixon and the Vietnam War: The End of the American Century*. Blue Ridge Summit, PA: Rowman & Littlefield Publishers, 2014.

Schweizer, Peter. *Reagan's War: The Epic Story of His Forty-Year Struggle and Final Triumph over Communism*. Westminster, MD: Doubleday Publishing, 2003.

Scott-Smith, Giles. *Politics of Apolitical Culture: Congress for Cultural Freedom, and the CIA and Post-War American Hegemony*. London: Routledge, 2002.

Scott-Smith, Giles. "Aristotle, US Public Diplomacy, and the Cold War: The Work of Carnes Lord." *Foundations of Science* 13, no. 3/4 (2008): 251–64.

Scott-Smith, Giles. "Confronting Peaceful Co-existence: Psychological Warfare and the Role of Interdoc, 1963–72." *Cold War History* 7, no. 1 (2007): 19–43.

Scott-Smith, Giles. "Maintaining Transatlantic Community: US Public Diplomacy, the Ford Foundation and the Successor Generation Concept in US Foreign Affairs, 1960s–1980s." *Global Society: Journal of Interdisciplinary International Relations* 28, no. 1 (2014): 90–103.

Scott-Smith, Giles. "Mapping the Undefinable: Some Thoughts on the Relevance of Exchange Programmes Within International Relations Theory." *Annals of the Academy of Political and Social Science*. No. 616 (2008): 173–95.

Scott-Smith, Giles. "Mending the "Unhinged Alliance" in the 1970s: Transatlantic Relations, Public Diplomacy, and the Origins of the European Union Visitors Program." *Diplomacy & Statecraft* 16, no. 4 (2005): 749–78.

Scott-Smith, Giles. "Networks of Influence: U.S. Exchange Programs and Western Europe in the 1980s." In *The United States and Public Diplomacy: New Directions in Cultural and International History*, edited by Kenneth Osgood and Brian Etheridge, 345–70. Leiden: Martinus Nijhoff Publishers, 2010.

Scott-Smith, Giles. "The Free Europe University in Strasbourg." *Journal of Cold War Studies* 16, no. 2 (2014): 77–107.

Scott-Smith, Giles. 2002. *Politics of Apolitical Culture: Congress for Cultural Freedom, and the CIA and Post-War American Hegemony*. Florence, KY: Routledge.

Selvaratnam, Viswanathan. "Higher Education Co-Operation and Western Dominance of Knowledge Creation and Flows in Third World Countries." *Higher Education* 17, no. 1 (1988): 41–68.

Sewell, Bevan, and Nataliya Petrova. *The US and Latin America: Eisenhower, Kennedy and Economic Diplomacy in the Cold War*. London: I. B. Tauris & Co. Ltd., 2002.

Siegelbaum, Lewis. "Sputnik Goes to Brussels: The Exhibition of a Soviet Technological Wonder." *Journal of Contemporary History* 47, no. 1 (2012): 120–36.

Simpson, Brad. "Indonesia's Accelerated Modernization and the Global Discourse of Development, 1960–197." *Diplomatic History* 33, no. 3 (2009): 467–86.

Sirat, Abdul Sarat. "Sharia and Islamic Education in Modern Afghanistan." *Middle East Journal* 23, no. 2 (Spring 1969): 217–19.

Sorensen, Theodore. *The Word War: The Story of American Propaganda*. New York: Harper & Row Publishers, 1968.

Swenson, Geoffrey, and Eli Sugerman. "Building the Rule of Law in Afghanistan: The Importance of Legal Education." *Hague Journal of The Rule of Law* 3, no. 1 (March 2011): 130–46.

Tang, Shiping. "Fear in International Politics: Two Positions." *International Studies Review* 10, no. 3 (2008): 451–71.

Tent, James. *Mission on the Rhine: Reeducation and Denazification in American–Occupied Germany*. Chicago: University of Chicago Press, 1982.

Thomas, Daniel. "Human Rights Ideas, the Demise of Communism, and the End of the Cold War." *Journal of Cold War Studies* 7, no. 2 (2005): 110–41.

Thomson, Charles A., and Walter H. C. Laves. , Walter H. C. *Cultural Relations and U. S. Foreign Policy*. Bloomington: Indiana University Press, 1963.

Tibi, Bassam. "Culture and Knowledge: The Politics of Islamization of Knowledge as a Postmodern Project? The Fundamentalist Claim to De-Westernization," *Theory, Culture & Society* no. 12 (1995): 1–24.

Tobia, Simona. "Introduction: Europe Americanized? Popular Reception of Western Cold War Propaganda in Europe." *Cold War History* 11, no. 1 (2011): 1–7.

Tomlinson, John. *Cultural Imperialism: A Critical Introduction*. Baltimore: Johns Hopkins University Press, 1991.

Tsipursky, Gleb. "Active and Conscious Builders of Communism: State-Sponsored Tourism for Soviet Adolescents in the Early Cold War, 1945–53." *Journal of Social History* 48, no. 1 (2014): 20–46.

Tsvetkova, Natalia, Ivan Tsvetkov, Ivan, Irina Barber. "Americanization versus Sovietization: Film exchanges Between the United States and the Soviet Union, 1948–1950." *Cogent Arts & Humanities* 5, no.1 (2018): 1–17.

Tsvetkova, Natalia. 2013. *Failure of American and Soviet Cultural Imperialism in German Universities, 1945–1990*. Leiden, Netherlands: Brill, 2013.

Tsvetkova, Natalia. "Americanisation, Sovietisation, and resistance at Kabul University: limits of the educational reforms." *History of Education* 46, no. 3 (May 2017): 336–43.

Tsvetkova, Natalia. "Education of Russia in Asia-Pacific Region: Forgotten Lessons from the legacy of the Soviet Union and Recent Experience of American educational Policy, Russian Council for International Affairs." Accessed August 04, 2019. http://russiancouncil.ru/inner/index.php?id_4=986.

Tsvetkova, Natalia. "International Education during the Cold War: Soviet Social Transformation and American Social Reproduction." *Comparative Education Review* 52, no. 2 (2008): 199–217.

Tsvetkova, Natalia. "Making a New and Pliable Professor: American and Soviet Transformations in German Universities, 1945–1990." *Minerva,* no. 52 (2014): 161–85.

BIBLIOGRAPHY   249

Tsvetkova, Natalia. "Universities During the Cultural Cold War: Mapping the Research Agenda." In *Entangled East and West: Cultural Diplomacy during the Cold War*, edited by Simo Mikkonen, Jari Parkkinen, and Giles Scott-Smith, 132–56. Berlin: De Gruyter Saur, 2018.

Tsvetkova, Natalia. "Why is Cultural Imperialism Impossible? The US and USSR Policy in German Universities during the Cold War." *Ab Imperio*. N no. 2 (2017): 144–75.

van Ham, Peter. "Power, Public Diplomacy and the Pax Americana." In *The New Public Diplomacy: Soft Power in International Relations*, edited by Jan Melissen, 47–66. New York: Palgrave Macmillan, 2007.

van Vleck, Jenifer. "An Airline at the Crossroads of the World: Ariana Afghan Airlines, Modernization, and the Global Cold War." *History & Technology* 25, no. 1 (March 2009): 3–24.

Vorobjev, Nikoly. *Higher Education in the Democratic Republic of Germany*. Rostov: University of Rostov Press, 1972.

Vowinckel, Annette, Marcus Payk, and Thomas Lindenberger. *Cold War Cultures: Perspectives on Eastern and Western Societies*. New York: Berghahn Books, 2012.

Wafadar, K. "Afghanistan in 1981: The Struggle Intensifies," *Asian Survey* 22, no. 2. A Survey of Asia in 1981: Part II (April 1982): 147–54.

Wagnleitner, Reinhold. *Coca-Colonization and the Cold War: Cultural Transmission of United States in Austria after the Second World War*. Chapel Hill: University of North Carolina Press, 1994.

Wagnleitner, Reinhold. "The Empire of the Fun, or Talkin' Soviet Union Blues: The Sound of Freedom and Cultural Hegemony in Europe." *Diplomatic History* 23, no. 3 (1999): 499–524.

Walker, Christopher. "What Is 'Sharp Power'?" *Journal of Democracy* 29, no. 3 (2018): 9–23.

Wendt, Alexander. "Constructing International Politics." *International Security* 20. N no. 1 (1995): 71–81.

Westad, Odd Arne. *The Global Cold War: Third World Interventions and the Making of Our Times*. Cambridge: Cambridge University Press, 2005.

Whyte, Jeffrey. "Psychological War in Vietnam: Governmentality at The United States Information Agency." *Geopolitics* 23, no. 3 (2018): 661–89.

Wilber, Donald. "The Structure and Position of Islam in Afghanistan." *Middle East Journal* 6, no. 1 (Winter 1952): 41–48.

Williams, Patrick. *Colonial Discourse and Post-Colonial Theory: A Reader*. New York: Columbia University Press, 2011.

Wishon, Jeremiah. "Soviet Globalization: Indo-Soviet Public Diplomacy and Cold War Cultural Spheres." *Global Studies Journal* 5, no. 2, (2013): 103–14.

Zake, Ieva. "Controversies of US–USSR Cultural Contacts During the Cold War: The Perspective of Latvian Refugees." *Journal of Historical Sociology* 21, no. 1 (2008): 55–81.

Index

Afghanistan 88. *See* Kabul University
    American advisors 91
    Soviet advisors 104
    studies 87
Americanization 119, 229. *See* Theories and
    Concepts
American studies 56, 63
Archival documents
    advisors 30

Bauer, Karl 51
Bergelin, Olaf 108, 110
Bogatyrev, Nikita 48

Constructivism. *See* Theories and Concepts
Cuba
    pedagogical institutes 216
Cultural Cold War
    studies 25
Cultural diplomacy 35, 39, 87, 97, 157, 188,
    190

Eisenhower, Dwight 157
English 162
Erlangen University 51, 55
Ethiopia 121
    professors 130, 139
    See Haile Selassie I University 125
    See Polytechnic Institute in Bahar
        Dar 136
    studies 124

Fear. *See* Theories and Concepts
Free University 62

Germany
    Marxism 68
    Old Professors 43
    political science 56
    professors 45, 70
    rectors 69
    social sciences 57
    Soviet advisors 81
Guatemala
    Del Valle University 204

Francisco Marroquin Universldad 206
Rafael Landivar Universidad 206
See San Carlos University 196

Habte, Aklilu 126
Haile Selassie I University 125
    Ethiopianization 130
    Faculty of Education 128
    rector 126
    students 134
Havana University
    Chair of Russian language 212
    professors 213
Havemann, Robert 77
Heidelberg University 51
Hochschule für Politische Wissenschaften,
    München 62
Holland, Howard 133
Humboldt University 78
Hund, Fredrich 48

Jaspers, Karl 47
Jena University 48, 74

Kabul University 89, 100
    English 96
    Faculty of Engineering 91
    purge 106
    rector 101, 104
    students 98, 114
Keefer, Daryle 161, 163
Kennedy, John 63, 90, 126, 157, 197
Knauer, G. 70
Kreibich, Rolf 69

Löwenthal, Richard 71

Munich University 51

Nixon, Richard 157

Pedagogical Institute of Foreign Languages in
    Hanoi 173
    Faculty of Russian 174
Political science 56

INDEX 251

Political Science
   Hochschule für Politische Wissenschaften,
     München 62
Polytechnic Institute in Bahar Dar 136
   Ethiopianization 145
   Soviet advisors 138
   students 148
Professors
   conservative professoriate 66, 78
   hostile attitudes 76
   Old Professors 43
   purge 50
   reemployment 52
   resignation 70
   resistance 117, 144, 201
   sabotage 111, 141, 171
   shortage 130

Reagan, Ronald 64
Realism. *See* Theories and Concepts
Response theory. *See* Theories and
   Concepts
Russian 65, 174

Saigon University 161
   English 162, 163, 165
   professors 171
   teachers 162
San Carlos University 196
   professors 201
   students 200
See, Harold 91
Sovietization 33, 119, 229
Soviet Union
   advisors 30, 113, 138, 183, 216
   Afghanistan 103
   Germany 44
   Marxism 59
   Pedagogical Institute of Foreign
     Languages in Hanoi 174

Polytechnic Institute in Bahar Dar 136
   Russian 65
   Vietnam 173
   visiting professors 79, 175, 180
Students 98, 114, 116, 147
   anti-americanism 134

Taylor, John 41, 55
Theories and Concepts
   Americanization 119, 229
   fear 32, 189
   poststructuralist theories 123
   response theory 34
   Sovietization 32, 33, 119, 229

United States
   advisors 30, 90, 131, 161, 201
   Afghanistan 89
   American studies 63
   Faculty of Education, Haile Selassie I
     University 128
   Faculty of Engineering, Kabul
     University 92
   Germany 40
   Kabul University 90
   Peace Corps 135
   political science 56, 62
   Vietnam 159
   visiting professors 55

Vietnam 156
   Pedagogical Institute of Foreign
     Languages in Hanoi 173
   Saigon University 160
   schools 179, 182
   teachers 166

Würzburg University 50

Zolotukhin, Pjotr 41, 59

Printed in the United States
by Baker & Taylor Publisher Services